FLY TYING
MADE CLEAR AND SIMPLE II
ADVANCED TECHNIQUES

Skip Morris

Frank Amato
PORTLAND

DEDICATION

I dedicate this book to Earl Yim, who worked hard to become a good fly fisher and fly tier late in his life, and did. Who sat at his tying vise under my direction to test my instructions and make them clean and concise. And who, unfortunately, died before he could see this book to which he contributed so much. Still, a missed book—what's that, compared with a long life among people you love and who love you? Earl had that. Way to go, Earl.

ACKNOWLEDGEMENTS

My thanks to the following fly-designers for helping me get their patterns right (in the order their fly patterns appear in the book): John Barr, Bob Clouser and Lefty Kreh, Hans van Klinken, Mark Engler, René Harrop, and Dave Whitlock. Also, a hearty thank you to my test-subjects, from whom I learned so much about how to teach tying: Earl Yim, Danny Barnes, and Carol Ann Morris (who also happens to be the illustrator and photographer for my books, and our cats' veterinarian, and my wife).

And I really must thank John Hagan, co-owner of Northwest Flyfishing Outfitters in Portland, Oregon, who urged me, several times over a dozen years, to write a follow-up to the original *Fly Tying Made Clear and Simple*. Dear John: *surprise*—I finally did it!

As with so many of my books, I owe thanks to Tony Amato for his tasteful layout and to Frank Amato for his moral support, good sense, and for simply being a good friend all these years.

My thanks to the members of my writers' critique group (named through a process incomprehensible to anyone outside the group), the Banerjets, for struggling through many of these chapters while unable to rely on even a shred of personal experience in tying flies—and, somehow, providing useful suggestions.

We've all heard that it takes a village to raise a child. Apparently it takes something like a village to create a fly-tying book. So, I offer a final single bow of gratitude to all you villagers who helped me with *Fly Tying Made Clear and Simple II.*

ABOUT THE AUTHOR

There are few names in the world of fly fishing so widely known and solidly established as Skip Morris. Skip has published eleven other fly-fishing books, including the genuine best-seller (currently in its 22nd printing) *Fly Tying Made Clear and Simple,* to which this book is a sequel. He's published hundreds of magazine articles on fly-fishing and fly-tying (along with a smaller number on jazz guitar). He is the instructor on six videos, has worked in television and radio as both a fly-fishing host and celebrity guest. He lives with his wife, Carol, amid the rivers and lakes and saltwater beaches of Washington State's wild and magnificent Olympic Peninsula.

CAROL ANN MORRIS

Carol Ann's photographs and illustrations have appeared in such magazines as *Gray's Sporting Journal, Fly Fishing & Tying Journal,* and *Fly Fisherman* and in several books. She took the front and back cover photos for this book along with all the scenic and fishing shots and painted all the instructional illustrations.

When she is not painting, taking photographs, or treating cats and dogs as a veterinarian, she is often fishing with her husband, Skip.

All inquiries should be addressed to:
Frank Amato Publications, Inc.
P.O. Box 82112
Portland, Oregon 97282
www.amatobooks.com
(503) 653-8108

Fly pattern/tying photos by Skip Morris
Scenic/cover photos and illustrations by Carol Ann Morris
Cover and book design by Tony Amato

SPIRAL SB ISBN-13: 978-1-57188-453-4   SPIRAL SB UPC: 0-81127-00289-4
Printed in Hong Kong

1 3 5 7 9 10 8 6 4 2

CONTENTS

INTRODUCTION

How do you talk about the merits of your own work without drifting into false modesty or outright boasting? If it can be done at all, my best guess is that it must be done by sticking to the facts. So...

Fact: the original *Fly Tying Made Clear and Simple* has remained among the top-selling fly-tying books in North America for over a decade and a half—many tying books have come and gone during that time.

Fact: this volume, *Fly Tying Made Clear and Simple II*, is truly a faithful follow-up to the first volume, researched, written, photographed, and organized carefully along the lines of the extremely successful original.

Fact: you can start directly with this book even if you've never read the original *Fly Tying Made Clear and Simple*. If you are a fly tier of at least modest experience you'll do fine. The critical tying points from the first book are reviewed here, and everything else is explained in full. This volume stands on its own.

Fact: *Fly Tying Made Clear and Simple II, Advanced Techniques* is much more than simply a continuation of the first volume; it springboards off the original *Clear and Simple* up into the lofty atmosphere of fly tying's current hottest techniques, materials, and fly patterns. You're going to like it up here—our craft is fascinating at this altitude. There is a realistic fly (the Anatomical Green Drake) with the gills and glossy back and other details of the real mayfly nymph it imitates. A shaggy pupa-fly with a body-core of shining, almost glowing glass beads (the Pettis' Pulsating Caddis Pupa). A streamer with a neat head of flared, packed, and sculpted hair (the Marabou Muddler) and another with a gleaming detailed head (complete with eyes, spots, gill slits...) and a body of brilliant strands that wave in the water (the Morris Minnow, Brown). Several sure-fire emerger-flies (the Quigley Cripple and Klinkhamer Special, among others). A dry fly with wings of buoyant CDC fibers (the CDC *Callibaetis* Spinner), another with a clean wing of trimmed water-resistant wool (the Woolly Wing), and another that simulates a grasshopper with elegant conviction (the Dave's Hopper) and has become the standard for it's purpose. Along with other fly designs just as varied and intriguing as all of these.

But the important thing is that every fly in this book teaches you specific techniques and tying strategies, and is

presented plainly and logically, with short sections that offer solutions to the problems you may encounter and suggestions for avoiding such problems in the future. With these sections even the most complex fly dressings can be manageable and fun.

Seems I'm slipping from fact into observation and opinion. That's fine; the bare facts were growing a bit dull anyway.

I wrote the original *Clear and Simple* to help the many who struggle with the craft (never mind the art) of tying flies. I know how they feel; I had my own struggles way back when I started tying as a kid. Developing my tying skills was tough enough without trying to make sense of those tying-instruction books from the 1960s and before. Truth is, many of those books were as confusing as I was confused.

So I get it, I really do understand—fly tying *is* confusing.

Which means I also get the requirements of my job as a writer of tying books: to make this craft/art easy to understand, and as smooth as possible to perform.

My sense is that the failings of those long-ago tying books fueled, and still fuel, my dedication to making fly tying accessible to everyone. I want to make fly tying not a struggle

but a joy for every retiree, teenager, housewife, house-husband, and working mother or father who takes a crack at it.

And here's how I accomplished that, this time around. I started by searching out tiers with the right level of experience to serve as test subjects. (The right level for the first *Clear and Simple* was straight-zero, no experience whatsoever; but this time I needed subjects with at least a modicum of tying experience, preferably who'd read the first book but hadn't moved much beyond it—exactly the sort I'd expect to pick up *Fly Tying Made Clear and Simple II.*)

I found them. Then I took a mountain of notes as I instructed them entirely with words—I never touched a hackle or a bobbin in the process. And none of my subjects saw one finished fly or even a photo of one. Together, eventually, we got the words right.

So, 17 years after the publication of *Fly Tying Made Clear and Simple,* and after a lot of experimentation with my test subjects, here it is: *Fly Tying Made Clear and Simple—II.* Actually, I'm glad I waited, because the past 17 years provided a wealth of experience, making this a better book than it would have been had I written it sooner. Still, it's about time.

—*Skip Morris*

PRINCE NYMPH

(and a refresher on basic tying techniques)

New Techniques: breaking lead, reinforcing herl, reinforcing hackle, creating weird biot-wings

The old Prince Nymph is still so popular that when I scan the bins of a fly shop or the pages of a fly-fishing mail-order catalog and *don't* find it, I'm genuinely surprised. About any list of standard trout flies, even a rather short list, will include the Prince.

It seems strange, though, that this fly caught on when you consider all the confusion that has surrounded it. Its primary material has long been in question—I've seen the body listed as dyed-black ostrich herl, peacock herl, and black chenille (although peacock herl seems to have finally won out). And even the name is uncertain—the fly has been known not only as the Prince or Prince Nymph but also as the Black Forked Tail and Brown Forked Tail (though Prince Nymph, and just Prince for short, is now fairly established). How does a fly you can't tie or name with confidence become a hit? I guess the Prince Nymph was just destined to take off.

By now you've probably looked at the photograph above and are wondering what in God's Creation this peculiar fly could possibly imitate. Relax—it imitates nothing. Nothing, that is, beyond the surreal vision of its creator, Doug Prince. The Prince Nymph is what fly fishers call an "attractor fly," one that really doesn't pass as anything a fish has ever seen. Regardless, attractor flies work, sometimes far better than imitations. Go figure.

The standard method of fishing the Prince is to get it down along the bed of a trout stream, drifting freely below a strike indicator. It gets some use in trout lakes, too, mostly down on a full-sinking line, but sometimes teased just under the water's surface for trout that are rising or searching for insects only a foot or two down.

As the pattern below states, the Prince Nymph can be tied on a broad range of hook sizes, and all are useful and effective. But sizes 14, 12, and 10 are probably the most popular, most common, and most versatile.

We'll use the Prince Nymph not only to learn a new pattern and new skills, but also to refresh the skills you developed while working through the original *Fly Tying Made Clear and Simple.*

In learning to tie the Prince, you will also learn how to reinforce herl (peacock here, but it's the same with ostrich) with tying thread—an important technique, since sparkling, emerald herl is so popular yet too fragile to last without help. Additionally, you'll learn how to make biot tails, a durable hackle collar, and those bizarre Prince Nymph hornlike wings.

PRINCE NYMPH

HOOK: Heavy wire, 2X long (or 1X long), sizes 16 to 6.
THREAD: Black 8/0 or 6/0.
WEIGHT: Lead or lead-substitute wire. For hook-sizes 16 and 14, 0.015-inch lead (or lead-substitute) wire; for sizes 12 and 10, 0.020-inch; for sizes 8 and 6, 0.025-inch.
TAIL: Dyed-brown goose biots.
RIB: Fine oval (or flat) gold tinsel (or substitute silver).
BODY: Peacock herl.
HACKLE: Brown hen-neck.
WINGS: White goose biots.

Essential Guidelines

You've seen most of these in the original *Clear and Simple*, but they're important and worth repeating. Consider reviewing them periodically as you work through the chapters.

1. When I refer to the "front" of a fly or hook, I mean the end with the eye; "forward" means towards the eye. "Up" the hook or shank also means towards the eye. When I refer to the "rear" of a hook, I mean the end with the bend; "back" means towards the bend. "Down" the hook also means towards the bend. So if I tell you to spiral the thread *back*...well, now you know.

2. Always wrap thread (or ribs or herl or *anything* that wraps around a hook) *away* from you over the *top* of the hook's shank and *towards* you *underneath* the shank, unless instructed otherwise.

3. Try to maintain *constant* and *consistent* tension on the thread and on any material you wrap onto a fly (except for those few special procedures that require momentary slack, like the light turn and the pinch). Even an instant of slack may loosen many of the previous turns and result in a fly with a short fishing life.

4. Unless there is a reason to do so (which is rare), use *heavy* thread tension at all times, fairly close to the breaking point of the thread. This will make a tight fly, one whose components stay in place rather than pulling loose or twisting around the hook.

5. If your thread breaks, immediately clamp your hackle pliers on the loose end and then let the pliers hang as weight. Restart the thread ahead of the break, wrap the thread back over the broken thread-end, trim the tag ends of both the broken and restarted thread, and continue tying the fly.

6. If I instruct you to wrap something back to or to perform a procedure at "the bend," I'm referring to where the straight shank first meets the curve of the hook's bend.

7. All instructions are for the right-handed, unless otherwise noted. Fact is, left-handers are used to converting right-hander's instructions, a necessity in a right-handed world.

8. Whenever I give you measurements—1/16-inch, 1/8-inch, and such—I've checked them carefully along a ruler. So when in doubt, use a ruler too.

1. Find a hen-neck hackle of appropriate size using a hackle gauge.

Selecting and Preparing the Hackle

The Prince Nymph will require a hackle, so if your hackle gauge mounts in your vise, as some do, your first step will be to select a brown hen-*neck* hackle of the proper size. Even if your hackle gauge doesn't require mounting in a vise, go ahead and find your hackle now anyway. (Hen-*saddle* is an acceptable substitute for hen-neck, but a bit soft for the job.) Because the hook will be size-10 and 2X long, and a hackle gauge is designed for hooks *IX* long, find a hackle for a hook of size-8. (Do this by winding likely hackles over the post of the gauge, and then checking each feather's fibers against the markings on the gauge until you find a hackle that's of suitable size. It's the length of the fibers from about halfway up the stem to near its tip or point, not butt, that you'll use.)

Strip all the longer and softer fibers from the lower half of the hackle—that is, strip fibers from the middle of the feather down to the nub-end you plucked. Set the hackle aside for now.

2. Strip the longer, softer fibers from the base of the hackle, so it looks like the one on the right.

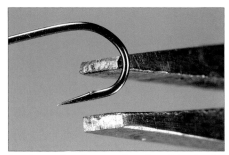

3. Smash down the hook's barb. Mount the hook in your vise.

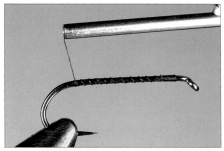

4. Start the thread just back from the eye. Trim off the end of the thread. Spiral the thread to the bend.

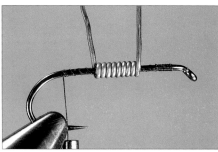

5. Wind lead wire up the hook's shank, covering the middle third.

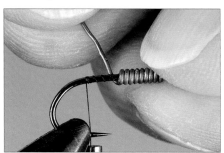

6. Break off the ends of the lead.

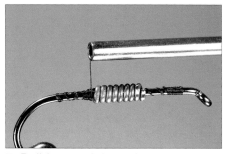

7. Build a small dam of thread against the rear end of the lead.

Selecting and Preparing the Hackle— Problems, Solutions, and Suggestions

1. The best way I know to gauge hackles is to bow the hackle neck, almost fold the skin so a row of hackles stands out. Experience helps me find one that's suitable usually in just two or three tries with the gauge. If it takes you considerably longer, don't worry, you'll catch on.

2. To find the section of fibers of about uniform length, which some tiers call the "sweet spot," slide the hackle over the gauge's post until you've identified where the longer, fluffier butt-fibers end and the sweet spot begins. The short cut is to simply assume that the sweet spot begins in the center of the feather—one inch up from the base of a two-inch feather, for example—and runs up to near the feather's point, or tip. That almost always comes close.

Adding Lead

Smash down the barb on a size-10, 2X long, heavy-wire nymph hook. (Shown here is a Daiichi 1710. Remember to smash the barb with flat-nose pliers. Avoid pliers with round or serrated jaws if possible. Never smash a barb in your vise jaws—that can chip the edges of the jaws.)

Mount the hook firmly in the jaws of your vise (as in the photos—the hook's point showing, the vise's grip not so shallow that the hook can slip, but not so deep that tying access is impeded).

Start the thread 1/16-inch behind the hook's eye, cut off the thread's end, and then spiral the thread back to the hook's bend. (Starting thread 101—four tight turns forward, six turns back over the first four.)

Hold the end of a stretch of 0.020-inch lead or lead-substitute wire in your left hand and the card or spool, on which the lead comes wrapped, in your right. (All instructions are for right-handers, remember? Left-handers, who'll have the vise facing left, just reverse hands.) Hold the end of the lead up close to the hook on the hook's near side with the card or spool on the far side. The lead wire should cross over the top of the hook. With your right hand, wind the lead wire in firm turns up the shank, each turn back up against the last. You want the lead windings to cover the center third of the hook's shank. (This, of course, means that one third of the shank at either end is *not* covered with lead.)

Rather than cutting the ends of the lead, as we did in the original *Clear and Simple*, we'll *break* off the ends, which is faster and neater. Hold the lead windings firmly with your left hand. Hold the end of the lead coming off the front of the windings in your right. Now pull firmly on the end of the lead as you rotate it in a few wide circles. This will weaken the lead next to the hook. Now give the lead a pull. It should stretch a bit, to a taper, and then break against the shank. This slims the end of the lead and curls it right down against the shank—there's no need to press the end down, because it's already down as neat and close as it can be.

Now hold the lead windings with your *right* hand, and break the lead as before while holding its end in your left hand. By not cutting off a length of lead but instead holding the card or spool, you wasted very little of the lead wire.

Wind the thread forward to the lead. Build ten to twelve turns of thread against the rear of the lead as a little dam, to keep the lead windings from spreading out as you tie over them.

Spiral the thread forward over the lead in just two or three sharply angled turns (if the thread isn't spiraled at a sharp angle, it just keeps dropping between turns of lead, spreading the lead and accomplishing nothing but mischief).

Build a tight thread-dam at the front of the lead wrappings, as you did at the rear.

Adding Lead—
Problems, Solutions, and Suggestions

1. Breaking lead requires a little practice—you want to make enough circles to weaken the lead, but you want it still strong enough to stretch a little as you pull it. Pull too soon and the lead won't break, pull too late and it won't stretch and taper. But if it's one or the other, the latter—the lead breaking too easily and failing to taper—is best. It's really no big deal if your lead doesn't taper, just a smidge neater if it does.

2. Lead wire is generally softer than non-toxic substitutes, so expect to use a different number of circles to weaken each.

3. Before you break the ends of the lead-wire, check to make sure you've left one third of the shank clear of lead at the front and one third at the rear—if you don't leave this much space, you won't have sufficient room later for the tails, hackle, and thread head. If, on the other hand, you leave *too much* space at the ends, the lead becomes a short lump under what will become a herl-body with an unappealing short-lump shape.

4. If the turns of lead aren't tight together but are instead spread out with gaps showing here and there, get right down with the finger and thumb nails of both hands and push the ends towards the center until the turns of lead compress together. And next time, angle the lead *slightly* back as you wind it onto the shank, so that its turns are forced together.

5. Make the little thread-dams at the ends of the lead small and *tight*, to keep the lead from spreading out later as you build the fly over it.

Binding on the Tails

Spiral the thread back to the bend, and then let the bobbin hang. (Last reminder: "at the bend" or "to the bend" always refers to where the straight shank first meets the curve of the bend.) From a strip of dyed-brown goose biots, cut off two biots right next to the quill. (The "biots" are the individual pointed blades.) Measure one biot along the hook. Find a point down from the sharp tip of the biot at which the biot equals one half to two thirds the length of the *shank*.

Hold the biot against the shank in your left hand so that this measured point lies at the bend, on your side of the hook. The biot should be flat against the side of the hook, with the wide, cut butt of the biot forward and the pointed end back, and the length of the biot in line with the shank. Note that a biot has a slight curve along its flat—you want the biot curving towards you, so the tails will spread apart.

Use the light turn to secure the butt of the biot against the shank. (The light turn is a technique for binding on materials that are at least slightly stiff. Wind a very light-tension, almost loose, turn of thread around the material and shank, and then pull the thread tight.) Without allowing a moment's slack, immediately add three more tight thread-turns. Wind the thread up the butt of the biot and the shank *to* the rear of the lead—not over or past the rear edge of the lead. Keep in mind that you are trying to build and taper the shank that is behind the lead up to the lead's diameter for a smooth body-foundation—the last thing you want is to bind anything *over* the lead and increase the lead's diameter. Trim off the butt of the biot closely.

8.
9.

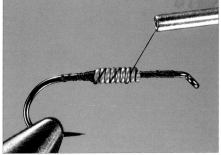

8. Spiral the thread forward over the lead in wide spirals.

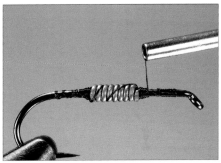

9. Build a second thread dam against the *front* of the lead.

10.

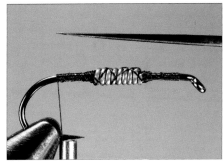

10. Measure a goose biot against the hook. Note where it equals one half to two thirds the shank's length.

11.

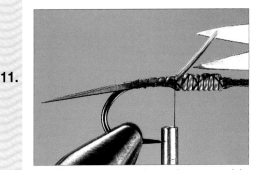

11. Bind the biot along the near side of the hook at its measured point. Trim off the butt of the biot.

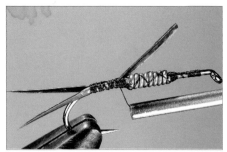

12. Bind a second biot on the *far* side of the hook, same length. Trim off its butt.

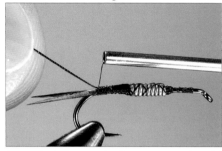

13. Bind the end of some oval gold tinsel right behind the lead; then bind the tinsel back to the bend.

14. Cut six herls from the stem and trim them back a little at their tips.

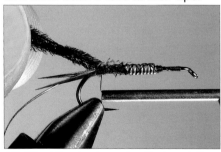

15. Bind the herls on by their cut tips, from lead to bend.

16. Dub a taper from the rear of the lead down to the bend. Dub another taper at the front of the lead.

12. Spiral the thread back to the bend. Measure the second biot, and then bind it along the far side of the shank, as you did the first biot. Now the biots should be of one length and curve away from one another. Trim off the butt of this second biot as you did the first.

Binding on the Tails— Problems, Solutions, and Suggestions

1. If using the light turn gives you trouble, try binding on the biots, one at a time, using a sort of side pinch (instructions are below).

2. After you bind on a biot with just two medium-light-tension thread-turns, you should still be able to adjust its angle by grasping the butt and tip of the biot (or maybe just the tip) and tugging. You can also pull it out a little longer or in a little shorter. Ideally, both the tails will end up right in line with the shank and of one length.

3. If you have the original *Fly Tying Made Clear and Simple,* you can always refer to it for additional instruction on such basic techniques as the light turn and the pinch. However, I've described such techniques here sufficiently for anyone with even modest tying experience.

4. If the biots tip down, it may be because you wound the thread down the curve of the bend a little. No big deal, just stop winding sooner next time, no further back than the end of the straight shank.

Adding the Tinsel and Building the Herl Body

13. Unravel some oval gold tinsel and set the spool on your bench, to your left. Bind the end of the tinsel atop the shank and up against the rear of the lead, using a light turn. Add four more tight thread-turns to really secure the tinsel. Hold the tinsel back just above the shank under light tension as you spiral the thread tightly down shank and tinsel to the bend. Add four tight turns of thread right at the bend to really secure the tinsel. Spiral the thread forward to the lead. Trim off the short tag-end of the tinsel, if necessary.

14. Snip six long herls from the side of an eyed peacock feather. (Use the herls with the longest fibers for the biggest hooks and the herls with the shortest fibers for the smallest hooks; medium-length fibers for middling hook sizes.) Even the tips of the herls and then trim off the last 1/2-inch of their fragile points.

Bind on the herls right up against the rear of the lead windings, using the pinch. (The pinch is a technique for binding on soft materials. Hold the material atop the shank, tug the thread up between your thumb-tip and the material, tug the thread down the far side between your fingertip and the material [leaving a little loose loop of thread on top], roll the tips of thumb and finger forward a little, pull down

15. tight on the thread.) Add five tight turns of thread. The herls should now be bound atop the shank with their cut tips up against the rear of the lead.

Hold the herls back and slightly above the shank under light tension as you spiral the thread down them and the shank to the bend. Add three tight thread-turns at the bend. Closely trim off the cut ends of the herls at the rear of the lead. Spiral the thread forward to the rear of the lead.

Spin some dubbing, any color, thinly along an inch or so of the thread— any dubbing, really, though fine, soft rabbit is probably as easy as any to manage. (Wax the thread if you prefer. Waxing thread is optional with soft dubbings, but a real aid with coarse or stiff dubbings like hare's mask or Buggy Nymph Dubbing.) Dub between the bend and the rear of the lead

16. until the space between them tapers neatly down from lead to shank. Try to narrow the dubbing from almost none at the tails up to match the diameter of the lead where the lead and dubbing meet.

Spiral *bare* thread to the front of the lead. Dub again, a taper from the lead down to 1/8-inch behind the eye (leaving 1/8-inch of bare shank behind the eye).

Wind the thread back to the bend. Hold the herls lightly towards you and raise your bobbin until the thread runs along the herls. Pull your bobbin towards you until there is about two inches more thread exposed than the length of the longest herls. Gently adjust the herls until they are all gathered together under even, light tension (*light* tension—doesn't take much to break peacock herl).

Now grasp the herls and thread together at the butt-ends of the herls and spin the butts in one direction (either direction). Keep switching hands and gradually spinning the herls and thread until they create a sort of fuzzy rope together (check the photo in caption #18 and try to match it). The finer tip-ends of the herls will spin first, and will break if you spin them too tightly, so expect to spin the thread and herl-butts some more after the tip-ends are wound onto the shank.

Hold the ends of the spun herls and the thread together as you wind them up the shank and lead, in close turns, to 1/8-inch behind the eye.

Separate out the herls and thread. The herls will remain tightly wound up the shank. Add a few tight turns of bare thread over the ends of the herls, then closely trim off the herls' butt-ends.

Cut the tinsel about five inches from the hook. Wind it up the body in six to nine evenly spaced ribs. Wind the tinsel in the normal direction since the herl is toughened by thread (though counterwinding a rib can toughen some fly bodies, and might add a little security if you care to counterwind). Bind the end of the tinsel at the front of the herl body with a few tight thread-turns. Trim off the end of tinsel closely (deep in the scissors' blades, if the tinsel is stiff or hard. And try always to protect the sharpness of your scissors' tips, mainly by using them to cut only soft materials).

Adding the Tinsel and Building the Herl Body— Problems, Solutions, and Suggestions

1. If you have trouble getting the tinsel bound firmly up against the rear of the lead, try using the pinch instead of the light turn.

2. Remember: never wind the thread or anything else back further than the rearmost turns of thread securing the tails. Doing so will kick the tails out of position. Winding close to or even atop those last turns is fine, but never *past* them.

3. The dubbing that tapers from lead to shank, that creates a smooth foundation for the body, must be dense and firm to do its job. You can check this by winding tight thread-turns over the dubbing—if it compresses down much, dub some more, or just build some layers of thread, until the transition down from the lead is smooth and gradual, and *firm*.

4. The herl you want for the body is from the *sides* of an *eyed* peacock tail feather. Don't use any of the herl in the eye itself. And don't use herl from a "sword" feather, which is much narrower herl than from an eyed feather, and with fibers too short for a Prince.

17.

17. Wind the thread back to the bend. Hold the herls by their butts out towards you along the thread.

18.

18. Spin the herls and thread together into a sort of fuzzy rope.

19.

20.

19. Wind the herl-thread rope up the shank and lead to just back from the eye.

21.

20. Separate out the thread and herls, add a few tight thread-turns, trim off the butts of the herls.

21. Wind the tinsel up the herl-body as ribs. Bind the tinsel, and trim it.

22. Bind the hackle, by its stripped stem, slightly ahead of the herl body The hackle should project forward over the eye. Trim off the hackle's butt.

23. Wind the thread *back* to the body. Wind the hackle *back* to the body.

24. Wind the thread forward in a few open spirals through the hackle.

25. Trim out the hackle's tip.

26. Pinch the hackle fibers back and down, top and bottom, and along the sides.

5. Peacock herl varies. Some herls are twice as long as others, and the density of the fibers along different herls runs from skimpy to plush. This means that the number of herls required for a size-10 Prince—or a size-10 anything—will vary too. Therefore, the six herls I told you to use for your Prince Nymph is a general recommendation; you might need as few as three or as many as ten.

Take a little time to look closely at herls from different eyed feathers, to get a sense of how herls vary.

6. How tightly should you spin the herl and thread together? Let the photos serve as a guide. And remember that if you spin the herls too tightly, they'll break; but if you spin them too loosely, the body will look loose and unkempt. There's plenty of range between these extremes that will be sound and look good, however.

7. If you run out of herl before it reaches to 1/8-inch behind the eye, separate out and bind the butts and then trim them off. Bind in a few new herls, spin them with the thread, and continue.

8. If you hold the tinsel at one angle to the hook throughout the wrapping of the ribs, your ribs will naturally be evenly spaced.

9. Tinsel is fairly strong; you can—and should—wrap it firmly. Otherwise the ribs will tend to slip loose when they catch on trout teeth.

Adding the Hackle

Wind the thread forward to about halfway between the front of the herl-body and the rear of the eye (requires only a thread-turn or two—not very far). Using a light turn, bind the hackle by its stripped stem to the shank at this halfway point. The fibered body of the hackle should project *forward* off the eye, the bare stem *back* over the body. Just the tiniest bit of bare stem should show between the thread and hackle-fibers. The concave (cupped) side of the hackle should face away from you. Bind the stem back along the shank to the front of the body. Closely trim off the stem. A little bare shank should remain behind the eye.

Clamp the jaws of your hackle pliers onto the last 1/4-inch at the tip of the hackle. Make sure the pliers lock onto the stem. If your pliers are the English style (all-metal, with a springlike loop for the finger), make sure they are aligned with the hackle's stem, the stem coming straight out in line with the pliers and jaws, as this will avoid bending or kinking the stem and keep it as strong as possible.

Wind the hackle *back* to the body in three or four turns, each turn up against the last.

Now hold the hackle pliers up and back with your left hand as you wind a couple of turns of thread over the tip of the hackle with the bobbin in your right hand. Continue holding the pliers as you wind the thread *forward* through the hackle in three or four open turns. Now the hackle's stem is crossed repeatedly by the thread, which really toughens the stem. Add a few thread-turns in front of the hackle. Let the bobbin hang.

Still holding the pliers in your left hand, find the tip of the hackle and trim it off. (Now you can set the pliers down.)

Pinch down the hackle-fibers between your right-hand thumb and first finger. Pinch top-and-bottom and along the sides. The fibers should now angle steeply back.

Adding the Hackle—
Problems, Solutions, and Suggestions

1. Double check to see that you've left an appropriate amount of space between the eye and the front of the herl-body (in this case, 1/8-inch) for the turns of hackle and the thread-head. If there's not enough room, bind back over the body to create more hackle-space. Or you can try compressing back the hackle after it's wrapped with your right-hand thumbnail and fingernail. Another solution (though not my favorite) is to form a hideous, gargantuan thread-head back over the hackle-fibers.

In any case, take note and learn, and if you left too little room this time just be sure you leave the appropriate space on your next Prince Nymph.

2. When you bind on the hackle, try to mount it on its side, the flats of the feather vertical—the hackle will handle best and look best if it is wound on its side, and starting with it mounted this way will insure it will remain so as you wind it. Remember that the torque of tightening the thread may roll the hackle, so allow for this by tipping the hackle a little before tightening the thread on it.

3. To avoid catching hackle-fibers in the thread as you spiral it forward through the hackle, zig zag the thread a bit a you wind it.

4. Ideally, you want to trim out the hackle's tip without cutting off any of the fibers of the hackle collar. I find that keeping the tips of the scissor blades barely parted, pulling the hackle tip back away from the other fibers, bringing the scissor tips straight in from the side, working slowly and carefully, and getting my nose right down for a close look all help me accomplish this.

Another approach is to hold the hackle-tip firmly back (with the hackle pliers), and then *saw* on the stem with one blade of your scissors. The blade's fine serrations will cut through with just a few strokes.

Binding on the Wings

Snip two white biots from a goose quill. Measure one biot along the hook. Find the spot on the biot's wide base, up from its point, at which the biot equals the *full length* of the hook (not just the length of its shank).

Hold the biot with this measured point just behind the eye. Set the biot flat *atop* the hook, its butt forward and its tip back, its point angled *away* from you slightly (see the top-view photo). The slight curve of the biot should be up (though some tiers prefer it down. No big deal either way). Use the light turn to secure the biot. Add three or four more tight thread-turns to really secure it.

Measure and bind the second biot atop the first, in the same manner you mounted the first biot. The second biot should angle out to the same degree as the first one but *towards* you—the opposite direction of the first biot. Add a few more tight thread-turns.

Now there should be two hook-length biots bound directly atop the hook just behind the eye. They should angle out a little to the sides and curve upwards. Trim off the butts of the biots closely.

27. Measure a goose biot along the hook. Find where the biot equals the length of the entire hook.

28. This is mostly a top view. Using a light turn, bind the biot flat *atop* the shank, angling slightly away from you.

29. Bind a second quill in the same manner, same length, but angling slightly towards you.

30. Side view again. Trim off the butts of the biots. Trim closely so the thread-head you build over them isn't outsize.

27.

28.

29.

30.

31. Cover the cut ends of the biots with tight thread-turns, build a thread head, whip finish the thread, trim the thread, add head cement to the head.

31.

Bind the cut ends with tight thread-turns. Build a tapered thread head over the butts.

Whip finish the thread; then trim its end closely. Apply head-cement to the thread head (*carefully*, so as not to get any in the eye or allow any to soak back into the hackles, and *sparingly*, for the same reasons). Stick the fly into a board and flip it regularly until the cement is cured, or use a fly-turning device.

It's always wise to check flies a minute or two after adding head-cement to see if it has crept into the hooks' eyes. If so, strip the fibers from the lower part of a hen-neck hackle or other small feather, push the stem down into the eye and then grasp the stem below the eye with tweezers (to keep the cement off your skin); draw the whole feather through the eye and out—the stem and tip-fibers will swab out the cement. Check the eye again a little later, and then clear it again if necessary.

Binding on the Wings— Problems, Solutions, and Suggestions

1. Because the wings are long—pushing the limit of biot-length with the largest hook-size for the Prince—cut right up to the quill when you trim off the wing biots. And save the longest ones for the biggest Princes.

2. If you find a biot rolling down the side of the shank as you tighten the thread, press a finger down directly on top of the biot and the light turn of thread holding it; then pull the thread tight. Maintain constant thread-tension and immediately add three or four tight thread-turns.

3. There is no consensus on an exact angle for the spread of the biot-wings—Doug Prince never gave one, to the best of my knowledge, and fly tiers are generally a freethinking and obstinate lot anyway. What you see in the photos is my personal preference. The bottom line is, if the spread of the wings is too shallow they'll look almost like a single wing, but if it's too wide they may interfere with the work of the hook's point. Just try to match the photos...at least until the urge to defy me and do it your own way takes over—you *rebel,* you!

4. If you find the biot-wings are angling up too much (*up,* that is, not *out*—they're supposed to angle out to the sides), use the triangle to draw the wings down and the hackle back; then wind the thread back over the base of the hackles a bit, creating a longer thread-head and forcing down the wings.

5. If one or both biots wind up angling too far out or not far enough, you should be able to tug them into position, especially if you haven't yet cut off the biots' butts. (If you have cut of their butts, tug them very carefully or you'll pull them out.)

PETTIS' PULSATING CADDIS PUPA (*Hydropsyche*)

New Techniques: making a glass-bead body, dubbing over glass beads, brushing dubbing, making side-legs

Thumb through Joe Warren's book *Tying Glass Bead Flies* and you'll see lots of options. Glass beads can be pushed together and blocked at both ends (as with the Killer Caddis, Olive in the chapter titled "Additional Nymphs"); a single bead can be mounted at the head of a fly (as with the Copper John and Anatomical Green Drake in other chapters); or beads can be secured one at a time with turns of bare or dubbing-layered thread (as with the Pettis' Pulsating Caddis Pupa (*Hydropsyche*) we'll tie here). And those are just a few common approaches. I've seen glass beads strung along wire or monofilament for extended bodies, beads hung along fly bodies like bubbles, and so on and so on... There seem to be no limits to this business.

So the Pettis' Pulsating Caddis Pupa (*Hydropsyche*) is really just an introduction to tying glass-bead flies. But it's a good fly for the job. It's certainly one of the best-established glass-bead flies, and the way its beads are bound is an approach used in quite a few other patterns, though sometimes with just bare rather than dubbed thread. Personally, I like the design. Some glass-bead flies look a bit contrived to me, as though the fly's designer had fallen too much in love with the bead concept for the good of his or her fly designs, but the beads in the Pettis' Pulsating Caddis Pupa (*Hydropsyche*) glow softly beneath a shaggy,

illuminated haze of dubbing, which strikes me as a plausible simulation of a real caddis pupa's bright, gas-swollen, bubble-crusted abdomen.

This version of Mr. Pettis's fly imitates the pupa of the *Hydropsyche* genus of caddisflies, which Eric Leiser and Larry Solomon, in their book *The Caddis and the Angler,* call "the most common of all the caddis on this continent," said continent being North America. And because *Hydropsyche* varies so much in size, it's hard to generalize about the most useful sizes for the Pettis' Pulsating Caddis Pupa (*Hydropsyche*), but I'll try. For western species, sizes 16 to 12 (in my experience) are all equally useful. Eastern and Midwestern species tend to be smaller, sizes 16 and 18 being typical.

You can fish the Pettis' Pulsating Caddis Pupa (*Hydropsyche*) just below the water's surface on a slow, mended wet-fly swing (with perhaps an occasional twitch of the fly); or cast it upstream, let it sink, and then allow it to rise at the end of the drift.

In learning Jim Pettis's fly you'll learn not only a good approach to making a glass-bead fly-body but also about brushing out dubbing (which results in fly with a body that is rough and lively) and how to add legs along a fly's sides.

PETTIS' PULSATING CADDIS PUPA (*Hydropsyche*)

HOOK: Heavy wire, short to standard length (curved shank scud/pupa hook preferred), sizes 18 to 12.

THREAD: Olive 8/0 or 6/0 (I prefer medium-brown).

ABDOMEN: Four to six orange glass beads, small. "Lava brown" Buggy Nymph Dubbing (or some other golden-brown semi-coarse dubbing) over the beads.

LEGS: Wood-duck flank-feather fibers (or mallard dyed to wood-duck color, a standard material).

THORAX: Dark-brown Buggy Nymph Dubbing (or almost any dubbing—Antron, rabbit...).

Mounting the Beads

We'll begin by learning how to slip beads efficiently onto hooks, so you don't spend a lot of your tying time on hands and knees searching for beads you've dropped.

Smash down the barb on a size-12 heavy wire, curved-shank hook. (The hook in the photos is a Tiemco 2457.)

Mount the hook in the jaws of your vise, close to the hook's eye. The hook's eye should be to your left and the bend to your right with the hook upside down and more or less horizontal (see the photo with caption #1).

Cup your left hand up close under the hook (right-hander's instructions, remember? Last reminder). Pick up one bead with your right hand and slip it over the hook's point, and then down onto its shank. Continue adding beads in this manner until you've got four on the hook. (That should be the right number of beads for this size-12 hook, but that could vary from three to five beads with different hook models and variations in beads from different companies. Just use enough beads to create an abdomen about the same length as the one in the photos.)

Now press a right-hand fingertip *lightly* against the hook's point—as long as your finger touches the point, the beads can't come off the hook. Keep touching that point as you grasp the hook, release the vise jaws, and invert the hook. Hold the beads up against the hook's eye as you mount the hook in your vise in the standard manner. That's it, no combing the carpet for beads, no need for a pillow to cushion the knees.

1. Mount the hook upside down near its eye in your vise, as shown.

2. Cup one hand under the hook as you slip the beads on, one by one. Remount the hook in your vise, in the normal way.

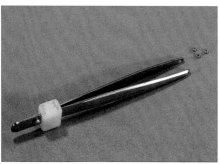

3. Some tiers prefer handling beads with these special tweezers, cupped inside their tips. Fly shops carry them.

Mounting the Beads— Problems, Solutions, and Suggestions

1. If you have trouble getting the beads onto the hook, well, at least you're not alone—lots of tiers wrestle with beads. Here are strategies that may help. First, use magnification even if you normally don't—finding the hole in a tiny bead is no cinch. Second, hold the beads in your palm; they're easier to pick up from a palm than a table. Third, try the special bead-nabbers with cupped jaws (shown in the photo with caption #3). Fourth, *slow down*. Things will go best if you take your time, and once everything smooths out, the process will gradually pick up speed.

2. Here's yet another way to handle the beads. Push the tip of your bodkin down into the hole of a bead lying flat on a table. Press your fingertip against the side of the bead; then lift the bead this way and push it onto the hook's point, with the hook mounted in your vise. With only the bodkin's fine point inside the bead's hole, there's plenty of room in there for the point of the hook. Of course, you can hold a cupped palm under the hook in case the bead drops.

Binding the Beads

Push the beads back from the eye, letting them rest down against the jaws of your vise. Start the thread on the shank, slightly back from the eye, and then cut off the thread's tag-end. Wrap the thread tightly back in close turns to 1/8-inch from the eye. At this 1/8-inch point, build a small tight dam, or collar, of thread large enough to stop a bead.

Slip one bead forward to the thread; then angle the thread steeply as you wrap it back *under* the bead to the shank behind. Add a couple of tight thread-turns behind the bead. The bead should now be secured.

Slide the next bead forward and secure it in this same manner. Now the second bead should be secured close up behind the first bead. Continue until all the beads are bound and the thread is hanging behind the last bead.

Binding the Beads— Problems, Solutions, and Suggestions

1. If the front bead slips past the thread-dam, build up the thread-dam with more tight thread-turns. Try to keep the dam narrow.

2. As you pass the thread back under each bead, you can keep the bead in place by just pressing a finger tip against its far side (as in the illustration).

3. Remember: once the beads are all bound, they should be quite close together, only slight spaces between. If they are too spread out, watch for this next time (and try suggestion #2 above).

Dubbing the Abdomen

Spin "lava brown" Buggy Nymph dubbing (or a substitute) up about three inches of the thread. The dubbing should be slightly heavy. Take a few turns of the dubbed thread behind the last bead, to fill out and taper the rear of the abdomen.

Advance the dubbing-covered thread *forward under* the rearmost bead to the slight space between this bead and the bead just ahead of it. Wind two to four tight turns of the dubbed thread between the beads— this should cover the beads somewhat.

Wind the dubbing-covered thread forward *under* the next bead; take two to four turns again in the sliver of space between the beads.

Continue working forward in this manner until all the bead-spaces are covered in dubbing and there is some buildup of dubbing against the front of the frontmost bead (so that this bead will later be covered with teased-out dubbing like the rest of the beads). Add a few turns of bare thread ahead of the dubbing to lock the thread in place.

4. Start the thread just back from the hook's eye; wrap it back 1/8-inch.

5. Push a bead forward and then take a turn of thread back under it. Add two tight thread-turns behind it.

WORKING THREAD BACK UNDER THE BEAD

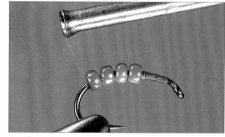

6. Continue binding beads with bare thread, one at a time, until they are all locked in place.

7. Spin dubbing onto the thread. Build a ball of dubbing behind the beads.

8. Wind the dubbed thread forward *under* the last bead. Add two to four turns of dubbing between the last two beads.

9. Continue working the dubbed thread forward under the beads, making two to four turns in each space between beads.

10. Tease the dubbing out to shaggy, all along the length of the abdomen. Tease out the sides, top, and bottom.

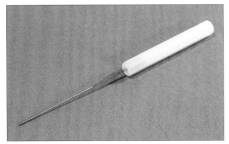

11. One tool for tugging out the dubbing is a dubbing teaser. It has tiny teeth on its end.

12. Dub moderately between the front of the abdomen and the eye.

13. Stroke the tips of some wood-duck fibers out to an angle that evens their tips, and then strip or cut them off.

14. Bind the fibers along the near side of the abdomen. They should project back a full hook's length.

Dubbing the Abdomen— Problems, Solutions, and Suggestions

1. Use heavy thread-tension as you wrap the dubbing, and make sure that tension is constant, allowing no slack. You want the thread well buried into the dubbing since we'll soon tease the dubbing out to shaggy, and this teasing could cut loose thread or cause it to slip out from between the beads.

2. You can take one to four turns of dubbing-layered thread between beads—just depends on whichever number of turns provides enough dubbing for a fuzzy abdomen (but not too fuzzy) when the dubbing is later teased out. My advice: remember how many turns you took, look at your fly once the abdomen has been teased out, look at the photos, and then decide how many turns of dubbed thread you want next time.

Teasing Out the Dubbing and Adding the Legs

10.
11. Add a few tight thread-turns in front of the abdomen, to secure the thread. Tease or pick the dubbing out along the abdomen to a shaggy effect. You can use a tool called a dubbing teaser (or a dubbing brush or dubbing picker or any such tool) or your bodkin or the tips of your scissors.

12. Spin dark-brown dubbing onto the thread and build up the thorax-area to about the diameter of the beads—but no more. Dub from the front of the frontmost bead up the shank, leaving a little bare shank behind the hook's eye.

13. Stroke out some fibers along the sides of a wood duck (or mallard-dyed-wood-duck-color) feather at an angle that evens the tips of the fibers. Cut or strip off the fibers. You want two sections of fibers for the legs, each section about half as wide as the hook's gape (the original gape, before the beads were added).

14. Measure the fibers against the hook. Note the point where they equal the full length of the hook. Hold the fibers against the near side of the abdomen so that this measured point lies at the rear of the abdomen. Use a modified pinch, a sort of *side* pinch, to mount the fibers on the near *side* of the abdomen. The fibers have a slight curve; mount them so they curve out away from the abdomen (though it's no big deal if they don't). Bind the butts of the fibers with several tight thread-turns.

In this same manner, bind the second set of fibers along the far *side* of the abdomen. Trim off the butts of all the leg-fibers closely.

Dub moderately over the length of the thorax, to cover the butts of the fibers and the thread-wraps holding them.

Build a small, tapered thread head, whip finish the thread, trim the thread closely, and add head cement to the thread head to complete the Pettis' Pulsating Caddis Pupa *(Hydropsyche)*.

15. Bind more fibers along the other side of the abdomen. Trim off the butts of all the fibers.

16. Dub moderately over the bound butts of the wood-duck fibers to just short of the eye.

Build a thread head, whip finish and trim the thread, add head cement.

Teasing Out the Dubbing and Adding the Legs— Problems, Solutions, and Suggestions

1. If you use a bodkin or scissors to tease out the dubbing, don't dig too hard or deeply, or you may cut the thread.

2. Make sure to tease out the dubbing *all* around and *all* along the abdomen. Get the top, sides, and underside, from the rear of the abdomen to its front. This way the effect will be complete.

3. Use only the hard, well-marked fibers from the wood-duck or dyed-mallard feather, not the soft fluff at the base of its stem. And if you use a real wood-duck feather, use the kind that is pale and lightly marked all over, not the kind with a heavy black and heavy white strip across its tip.

4. Building up the abdomen before adding the legs serves a purpose—it keeps the legs from bowing way out against the front bead of the abdomen. You do want the legs to stick out, but only a bit. So make sure you dub over the abdomen-area before adding the legs, and if their angle is severe, add more dubbing next time. (Conversely, if the legs lie flat against the body, build *less* dubbing next time.)

5. If the fibers resist being stripped from the stem, you'll probably lose the evenness of their tips during the wrestling match that follows. So if this is a problem, *cut* the fibers free, rather than strip them.

6. I've found it trickier, for some reason, to get the right length on the legs when they're mounted on the sides rather than, as with some flies, on the underside. So I measure twice and I suggest you do the same. A good test: pinch the leg-fibers in against the sides of the body— the tips of the fibers should reach a little past the far edge of the bend.

7. Having trouble mounting the legs with a side-pinch? Try a light turn.

8. After a set of legs is mounted with just a couple of light-tension thread-turns, you can work the leg-fibers up or down the sides, pull them to shorter or longer, or adjust their angle by grasping the tips of the fibers in one hand and the butts in the other and then giving them a few gentle tugs. Once you like their position and length, bind them firmly with several tight thread-turns.

9. If you're thinking of using the cut butts, the ones left over from the section of fibers that makes the first set of legs, to make the second set of legs—stop even *thinking* that. The cut butts will be thicker and stubbier than the fine tips, and if you use them for legs the resulting fly will look plain ugly.

10. Run out of room to make the thread head? The solution is the same as always: leave an eye's length of bare shank for the head. When you add the first layer of dubbing, the legs, the final layer of dubbing— don't cover that last little stretch of bare shank.

BITCH CREEK

New Techniques: creating rubber-strand antennae and tails, standard weaving

Woven flies, with their pale undersides, dark backs, and interlocking fingers of color are fascinating and nearly irresistible to fly tiers. Many are a hit with trout, too.

I'm pretty sure the first woven flies I saw were Dan Bailey's Light and Dark Mossbacks. They were uncommonly lifelike fly patterns for their time, the time of the Woolly Worm and Grizzly Wulff. I thought them quite remarkable.

I still think so. Which is why I'm surprised more such designs haven't emerged over the decades since the Mossbacks caught on. Nonetheless, there are a few popular woven fly patterns, the Bitch Creek chief among them.

Weaving chenille (or yarn or floss or anything else) is one of those techniques that might baffle you a little at first, but then, once you've got it working, will seem so plain you'll wonder why it was ever a big deal.

It seems an ever-increasing number of new nymph patterns—especially attractor patterns and imitations of stonefly nymphs—are sprouting rubber-strand tails and antennae. You'll learn how to make such components through learning the Bitch Creek.

The Bitch Creek's orange belly and dark back make it a natural for imitating the nymph of the giant western salmonfly (although the fly's white tails and antennae are a leap from the natural's, which are blackish brown). But the Bitch Creek probably functions as an attractor pattern about half the time, maybe more. I suspect anglers often have no idea what the trout take it for and don't care, so long as the trout take it.

I tie and fish the Bitch Creek mostly in sizes 8 and 6, though I can think of big-fish waters where sizes 2 and 4 might be best. And size 2 is still reasonable for imitating the massive salmonfly nymph.

Take your time with the weaving of this fly—weaving is a tricky technique to explain, and tricky to grasp even with a good explanation. But essentially, and mercifully, it's also a pretty straightforward process.

BITCH CREEK

HOOK: Heavy wire, 3X, or 4X long, sizes 10 to 2.
THREAD: Black 8/0, 6/0, or 3/0.
WEIGHT: Lead or lead-substitute wire.
ANTENNAE: White rubber strand, medium thick.
TAILS: White rubber strand, medium thick.
ABDOMEN: Orange and black chenille, woven.
THORAX: Black chenille.
HACKLE: Brown, one, spiraled. (A big dry-fly neck-hackle with its thick, tough stem is my favorite. Some tiers prefer rooster-saddle hackle.)

Adding Lead, Binding on the Antennae and Tails

Smash down the barb on a size-6, 3X or 4X long, heavy wire nymph hook. (The hook shown is a Daiichi 1720.) Mount the hook in your vise. Start the thread just back from the hook's eye, cut off the free end of the thread, and spiral the thread tightly back to the hook's bend.

Wind 0.025-inch lead or lead-substitute wire up the hook's shank, each turn back against the last, from about 1/8-inch ahead of the bend up to about 1/8-inch short of the eye. Cut or break off the ends of the wire. All pretty much as you did with the Prince Nymph.

Bind the lead, as with the Prince Nymph. (If you need more detail on adding lead wire and binding it, refer back to pages 8 and 9 under "Adding Lead" in the chapter titled "Prince Nymph.")

Next, we'll add antennae and tails. So that you understand what you are trying to accomplish, here is how they should end up: both the antennae and tails should appear as white rubber-strands projecting off the front of the hook (antennae) and the rear (tails); two tails, two antennae, each pair in line with the shank from a side-view and split into a neat "V" from a top-view.

Snip off two sections of medium-diameter white rubber-strand, each about three-inches long. Wind the thread forward to right up against the rear of the eye. Double one rubber-strand section so its ends are together; this will form a loop—the rounded end of the loop will be the center of the strand.

Spiral the thread up to the eye. Using a sort of side-pinch, bind the rubber-strand section, at its center, on the far side of the shank, up against the rear of the eye. Add six tight thread-turns to really secure the strand. Hold the rear end of the bound strand back as you spiral the thread back to the front of the lead.

Wind the thread forward to halfway between the lead and the eye. Pull the rear end of the strand (the end projecting back along the lead) up and forward, then down, under moderate tension on the *near* side of the hook. Hold it there in your right hand. Bind it on the near side of the hook with a few tight turns of thread, by repeatedly draping the bobbin over the hook, letting it hang on down the far side of the hook, and then pulling the thread tight. The rear of the strand should now cross over the shank and angle down to the near side of the shank, where it is bound with these last thread-turns between the lead and eye.

Hold the strand out (or back) and wind the thread forward until it is up against the rear of the eye. Pull the strand straight forward along your side of the shank, and then bind it behind the eye with six tight thread-turns (again, by draping the bobbin over the hook at first with your left hand, until the thread is holding the strand secure; then adding the final turns while holding the bobbin in your right hand).

Now adjust the strands, if they tip down or up, so that they are level with the hook (at least level at their bases; their tips will droop downward under their own weight). Adjust them by pulling aggressively on them, one at a time, to shift their positions.

I prefer to trim the strands now, to get them out of my way for the rest of my tying; though you can trim them later if you prefer. Draw both strands together and then stroke your grasp *lightly* straight out towards their tips. Measure your open scissor-points against the hook to find two thirds to three quarters of the shank's length. Hold the points alongside the strands to determine this point; then snip them there. The result: two rubber-strand antennae.

1.

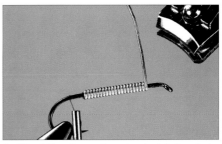

1. Start the thread and wind it back to the bend. Add lead in the usual manner, but leave 1/8-inch of bare shank at each end.

2.

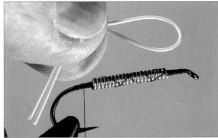

2. Bind the lead as usual. Double a section of rubber-strand to find its center.

3.

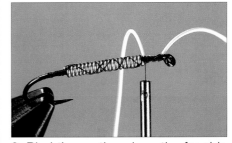

3. Bind the section along the far side of the shank from the eye to the lead.

4.

4. Swing the rear end of the strand forward and bind it along the *near* side of the shank.

5.

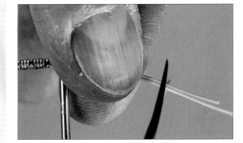

5. Draw the strand-tips lightly forward and trim them to length.

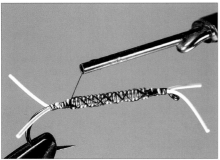

6. Spiral the thread to the bend and create rubber-strand tails as you created the rubber-strand antennae.

7. Bind the end of some black chenille along the far side of the hook, just from the lead to the bend.

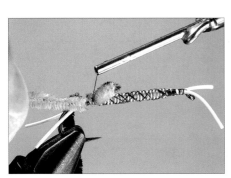

8. Bind the end of some orange chenille along the near side of the hook, from the lead to the bend.

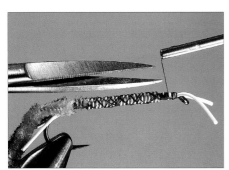

9. Trim off the stub-ends of the chenille. Spiral the thread to the eye, whip finish the thread, and trim it.

Now you'll follow essentially the same steps you used for creating the antennae to make the tails. Here's how.

Spiral the thread back to the bend. Double the second section of rubber-strand to find its center. Bind the strand on the far side of the shank at the bend; then bind it forward along the shank to the rear of the lead. Spiral the thread back to halfway between the bend and the lead windings. Draw the

6. forward end of the strand back and downward and bind it along the *near* side of the shank. Hold the end of the strand back along the near side of the hook and wind the thread tightly back to the bend. Add six tight thread-turns at the bend. Wind the thread tightly up the shank and doubled strand to the rear of the lead.

Trim the ends of the strands to the same length as the antennae. Adjust the angle of the strands to horizontal, if necessary, by tugging on each.

Adding Lead, Binding on the Antennae and Tails— Problems, Solutions, and Suggestions

1. Rubber-strand generally comes in a sheet, from which you peel individual strands off the side. To get a strand started, hold the sheet down flat on a flat surface (a surface you don't mind scratching). Push the tip of a bodkin (or one scissor blade) into the very edge of the strand-sheet about a half-inch from the end; the bodkin should catch in the groove next to the outside strand. Hold the bodkin down firmly as you slide it out to the end of the sheet. Now the tip of one strand should be free from the sheet. Just hold the end of the strand and peel it off the sheet.

2. Don't let binding rubber-strand onto the side of a hook's shank with a modified pinch shake you—it isn't hard. Just follow the guidelines for a standard pinch, but tip it to the side (or, with a rotary vise, turn the hook on its side).

3. When you bind on the rubber-strand for the antennae, make sure you bind it from up close to the rear of the eye and back to right up against the front of the lead—if you stop winding thread short of the eye, you will leave a gap of bare shank in the finished fly, and short of the lead will leave another kind of gap, one that will make the body irregular.

4. Before you adjust the angle of the antennae by tugging on each, try trimming them to the same length. This needn't be the final length, but if one is longer than the other it will droop more under its additional weight, making the adjustment difficult to judge. Same with tails.

5. When you cut rubber-strand, do so with a quick, sure snip. If this fails to make a clean cut, your scissors are probably dull, loose, or both, and due to be replaced.

Weaving the Abdomen

Spiral the thread to slightly back from the rear of the lead windings. Trim off two lengths of "small" (small-diameter) chenille, one length black, the other orange. (Five-inches of each seems to work well with this hook-size at first; after you've woven a while, you can cut the chenille an inch shorter.)

7. Using a sort of side-pinch, bind the end of the black chenille against the far side of the hook, close behind the lead windings. Hold the chenille slightly out and to the side as you spiral the thread tightly down it and the shank to about 1/32-inch short of the bend. Add five tight thread-turns there to really secure the chenille.

Bind the orange chenille (using a side-pinch) on the near side of the

8. shank, just behind the lead, and then spiral the thread down it as with the black. Add a few tight turns at the bend.

Trim off the stub-ends of both strands of chenille. You want the cut ends of the chenille up against the rear of the lead windings.

9. Spiral the thread up to just short of the eye (and behind the antennae), whip finish the thread, cut the thread. (You can't properly weave without first cutting the thread.)

Look at the completed Bitch Creek on page 20. Note how the body has orange beneath and black on top, with the two colors overlapping in a row of locks along the sides. *That* is the result you want from weaving.

So, let's weave. Start by turning your vise so its head points directly away from you. (I turned my vise to more of a 45 degree angle for the photos, so you could best see the process.) Hold the end of the orange chenille in your right hand and the end of the black chenille in your left (same for left-handers—don't switch hands). Hold the lengths of chenille straight out to their respective sides.

Swing the orange chenille (in your right hand) *under* the hook, and to your *left*, and then *up* against the far side of the hook. The orange strand should now come straight up from the left side of the hook, in front of the black. (Remember: the black chenille has been, and remains, straight out from the left side of the hook.)

In order that the woven abdomen is neat and secure, you must keep constant firm tension on both lengths of chenille—one moment's slack and the woven body will loosen.

Still holding the orange chenille straight up on the left side, swing the black chenille (in your left hand) forward, and then over the *top* of the hook and to your right. Stop when the black chenille is straight out to the right. See?—now the orange is underneath and the black is on top and they are interlocked on the left side of the hook.

Remember: always work the black chenille over the top of the shank and the orange under the shank.

With a little experimentation and wrist-bending, you can continue weaving without ever releasing the ends of the chenille or switching hands with them—honest. And you can hold each strand of chenille at whatever point along it works best; you don't have to hold it by the end.

Continue holding the black chenille straight off to your right, over the top of the hook. You should still be holding the orange chenille straight up on the left side of the shank. Swing the orange chenille forward and down along the left side of the hook. Now swing it *under* the hook and to your right. On the right side of the shank, swing the orange straight up again, in front of the black chenille.

Continuing holding the orange up on the right side of the shank; swing the black chenille over the top of the hook to your left.

Swing the orange under the shank and up the left side until it's straight up again. Swing the black over the top of the shank until it is horizontal and out to your right again. Swing the orange chenille under the shank and towards you, then up on the right. You should now have three locks, two on the left side of the shank, one on the right side, and the fourth lock half completed.

Got it? Just keep weaving the abdomen of the fly in this manner until the chenille covers the rear two thirds (or slightly less) of the shank.

As you continue weaving, remember to occasionally pull back on the ends of the chenille to tighten the weave. And, watch that you keep the locks along the sides, not slipping down beneath or up on top.

10.
11.
12.
13.
14.
15.

10. Turn the vise-head so that it points straight away from you (though it's at more of a 45° angle here).

Hold the orange chenille in your right hand, the black in your left. Hold the lengths of chenille out to their respective sides.

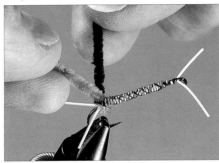

11. Swing the orange chenille under the shank, and then straight up on the left side of the shank.

12. Swing the black chenille forward, then over the top of the shank to your right. One lock completed.

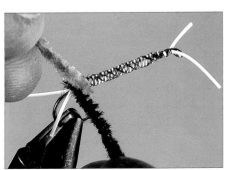

13. Swing the orange chenille forward, down, and under the shank to come straight up on the right side.

14. Swing the black chenille forward around the orange, then over the top of the shank to your left.

15. Continue the weave up two thirds of the shank. Pull the ends of the chenille straight down.

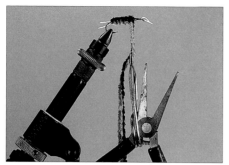

16. Clamp English hackle pliers on the chenille. Weight the pliers.

17. Restart the thread just behind the eye. Spiral it back, and then bind the ends of the chenille. Trim off the ends of the chenille and bind the cut ends.

18. Bind some black chenille atop the shank. Trim off the tag-end.

16.

Pull straight down on the two ends of the chenille, and adjust the tension on them until it is equal on both. Clamp a pair of English hackle pliers (the all-metal kind with the coil in the end, as shown in the photograph) onto the ends of the chenille. Hang something with a little weight from the pliers, to keep the weave from loosening. (Here, I hung some diagonal pliers from the hackle pliers.)

17.

Restart the thread just behind the eye. Trim off the tag-end of the thread. Spiral the thread back to the front of the woven abdomen. Draw the ends of the chenille forward and bind them at the front of the woven abdomen under eight tight thread-turns—this should secure both ends of the chenille. Just keep working the bobbin over the ends of the chenille, holding those ends out of your way as needed.

Trim off the ends of the chenille. Bind the cut ends thoroughly.

Weaving the Abdomen— Problems, Solutions, and Suggestions

1. For a thicker and slightly flattened abdomen, bind both lengths of chenille down the sides of the lead and back to the bend.

2. While weaving, keep firm tension on both strands of chenille, to create a tight, secure abdomen. Keep the tension *constant*—a moment's slack will result in a loose weave.

3. To keep the weave from slipping forward, tug both strands of chenille sharply back right after making each interlock.

4. Stop after each interlock of the chenille and check to see if the colors are even along the sides. You may have to briefly stand to check the far side of the hook.

5. If you want to skip clamping the English hackle pliers on the chenille before restarting the thread, make sure you set the bobbin in a handy place, with a few inches of thread hanging from the bobbin's tube, *before* you weave. After the body is woven, hold the ends of the chenille straight below the hook in your left hand, under firm tension. Pick up the bobbin in your right hand, and catch the end of the thread in the free fingers of your left. (You can wrap the thread around a finger, if that helps.) Now, start the thread on the shank, wrap it back over the ends of the chenille, trim the chenille and the tag end of the thread. When you cut the ends of the chenille and the thread, be careful *not* to cut the working thread.

6. Weaving is tricky at first—no doubt about it. Especially the working of your hands to make weaving happen without releasing the ends of the chenille. So be forgiving towards yourself. And patient. Once you've got it, though, you'll wonder how weaving could ever have seemed that difficult; I can almost guarantee it.

Building the Thorax

The woven abdomen should cover at least half but no more than two thirds of the shank. If it is longer than this, you can just wind the thread back over the woven abdomen a bit. (If it covers *less* than half the shank...well, it shouldn't. Just complete your short-abdomen fly and follow the instructions more closely next time.)

18.

Using the pinch, bind the end of some black chenille about 1/16-inch back from the eye (same thickness of chenille you used for the woven abdomen). Add a few tight thread-turns. Hold the chenille back along the top of the shank and bind it to the shank with tight turns of thread, right back to the front of the abdomen. Trim off the front stub-end of the chenille.

Select a brown hackle using your hackle gauge. The hackle should match a size-6 hook. (See the Bitch Creek pattern, or dressing, on the first page of this chapter for choices of hackle-type.) Strip the overlong and especially soft fibers from the base of the hackle's stem. Bind the hackle by its stem directly in front of the abdomen, using a light turn. About 1/16-inch of bare stem should show between the fibers and the thread-wrappings. Add a few tight thread-turns to really secure the stem. Wind the thread up the stem and shank to 1/16-inch back from the eye. Trim off the butt of the hackle's stem closely.

19.

19. Bind the stripped stem of a hackle in front of the abdomen. Trim off the stem. Wind the chenille to the eye, bind it there, and trim it.

Wind the chenille up the shank to about 1/16-inch short of the eye, each turn of chenille back up against the last. Bind the end of the chenille just short (yes, about 1/16-inch, *again*) of the eye. Trim off the end of the chenille; cut closely.

Lock the tip of the hackle in the jaws of your hackle pliers. Wind the hackle forward in three to five open, evenly spaced spirals to the front of the chenille thorax. Bind the tip of the hackle with a few tight thread-turns. Trim off the hackle's tip, build a tapered thread-head, whip finish and trim off the thread, add head cement to the thread-head.

20.

20. Wind the hackle forward in open spirals, bind it at the eye, trim off its tip, build and complete the usual tapered thread-head.

Building the Thorax— Problems, Solutions, and Suggestions

1. You can make the thorax slightly flattened (like the thorax of a real stonefly nymph) and fuller if you bind the black chenille down one *side* of the shank along the thorax-area, snip the stub-end off (you'll need a slightly long stub-end), and then bind the stub-end along the other side and then trim it. When you then wrap the chenille over this base, the resulting thorax will be a little wider and more flattened than usual.

2. If you want to cut down the bulk of the chenille where it's bound behind the eye, in order to create a smaller thread-head, strip the fuzzy fibers off the short front end of the chenille, leaving just the thread-core. If you have trouble holding the thread-core as you bind it behind the eye, try holding the end of the core in English hackle pliers.

3. Try winding the hackle in the depression between turns of the chenille. The fuzz of the chenille will obscure the depression, but it's there, just visible, and the hackle will tend to slide securely into them.

4. A very efficient way to build the thread head is to first draw the hackle-fibers back out of your way with the thumb, first finger, and second finger of your left hand. You can even draw back the hackle-fibers *and* the antennae, and then pop free the antennae with your bodkin or closed scissor blades.

5. Because the base of the antennae, the end of the thorax-chenille, and the tip of the hackle are all bound behind the eye, a large thread-head is almost unavoidable. No problem, just try to make it a large *neat* thread-head.

WEAVING A FLY BODY

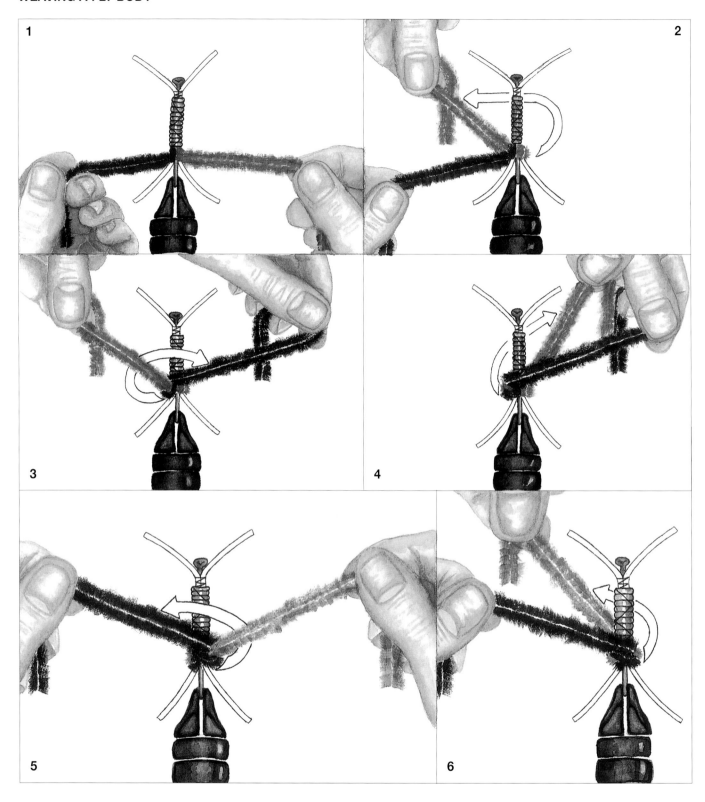

COPPER JOHN

New Techniques: making a bead-head fly, constructing the unique Copper John wing case, topping a wing case with epoxy glue

In what seemed no time at all, the Copper John leapt from John Barr's minor experiment to likely the most popular nymph in North America. John, a Colorado fly fisher and fly designer, wanted a bright, enticing little nymph that would sink quickly on what is often called the "hopper-dropper system," a smallish nymph dangled off the hook-bend of a big, buoyant dry fly, typically an imitation of a grasshopper.

Now, just a few years later, Copper Johns are fished not only with the hopper-dropper system but also dead drift below strike indicators and even below floating lines from long leaders to hover and jiggle just above the beds of trout lakes. The fly is currently tied in several colors and on hooks from a substantial size-12 with a long shank down to size-20. It's in every catalog, and fly shops typically stock plenty of Copper Johns.

John has created all sorts of effective attractor and imitative fly patterns. You can explore them in his book *Barr Flies.*

As for the tying of the Copper John, the tails are, essentially, the tails of the Prince Nymph, so nothing new there. After that, however, things get interesting. The softly gleaming coil of its copper-wire abdomen is an intriguing anomaly (only one other popular fly I know, the Brassie, incorporates it) and simple to construct; but we'll learn how to make it taper smoothly and lie neatly compacted. The peacock-herl thorax and partridge (or hen-back) side-legs are conventional enough, but the wing case is unique, requiring some care and strategy in its construction. Its topping of epoxy is an approach pioneered by fly-tying and lake-fishing authority Hal Janssen, further continued by Mike Mercer, an inventive tier and fly-fishing author.

The Copper John remains most popular in its standard color scheme, as we'll tie it here. Sixteen to 12 seem to be its most useful sizes.

COPPER JOHN

HOOK: Heavy wire, 2X long for sizes 18 to 12; standard dry-fly hook for size 20.

HEAD: Gold metal bead. For size 20, 5/64-inch; for sizes 18 and 16, 7/64-inch; size 14, 1/8-inch; size 12, 5/32-inch.

WEIGHT: Lead wire. None for size 20; 0.010-inch for size 18; 0.015-inch for sizes 16 and 14; 0.020 for size 12.

THREAD: Black 8/0 or 6/0.

TAILS: Dyed dark-brown goose biots.

ABDOMEN: Copper wire. Small for sizes 20 and 18; medium-fine (currently called "Brassie") for sizes 16 and 14; medium for size 12.

WING CASE: One strand of pearl Flashabou over brown Thin Skin, topped with epoxy glue.

THORAX: Peacock herl.

LEGS: Natural-brown partridge or mottled-brown hen back.

1. Mount a bead on the hook and slip it up to the eye. Mount the hook in your vice. Wind a layer of lead from mid-shank to the gold bead.

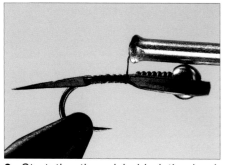

2. Cut or break off the ends of the lead. Push the lead up into the hole in rear of the bead.

3. Start the thread behind the lead. Bind a biot along one side of the shank for a tail. Bind the biot's butt up to the lead and no further.

4. Bind a second biot along the other side. Trim their butts at the lead.

Mounting the Bead, Adding the Lead, and Mounting the Tails

1. Smash down the barb on a size-12, 2X-long hook (The hook shown is a Tiemco 5262, John's choice), and then mount the hook upside down in your vise, in preparation for adding the bead. (For more on mounting beads, see the chapter titled "Pettis' Pulsating Caddis Pupa *(Hydrosyche).*") Slip a 5/32-inch-diameter gold metal bead over the point of the hook, then down to the shank. The small end of the bead's hole should be forward, so it will end up against the eye.

Remove the hook for your vise, and then remount the hook in the normal upright position.

Wind some 0.020-inch-diameter lead or lead-substitute wire up the hook's shank, each turn back against the previous turn, from the center of the shank (the center of the *bare* shank, the stretch between the bend and bead) right up to the bead.

2. Break or cut off the ends of the wire; push the ends of the wire down flush, with your thumbnail or closed scissor blades, if they stick out at all.

Push the coiled wire to slide forward until it is snug up inside the bead. The wire wrappings should now cover slightly less than half the hook's shank behind the bead. (The holes in beads vary from brand to brand—if the lead slips forward into the bead, let it; if the lead won't fit into the hole, no problem. The lead windings can be a little shorter or longer and really have no effect on the looks or function of the finished fly.)

3. Start the thread behind the lead, cut off the tag-end of the thread, and then wrap the thread back to the bend.

4. Snip off two dyed-brown goose biots; bind them onto the shank as tails (as you did with the Prince Nymph). The biots should extend from the bend about one-half to two thirds the shank's length, and should curve out to the sides, away from one another. Bind the butts of the biots right up to the rear of the lead. Trim off the butts of the biots flush with the lead.

Let's pause for a strategy session. You want the shank behind the lead built up to the diameter of the lead—no larger, no smaller. The shape of the foundation largely determines the shape of the completed abdomen; the neater and smoother the foundation, the cleaner the abdomen you make over it. So keep this in mind as you bind on the tails and the copper wire to come. After binding on the copper wire you may still need to build up the abdomen-area with thread. You want the foundation to taper from finer at the tails up to wider where it meets the lead windings.

Mounting the Bead, Adding the Lead, and Mounting the Tails— Problems, Solutions, and Suggestions

1. When you push the lead windings up into the bead, push them mostly from *behind*, so the turns of lead stay compact, and do not spread apart.

2. Some tiers prefer to measure the biots and then trim off their butts *before* binding them on the sides. They feel that this way, the butts are easier to trim and that getting their length right is easier too. Try this, if you like; but try my way too.

Building the Copper-Wire Abdomen

With the thread hanging just behind the lead windings, hold the end of about six inches of "medium"-diameter copper wire in your left hand. Hold the end of the wire atop the shank, its end up against the rear of the lead windings, with the wire in line with the shank. Use the light turn to bind the wire there; then add eight to ten tight thread-turns to really secure it. Hold the wire back and slightly up as you wind the thread tightly down the wire and the shank to the bend. At the bend, add a few tight thread-turns.

Spiral the thread forward to *slightly* (just a thread-turn or two) past the center of the shank (that is, the center of the shank that lies between the bend and the rear of the bead. If that means the copper wire later climbs onto the lead, fine). Let the thread hang. Wind the copper wire in touching turns up to the slightly past the middle of the shank, where the thread is hanging.

Bind the end of the wire on top of the shank with eight tight turns of thread. Trim off closely the end of the wire.

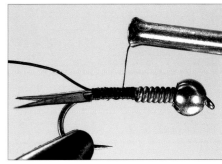

5. Bind the end of some medium-diameter copper wire from the lead to the bend. Really secure the wire.

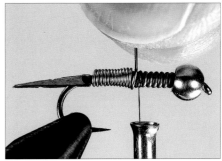

6. Wind the copper wire to the lead, each turn neatly back against the last.

Building the Copper-Wire Abdomen— Problems, Solutions, and Suggestions

1. The "medium"-thick copper wire for the abdomen of our size-12 Copper John is pretty stiff. This stiffness makes the wire a bit tricky to handle and can result in exposed thread near the bend and tails knocked out of position—the sort of stuff that makes fly tiers cringe. So remember how stiff your copper wire is when you bind it and the tails on—and really bind everything *tightly,* with plenty of thread-turns. Plenty of tight thread-turns will allow you to be aggressive with the wire, without the tails slipping around.

2. To make the turns of wire compact, keep the wire angled back slightly, so each turn pushes back against the previous turn.

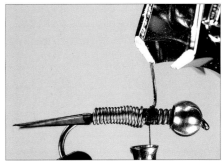

7. Bind the end of the wire. Trim off the end.

Building the Thorax and Wing Case

Spiral the thread forward to barely short of the bead. Hold a single strand of pearl Flashabou down flat atop the thorax-area, directly in line with the shank. One end of the Flashabou should project forward over the bead, the bulk of it back over the abdomen. Use the light turn to bind the strand atop the thorax-area. Wind four tight turns of thread over the Flashabou to really secure it. Hold the Flashabou strand back and slightly up with light tension as you wind the thread back over it from the metal bead to the front of the copper-wire abdomen. Add a few tight turns of thread. Trim off the forward tag-end of the strand.

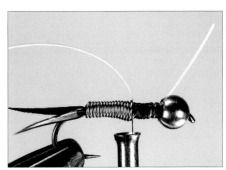

8. Bind a single strand of Flashabou atop the thorax-area. Trim off the front tag-end of the strand.

9. Cut a strip of Thin Skin. Bind one end atop the thorax-area, and atop the Flashabou strand. Trim off the front stub-end of the Thin Skin.

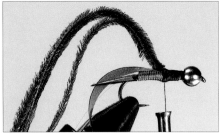

10. Bind a few peacock herls along the thorax-area.

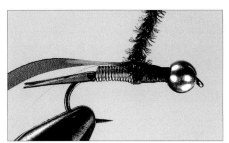

11. Spin the herl and thread together as a sort of fuzzy rope.

12. Wind the herl-rope up the thorax-area up to the bead.

9. Cut a strip from a sheet of brown Thin Skin. The strip should be no slimmer than half and no wider than two thirds the width of the hook's gape. (If you cut the strip about two inches long, you can use it for tying several Copper Johns.) Strip the Thin Skin off its white backing. Use a sort of modified pinch to press the edges of the strip down around the lead, and then bind the end of the strip atop the thorax-area with a few tight thread-turns. The strip should now be bound with one of its ends just behind the bead and the other end extending back in line with the shank, over the shank. Continue holding the strip down around the top of the lead. Slide your fingers back as you bind the strip back to the front of the wire-abdomen. Wind the thread back over the copper-wire abdomen, just a little, to *exactly halfway between the bend and the bead.* Add several tight thread-turns there. Trim off the short stub-end of the strip closely (if necessary), and then bind it.

10. Even the tips of four full, fairly long-fibered peacock herls. Snip off the fragile tips at least 1/4-inch down from their points. Wind the thread back to the front of the copper-wire abdomen, and then let the bobbin hang. Using the pinch, bind the herls atop the thorax, right in front of the abdomen. Bind the herls close to their trimmed ends, so little of their length is lost. Add a few tight thread-turns at the front of the abdomen to really secure the herls. Bind the herls well up the thorax-area. Trim off the stub-ends of the herls, and then bind those ends.

11. Wind the thread back to the rear of the thorax-area, and then spin the herls and thread together into a sort of herl-rope. (See the chapter titled "Prince Nymph" for details on this technique.)

12. Wind this rope up the thorax in close turns. Stop when the herl-rope is snug against the rear of the bead.

13. Unfurl the herl from the thread. Bind the herl with a few tight thread-turns up against the rear of the bead. Trim off the butts closely.

14. Pull the strip of Thin Skin forward and down over the top of the thorax while holding the strip in your right hand, under *light* tension. Work the bobbin over the front of the strip with your left hand and let it hang on the far side of the hook. Regrasp the bobbin beneath the hook in your left hand and swing it up and over for a second turn of thread (still holding the strip in your right hand). Pull down on the bobbin to tighten the thread-turns; then release the strip from your right hand. Build a thread-collar of five tight thread-turns right up against the rear of the bead.

Stretch the end of the Thin Skin strip forward lightly and trim it off closely.

15. Draw the single strand of Flashabou up, forward, and down over the strip of Thin Skin. Make sure the strand is flat, not twisted. Bind the Flashabou as you did the Thin Skin; then trim its end closely. One lone, shining strand up the center of a brown wing case—that's the proper effect.

13. Separate out the herls from the thread and trim them off.

14. Bind the Thin Skin at the bead as a wing case. Trim off the end of the Thin Skin.

15. Pull the Flashabou forward over the Thin Skin and bind it against the bead. Trim off the end of the strand.

Building the Thorax and Wing Case—Problems, Solutions, and Suggestions

1. Just before you bind on the Flashabou and Thin Skin is an excellent time to check your fly's proportions. The abdomen should end very close to halfway between the bend and the rear of the bead. By now, you'll mostly be checking to learn, to see if you'll need to make adjustments in the next Copper John. But you may still be able to reduce a little length in the abdomen on the fly now under construction, if you want to.

2. If you take the extra few seconds required to get the strand of Flashabou mounted directly atop the hook and straight in line with it, it will run neatly up the center of the wing case later.

3. If the strip of Thin Skin is shifting down the far side of the lead as you bind it, try holding the strip firmly close behind the thread as you tighten the thread. An alternate approach is to tip the strip a little to your side so that thread-torque shifts it right up on top.

4. If you don't have or can't easily obtain brown Thin Skin for the wing case, substitute a strip of Bug Skin or possibly even one of the synthetic wing materials. Whatever you use should be tough and bond well with the epoxy you'll later add. Natural fibers, such as a section of pheasant tail or duck quill, will look good and take the epoxy well, but aren't as tough as Thin Skin (though pheasant tail *is* pretty durable). Many tiers now form the wing case *entirely* from Flashabou or Krystal Flash—a bit loud, but there must be a reason this approach is catching on.

5. Keeping the epoxy (which you'll soon add) atop the wing case and out of the peacock herl and partridge legs will make the fly look best and fish best. One way to hedge your bet is to keep the strip of Thin Skin thin—if it's wide it will tend to touch, and therefore bleed epoxy into, the partridge legs we'll add next. So try keeping the strip only half the width of the gape or just *slightly* wider than half.

6. Take a few extra seconds to reach in with the very tips of your scissors and trim the ends of the Thin Skin and Flashabou down *close*. You'll later be covering those cut ends with thread wraps, and if the ends are long you'll fail to cover them, or be forced to build a massive and alarming thread-collar.

Adding the Legs and Coating the Wing Case

Strip the fluff from the base of a natural-brown partridge flank feather (or mottled-brown hen-back feather), leaving only the firmer, cleanly marked fibers. Separate out a section, about 1/4-inch wide, of the longer fibers. Stroke the fibers out to an angle that squares their tips. Either strip or cut the fibers (right at their base) off the stem.

Measure the fibers to find the point at which they are one half to two thirds the length of the hook's shank. Hold the fibers against the near side of the abdomen, horizontal, so the measured point lies against the rear of the bead. Use a sort of side-pinch (or a light turn) to bind the fibers at the front of the thorax, against the side of the bead. Add a second moderate-tension turn of thread.

Now adjust the bunch of fibers. If the fibers are too high where they are bound on, close to the edge of the Thin Skin, grasp the tips and butts of the fibers and tug them down away from the wing case. If the tips of the fibers angle slightly down or up, fine. But if the tips *really* angle up or down, tug them to horizontal.

Add four tight thread-turns right against the rear of the bead to really secure the partridge fibers.

16. Strip the fuzz from the base of a partridge (or hen-back) feather. Strip off some of the side fibers. (Like the feather on the right.)

17. Bind a section of the partridge fibers on one side of the thread collar.

18. Tug the section to proper length and position, if necessary.

16.

17.

18.

19. Bind a second section of partridge fibers on the other side.

20. Trim off the butts of the partridge. Whip finish and trim the thread.

21. Carefully run a bulge of epoxy glue up the center of the wing case.

Either mount the fly on a rotating device or in a board you regularly flip over until the epoxy sets up.

Once the epoxy is hard, add head cement (or epoxy) over the whip finish. Rotate or flip the fly over repeatedly until the epoxy sets up.

19. Measure and bind another section of partridge fibers along the far side of the hook, just as you did the first bunch. Tug the fibers down again, if they are too close to the edge of the Thin Skin, and make sure they aren't angling sharply up or down. Add a few more tight thread-turns to lock the fibers into position.

20. Trim off the butts of all the fibers closely. Build a collar of thread against the rear of the bead, covering (or mostly covering) the butts of the partridge and the butt of the wing case. Whip finish the thread and then trim it.

21. Mix some epoxy glue—plain slow-cure epoxy glue, the kind you can buy at a hardware store, *not* epoxy *finish,* as you'd use on the thread-windings of a fly rod. Use good ventilation (working outdoors with a cross-breeze is best) and seek out epoxy with low chemical-odors (my current choice is Devcon 2-Ton Crystal Clear Epoxy, but there are others). Pick up a dab of epoxy with the point of your bodkin or a sharp toothpick. Tease a line of epoxy up the center of the strip of Thin Skin, over the strand of Flashabou; the epoxy line should cover the middle half of the wing case. (If you feel brave, you can work the epoxy close to the edges—careful, though, that it doesn't seep into the peacock or partridge!) The epoxy should rise as a clear, elongated little hump from the very rear of the wing case right up to the thread collar.

You can set the fly upright with the shank horizontal, and the epoxy will probably set up fine. But I prefer to rotate the fly on one of those contraptions made for the job, or just stick the fly in a board and turn the board over regularly until the epoxy is firm.

The next day, when the epoxy is fully set, add head cement (or a little more epoxy) to the thread collar. (If you had added epoxy to the wing case and collar at the same time, it would have flowed off the wing case onto the collar, then spilled over into the legs and thorax resulting in a rigid little twig of a fly.)

Adding the Legs and Coating the Wing Case— Problems, Solutions, and Suggestions

1. To get an appropriate density for the legs, you can count fibers the first time or two. Ten to fifteen partridge or hen-back fibers in each leg-bunch looks good on a size-12 hook. Study the photos, too.

2. If you're having trouble handling the partridge (or hen-back) legs, make sure you use the longest fibers from the base of the feather.

3. Measure epoxy glue carefully—you'll need to come fairly close to 50/50 on the amounts of the syrupy A and B components. Also, make sure you mix the components thoroughly. (If a batch sets up dull or tacky, measure and mix more carefully next time.)

4. Though I said this earlier, it's worth repeating: make sure the epoxy doesn't wick into the thorax or legs, and your best insurance against this is to keep the epoxy short of the edges of the Thin Skin and to use no more epoxy than required to create a modest hump.

5. Another point worth repeating: never coat the thread collar at the same time you coat the wing case—you'll be begging for an epoxy disaster if you do.

6. Many tiers run the epoxy dome forward to partway over the bead and back atop the last few turns of copper wire in the abdomen. This results in a larger wing case and, possibly, an epoxy dome that is slightly more secure.

ANATOMICAL GREEN DRAKE

New Techniques: making a trimmed-feather tail, a dubbing loop, an overlaid back, and splayed fiber-legs, and tying a semirealistic fly

Not for the timid tier, this one. The Anatomical Green Drake is something of a "realistic" pattern, the kind that looks more like an insect than an artificial fly. The structural details that create this effect usually make such a fly pattern challenging to tie, and so it is with the Anatomical Green Drake. In this case, those details are a fringe of abdominal gills, three distinct and neatly splayed tails, two outstretched rows of legs, and a shiny exoskeletal back.

But if you work your way through the tying of this fly carefully, patiently, and refer to the "Problems, Solutions, and Suggestions" sections whenever difficulties arise, all should go well. Through the four previous fly patterns, and all of the original *Fly Tying Made Clear and Simple*, you've been training for this. You can handle it.

Why, though, do tiers tie such intricate flies as the Anatomical Green Drake? In my experience there are two standard answers: (1.) because they believe that flies convincing to the eye of the angler are convincing to the eye of a trout, and (2.) because some tiers just like a challenge. You can't argue about (2.), but (1.) has *long* been under debate.

I have a simple philosophy about realistic flies: The plausible detail can't hurt, and it might help. Perhaps where trout are wise to the fly fisher, have felt the sting of a

barbless hook or two, a more credible fly might succeed where a rougher "impressionistic" fly would fail. So, if I'm certain (or, rather, *believe* I'm certain) which real nymph the trout are on, I'll try a realistic imitation. If that fails...well, at least I know that the problem isn't the fly.

But realistic patterns vary, and not all of them interest me. I'm no fan of rigid little lifelike imitations—I want a fly that *moves*, one whose legs and tails and thorax are pliant hen-saddle, partridge, herl, or shaggy fur dubbing, not twig-like hackle quill or raffia lacquered to brittle hardness. A few glossy hard spots are okay, and may even add realism, but I want any underwater fly to have plenty of supple parts.

My Anatomical Green Drake (like its cousins the Anatomical *Baetis*/PMD and the Anatomical *Callibaetis*) is just the sort of soft and lively realistic nymph I trust. I fish it dead-drift below a strike indicator along a streambed just before or sometimes during a hatch of the western green drake mayfly. Every time I picture the fly, resembling the real nymph, drifting naturally among rocks and twisting currents, its segmented, gelatinous back glistening, its speckled legs and tails and its gills waving, I feel a little surge of confidence.

Regarding hooks, I tie and fish my Anatomical Green Drake mostly in sizes 12 and 10.

ANATOMICAL GREEN DRAKE

HOOK: Heavy wire, 2X long, sizes 12, 10, and 8.

BEAD: Black metal, 7/64-inch (or 1/8 inch) for size-12; 1/8-inch for sizes 10 and 8.

WEIGHT: Lead or lead-substitute wire, 0.015-inch for sizes 12 and 10; 0.020 for size 8.

THREAD: Brown (or green) 6/0 or 8/0.

TAILS: Dyed-olive (or dyed-brown) partridge.

BACK: Brown 1/8-inch Stretch Flex or Scud Back (or Medallion sheeting).

RIB: Fine copper wire (or 4m Uni-mono or 6X tippet).

ABDOMEN AND GILLS: Dyed-green and -brown ostrich herl.

WING CASE: Same as the back.

LEGS: Dyed-olive (or dyed-olive-brown or -brown) partridge.

THORAX: Arizona Synthetic Dubbing in "peacock."

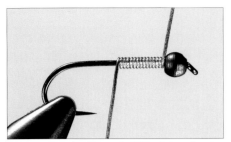

1. Mount the bead. Wind lead wire from mid-shank to the bead.

2. Break or trim off the ends of the lead. Push the lead up into the bead.

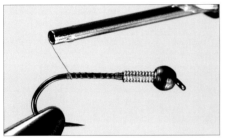

3. Start the thread right behind the lead. Spiral the thread to the bend.

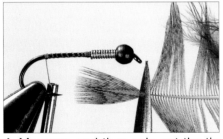

4. Measure, and then snip out the tip of a partridge feather for the tails.

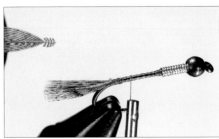

5. Trim up the tip's cut base along both sides of the stem about 1/16-inch. Bind the tip atop the bend. (Note the properly trimmed stem in the upper left of the photo.)

The Bead, Lead, and Making the Tails

1. Smash down the barb on a heavy wire, 2X long, size-10 hook. (The shank can be slow-curved or straight. The completed Anatomical Green Drake on the previous page was tied on a curved-shank Daiichi 1260 and the hook in the tying steps is a Daiichi 1710). Mount a 1/8-inch black-metal bead on the hook, and slip the bead (small end of the hole forward) up to the hook's eye. (All this bead business is described in detail in the chapter titled "Pettis' Pulsating Caddis Pupa (*Hydropsyche*).")

Wind a compact layer of 0.015-inch lead or lead-substitute wire from the center of the *exposed* part of the hook's shank (the shank behind the bead) up to the rear of the bead.

2. Cut or break off the ends of the lead (and press the ends down flush, if necessary). Push all the lead forward, so it slides into the hole in the back of the bead. The result should be that the bead is locked up against the eye and the lead extends less than halfway to the bend (as in the photo with caption #3).

3. Start the thread up against the rear of the lead—but don't wind thread up *over* the lead. You'll be working to build the area behind the lead up to the lead's diameter, and increasing the lead's diameter with thread-windings will only put you in a losing race. Cut off the tag-end of the thread. Wind the thread back to the bend.

4. Hold a dyed-olive partridge feather alongside the hook, the stem in line with the shank, for measuring. Note the point on the stem where the tip-end of the feather equals one half the length of the *entire hook*. Stroke back the fibers from this one-half point and snip off the tip of the feather there. Cut only the stem (try to avoid cutting fibers). Set the remaining body of the feather aside for later.

Next, trim the base of the feather-tip. Trim up closely along both sides of the stem, leaving a row of 1/16-inch-wide stubble along each side. The stubble should reach only about 1/16-inch up the tip's cut base. (The base is where you cut the stem, not the rounded end towards which the fibers all cant.)

5. Hold the feather-tip by its flats, between your left-hand thumb and first finger (right-handers instructions, of course). Hold the tip so the full 1/16-inch of its trimmed base is lying atop the rear of the shank, over the thread. Your thumb should be on top of the feather and your fingertip beneath it. The feather should be in line with the shank from all angles, and its slight curve should be up. Use a light turn to bind the feather on top of the shank; then immediately add several tight thread-turns to really secure it.

Now is the time to trim the feather-tip into tails—while you can still easily replace it if you make a mistake. Look straight down onto the top of the feather's stem from the rear of the fly. Cut carefully along one side of the stem down towards the base of the feather, leaving three (though it could be two to four) fibers intact next to the hook. (You'll need good scissors for this, preferably the kind with tiny serrations to grip the fibers.) Do the same on the other side. Now there should be three spread tails—the center tail is the stem lined with very short stubble, and the side tails are each three or four fibers projecting from the feather's base.

The Bead, Lead, and Making the Tails— Problems, Solutions, and Suggestions

1. Some measuring is more important than other measuring— measuring the feather-tip is the former. So measure twice before you cut; then measure one more time in case you need to trim off a little more. If you cut it too short, either cut another feather-tip or live with a short-tailed nymph this time around.

2. If you're tempted to simply strip the fibers from the base of the feather-tip...don't do it! The short-cut fibers help keep the stem from shifting when you bind it. A bare stem tends to roll onto its side.

3. Don't hesitate to measure the 1/16-inch trimming at the feather-tip's base against a ruler. You must provide enough trimmed stem for the thread to really grip, yet you don't want to trim so much that the tails are too short.

4. You can do all the trimming of the feather-tip—making it into three tails with a stubbly base—*before* binding it on if you prefer.

5. A good *safe* way to trim next to the fibers you plan to leave as tails is this: stroke the tail-fibers out, away from the fibers you want to cut, then reach *straight down* into the flat of the feather with the very tips of your scissors, catch the last few fibers you want to cut in the blades, and cut them, right next to the fibers you want to leave as tails. This will leave a little safety gap when you cut in line with the stem. And cutting straight down makes it easy to avoid cutting off any of the fibers meant for tails.

6. When you bind the stem of the tail-feather with the light turn, your thumb and finger should be right up close to the hook. The flexible stem of the feather-tip will be difficult to control if you hold it out from its base.

7. If the feather-tip rolls off the top of the shank, or tilts off to one side, try holding the feather down on your side of the shank slightly so that the tightening of the thread pulls the feather right up on top, and angle the near edge of the feather down a little so that it turns up to level.

Making the Abdomen

Wind the thread forward to just short of the lead. Trim off about a 1 1/4-inch length of 1/8-inch-wide Stretch Flex. Trim the Stretch Flex (or the like) down its length to about two thirds its original width.

Hold one end of the Stretch Flex against the rear of the lead, flat atop the shank, and bind it with the pinch (a pinch that wraps the Stretch Flex around the top of the shank). Add a few tight thread-turns. Hold the rear end of the Stretch Flex back over the shank under light tension as you spiral the thread tightly down it and the shank to the bend. Add a few tight thread-turns at the bend. Be sure you don't wrap the thread back too far and push the tails out of position.

6.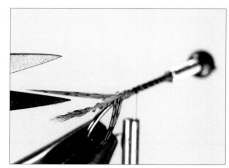

6. Trim closely along both sides of the stem, leaving three fibers on each side; the result: three tails.

7.

7. Snip some 1/8-inch Stretch Flex down its length, leaving it about two thirds its original width.

8.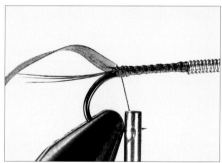

8. Bind the Stretch Flex from the rear of the lead to the bend.

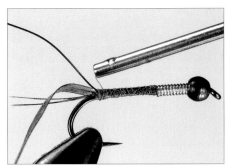

9. Bind fine copper wire from the lead back to the bend.

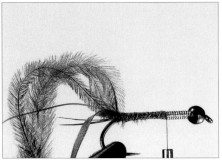

10. Snip off the pointed tips of three ostrich herls. Bind the herls from the lead to the bend.

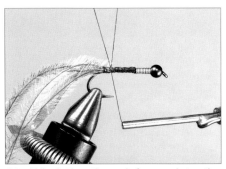

11. Wind the thread forward to the lead. Draw 16 inches of thread off the spool. Double the thread back to the hook and bind over it back to the bend.

9. Spiral the thread up to the lead again. Use the light turn to bind the end of some fine copper wire against the rear of the lead, atop the hook. Add a few tight thread-turns. Hold the wire back over the shank in line as you spiral the thread tightly down the wire and shank to the bend. Add a few tight thread-turns (but not past the tails).

10. Spiral the thread up to just short of the lead, *again*. Even the tips (not the butts, where they were attached to the stem) of two olive ostrich herls and one brown one. Snip off the very tips, about the last half-inch. Using the pinch, bind the tips together atop the shank; the cut tips should abut the lead (just as the ends of the Stretch Flex and copper wire do). Add a few more tight thread-turns to really nail down the ostrich; then hold it back under light tension and slightly raised as you spiral the thread down herls and shank to the bend. Add three tight thread-turns.

11. Spiral the thread up the shank to the rear of the lead. Pull the bobbin back until about 16 inches of thread are exposed. Catch the thread at its center with the first finger of your left hand; then swing the bobbin back to the hook—you want the thread to lie atop the shank at the rear of the lead. Maintain constant light thread-tension throughout this process. Wind a few tight thread-turns around the shank. Now the 16 inches of thread form a loop with both its ends coming from about the same spot on the shank (just behind the lead). Continue holding the loop towards you (wrapped over your first finger) under light tension as you wind the thread tightly down the shank to just short of the bend—now both ends of the loop are secured under turns of thread.

You just formed what most tiers call a "dubbing loop," a loop of tying thread that is normally twisted with a line of dubbing inside or with dubbing spun up one side of the loop. You won't use it with dubbing here, but it's still a dubbing loop in most tiers' minds.

Spiral the thread up the shank and lead to *slightly* past halfway to the bead.

12. From now until you're finished working with the thread-loop and herls, maintain *constant* light tension on the thread-loop.

Wind the three herls lightly up one side of the thread-loop. Five to eight turns should do it—just try to get most of the length of the herls wrapped on.

13. Holding the loop under light tension, pinch the sides of the loop together. Hook the two arms of a dubbing whirl or the single hook of a dubbing twister in the end of the loops as you remove your finger. Make sure you keep tension on the loop and its sides pinched together throughout.

14. The loop is longer than the herls, which allows you to drape the bare thread at the end of the loop over the crook in your bent first finger (whichever first finger you prefer) and let your dubbing whirl or twister hang.

12. Spiral the thread forward to barely past halfway up to the bead. Lightly wind the herls a few times around one side of the thread loop.

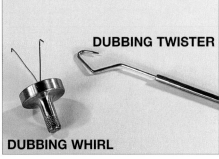

13. Use either a dubbing twister or a dubbing whirl for the next step.

14. Hook the tool into the end of the loop. Drape the loop over your finger, and let the tool hang.

So, go ahead—drape the dubbing loop over your finger. If you are using a dubbing *whirl*, give it a sharp flick and let it spin like a top.

If you're using a dubbing *twister*, lock its hooked end in the loop, and then remove the dubbing loop from your crooked finger. Rotate the twister a few times—just enough to lock the ends of the loop together—and then rotate the twister between thumbs and forefingers of both hands repeatedly. With either tool, you want the herl and thread twisted into a sort of tight fuzzy rope. (But don't twist the loop *too* tight or it will become fragile. As soon as it resembles the twisted loop in the photo with caption #17, stop twisting.)

Clamp the jaws of a pair of English hackle pliers (the plain all-metal ones shown in the photos) onto the twisted loop just down (towards the hook) from the whirl or twister.

Slip the whirl or twister out of the end of the loop—English hackle pliers grip hard, so the loop should stay tightly twisted.

Make sure the copper wire and Stretch Flex are back out of the way (the thread should still be hanging slightly ahead of halfway between the bend and bead), and then wind the herl-rope up the abdomen in touching turns. To bind a minimum of herl-fibers you can stroke back the fibers from each turn of the rope before adding the next turn. It may help further to stroke the fibers with damp fingers. (Damp—not *dripping* fingers. If the herl is really soaked it will turn to mush and be hard to work with.) Use water from a bowl—not saliva—to wet your fingers.

Bind the ends of the herl-rope with a few tight turns of thread, where the thread is hanging. Trim off the end of the herl-rope.

Pull the copper wire off to the far side of the hook. Pull the Stretch Flex forward and down over the top of the herl-abdomen. The Stretch Flex should be under tension, but only *light* tension. Bind the Stretch Flex at the front of the abdomen with plenty of tight thread-turns, at least ten. Draw back the forward end of the Stretch Flex, spiral the thread forward to just short of the bead, lower and bind the Stretch Flex securely just behind the bead, and then trim off the end of the Stretch Flex.

15.
16.
17.
18.
19.
20.
21.
22.

15. Just give a hanging dubbing whirl a spin, like a top, and let it go.

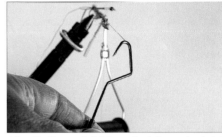

16. Pull a dubbing twister straight towards you, in line with the loop, and rotate it between thumb and finger.

17. Here is how the twisted thread-loop and herl should look.

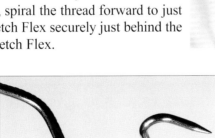

18. When the loop and herls are well twisted, clamp a pair of English hackle pliers onto the thread.

19. Remove the tool from the loop. The pliers will hold the twist.

20. Wind the herl-rope up the shank in touching turns to just past mid-shank.

21. To keep the fibers out and full you can stroke them back after each turn of the herl-rope you wind on. Bind and trim the rope's end.

22. Pull the Stretch Flex forward over the abdomen. Bind the end of the Stretch Flex up to the bead; then trim it off.

23. Wind the copper wire up the abdomen in five to eight ribs. Bind the end of the wire and trim it.

Trim the herl-fibers from the underside of the abdomen.

23. Take up the copper wire and wind it up the abdomen in five to eight ribs. Try to keep the space between the ribs consistent in width, and try to keep the ribs parallel.

The challenge is to keep from binding down the herl under the turns of wire, leaving it full along the side to suggest gills—my test subjects have convinced me that this is the trickiest part of tying this fly. So I'll put my suggestions for winding the rib here, where you can't miss them and where they can help you *as* you tie, rather than after, in the "Problems, Solutions, and Suggestions" section.

Here are my suggestions: Try pushing the point of your bodkin straight up into the ostrich fibers to part them before winding the wire through as a rib; wind the wire neatly into the part. Since you dampened the ostrich before winding it, make sure it is dry and fluffy before winding the rib through it—damp herl will almost surely get trapped under the rib. One problem may be that the Stretch Flex has pushed the herl down one side. If so, undo the windings holding the Stretch Flex and then reposition it square on top before binding it again at the front of the abdomen. Perhaps the Stretch Flex is simply too wide for the abdomen you've made; if so, then trim along both edges of the Stretch Flex to make it a little slimmer. Do this before you bind it at the front of the abdomen. You can even trim the Stretch Flex to a slight taper, a little narrower at the bend than at the front of the abdomen.

Any or all of these suggestions will help you build an abdomen with full and consistent herl-gills running up its sides.

23. (cont.) Okay, back to our fly under construction. When the rib-wire reaches the front of the abdomen, bind it there with plenty of tight thread-turns and then cut off the end of the wire. (For insurance, you can bind the end of the wire a little way up the shank with tight thread-turns.) Stroke the ostrich fibers upward along both sides of the abdomen. Reach in carefully with your scissors' tips and trim the underside of the abdomen to flat—careful you don't trim off the fibers along the sides! Don't get greedy about this trimming; it's better to have gills and a somewhat fluffy underside on the abdomen than a clean underside and scanty gills or none.

Making the Abdomen—
Problems, Solutions, and Suggestions

1. Make sure that you bind the butts of the Stretch Flex, wire, and herls right up against the rear of the lead (so there's no gap) but not up *onto* the lead (so there's no lump in the foundation you're creating).

2. To keep the herls from unwinding from the dubbing loop as you prepare to twist the loop, drape the loop over your bent finger with the last turn of the herls right *on* the finger. Hold the end of the loop down under light pressure (the weight of a dubbing whirl provides enough pressure). Now the herls will stay pinned in place while you go about your tying.

3. Just before (or even just after) you bind the Stretch Flex at the front of the abdomen is an excellent time to check your fly's proportions. Check to make sure the abdomen ends very close to halfway between the bend and the rear of the bead.

Looking at the big picture, the completing of the abdomen or body is usually an excellent time for considering the proportions on many fly patterns—enough of the fly is built that you can judge, but there's still time to adjust.

Making the Thorax

Spiral the thread to just short of the bead. Snip off about an inch and a half of 1/8-inch-wide Stretch Flex. Do *not* trim down the width of *this* length of Stretch Flex. Use a modified pinch (pushing the edges of the Stretch Flex down around the lead) to bind the end of the Stretch Flex atop the hook right behind the bead. Add a few tight thread-turns there. Hold the Stretch Flex back and slightly raised as you wind the thread down it to the front of the abdomen (the rear of the thorax-area). Add a few tight turns of thread to secure the Stretch Flex. If any of the Stretch Flex extends onto the bead, trim it off closely.

Wind the thread forward to slightly—*barely*—short of halfway between the abdomen and the rear of the bead. Strip the fluffy fibers from the base of a dyed partridge (or hen-back) feather. (You can probably get the fibers you need from the remaining body of the partridge feather whose tip you used for the tails.) Stroke the fibers along both sides of the feather's stem out to an angle that evens their tips. Strip the fibers off one side of the stem, then off the other. Leave unstripped the shorter fibers near the feather's tip—too short—and the fluffy ones at its base. Combine all the stripped fibers into one bunch, with all tips fairly even.

Hold the fibers over the hook to measure them, the fibers parallel with the shank and their tips even with the far edge of the eye. Note where the fibers equal half to two thirds the entire *shank's* length.

Hold the fibers atop the thorax-area and bind them, using the pinch, at the half-to-two-thirds point you measured. The fibers should be bound where the thread was hanging (just behind the center of the thorax). Wind tight thread-turns back over the butts of the fibers to just short of the abdomen.

Trim off the butts of the fibers closely.

Grasp the tips of the fiber-bunch and pull the fibers up, and then firmly back. Press your thumbnail down against the base of the fibers; then roll it back to crease the fibers upright at their base.

Hold the fibers back and add tight turns of thread against the front of the fibers. When you release the fibers, they should stand straight up.

Spiral the thread back to the rear of the thorax-area. Spin Arizona Synthetic Peacock Dubbing (or Arizona Synthetic *Bronze* Peacock Dubbing, or any dark-green, dark-olive, or olive-brown dubbing) fairly thinly onto a few inches of the thread. Dub the whole thorax from the front of the abdomen to right up against the rear of the bead. Dub around the standing partridge fibers in the process.

24.

24. Wind the thread forward; bind the end of some 1/8-inch Stretch Flex from the bead back to the abdomen.

25.

25. Measure partridge fibers to half to two thirds of the shank's length.

26.

27.

28.

29.

30.

26. Use the pinch to bind the fibers atop the hook just short of halfway up the thorax-area.

27. Trim off the butts of the partridge fibers.

28. Pull the fibers straight up and crease them firmly at their base with your thumbnail.

29. Add tight thread-turns up against the base of the fibers until they stand upright on their own.

30. Dub the thorax-area, right up to the bead.

31. Look straight down the hook from the front, and divide the fibers in half with your bodkin.

32. Push the fibers firmly down to the sides. Press down hard on the fibers at their base with the flat of your thumbnail or your scissors' closed blades to splay the fibers.

33. Pull the Stretch Flex up, forward, and down atop the thorax. Bind it against the rear of the bead with a narrow thread-collar. Stretch and trim off the Stretch Flex. Whip finish and trim the thread, add head cement to the whip finish.

31. Lower your head and angle it so you're looking straight down the hook; you should be looking directly at the hook's eye. Push your bodkin straight back into the center of the standing fibers.

32. Push the bodkin to one side, separating the fibers into two equal groups. Grasp one group and pull it firmly out to its side. Pull the other group of fibers out to the other side. Now press straight down into the center of the divided fibers firmly with the flat of your thumbnail or the side of your closed scissor blades, to really set the fibers down and splay them.

33. Pull the Stretch flex up and then down atop the dubbed thorax and flattened partridge fibers. Apply only moderate tension to the Stretch Flex—pulling it *tight* will only thin and weaken it. Continue holding the Stretch Flex down and forward with your right hand (as always, right-hander's instructions) as you work a few thread-turns over the Stretch Flex and shank with your left hand (accomplished by draping the bobbin over the top and then pulling it down to tighten the thread each time. Add several tight thread-turns as a collar against the bead. Raise the Stretch Flex firmly, so it thins and stretches, and then cut it close to the bead with the very tips of your scissors.

Add some more thread-turns to the thread-collar to cover the cut end of the Stretch Flex. Make a whip finish on the thread-collar. Trim the thread closely. Add head cement to the thread collar to complete the Anatomical Green Drake.

Making the Thorax—
Problems, Solutions, and Suggestions

1. With a little care (and luck) you were able to preserve most of the fibers remaining on the partridge feather whose tip you used for making the tails. If so, you can grasp the very end of the stem, where it was cut, in the jaws of English hackle pliers and stroke the fibers out to an angle that evens their tips, and then strip them off and use them for the Anatomical Green Drake's legs.

2. It's important that you bind the legs on *barely* short of halfway from the abdomen to the bead. So, once the leg-fibers are bound on, double check this, and then adjust it, by adding or unwinding turns of thread, if necessary.

3. The partridge-legs will splay best if you set them *straight up* with the tight thread-turns against their base. If the partridge angles forward or back, the fibers will tend to bunch together at the sides after you divide them.

4. If you use the Arizona Synthetic Dubbing I use for this fly (rather than a substitute such as Antron dubbing, rabbit...), you'll find it's a bit stiff—stroking fly-tying wax along the thread can really help you manage this dubbing.

CHARTREUSE AND WHITE CLOUSER MINNOW

New Techniques: mounting barbell eyes, making a hair wing with Mylar strips, tying Clouser-style streamers

The Clouser Minnow (originally the Clouser *Deep* Minnow) is so popular, so versatile, so widely trusted for so many fish species that you just *have* to learn to tie it. I myself have caught on it striped bass, crappie, smallmouth bass, rock bass, flounder (honest!), brook trout, silver salmon, largemouth bass, bluegill, sea-run cutthroat trout, black rockfish, and, I'm sure, a few species I've forgotten. The wise fly fisher always carries a few Clousers.

Bob Clouser showed an early version of his Minnow to his friend, fly-fishing icon Lefty Kreh. Together they refined Clouser's prototype into the current design. Tied in various sizes and colors the Clouser Minnow can imitate smallmouth fry, shiners, gobies, and all sorts of small fishes upon which trout and bass and bonefish and other species feed.

But Clousers in such unnatural colors as chartreuse, bright-orange, and purple are—at least in my experience and from my exceedingly modest research—fully as popular as their imitative kin. Lefty Kreh says in his book *Advanced Fly Fishing Techniques* that a Clouser with a white belly and a chartreuse wing has been "very successful" for him "with both largemouth and smallmouth bass." Lefty's word should be good enough for anyone. It's certainly good enough for me, so we'll tie it in these colors. And though I can't say I've yet fished the Chartreuse and White Clouser for freshwater

bass, I have caught scads of fine silver salmon and black rock fish on it in the salt water of the Pacific Northwest.

The most useful size-range and colors for the Clouser Minnow are hard to pin down, simply because the fly works on so many species. I tend to tie it small for smallmouth and a bit larger for largemouth bass, with a dark wing, gold or bronze Krystal Flash and Flashabou under-wing, and white belly in sizes 10 to 6, though many prefer big Clousers for both species. Lefty recommends a size-1/0 hook for bonefish. And I've had solid success fishing sizes 1 and 1/0 for black rockfish running from one to four pounds and Pacific salmon to twelve.

Lefty, who tells us in *Advanced Fly Fishing Techniques* that "in three years" the Clouser Minnow took for him "fifty-eight species of fish around the world," sums up in that same volume the general matter of colors for the fly (what he calls the "underwing" is what I call the belly): "The most effective pattern colors for the Clouser Deep Minnow, I think, are an underwing of white or smoke, with an over-wing of chartreuse; a white underwing with dove gray over-wing; a white underwing with tan or brown over-wing." Take it from Lefty, and Bob Clouser, and, for that matter, from me: the Clouser Minnow belongs in your fly boxes. And if it's there, you'll use it sooner or later, and be glad you did.

CHARTREUSE AND WHITE CLOUSER MINNOW

HOOK: Heavy (or standard) wire, 3X or 4X long, down- or ring-eye, sizes 10 to 2/0.

THREAD: Chartreuse (or white) 8/0 or 6/0, or, for size-6 and up, 3/0.

EYES: Lead or lead-substitute barbell eyes. For hooks size-10 and 8, 1/8- inch diameter; for size-6, 5/32-inch diameter; for size-4, 6/32-inch; size-2, 7/32-inch; for larger hooks than these—big. (These are my general recommendations, but don't be bound by them.)

BELLY: White buck tail.

UNDER-WING: Pearl Krystal Flash and pearl Flashabou (but options include gold, brown, yellow—really, any color for this or other Clousers).

WING: Dyed-chartreuse buck tail.

1. Eyes for Clouser Minnows, from the left: lead, pre-painted lead, nickel-plated lead. Others come and go.

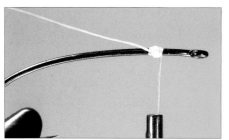

2. Start the thread and build a ball of thread about 1/8-inch back from the eye. Cut off the end of the thread.

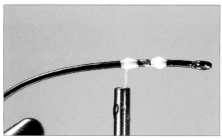

3. Wind the thread back another 1/16-inch and build a second-thread-ball.

4. Bind barbell-eyes atop the shank between the thread-balls. Wind from the rear of the eye-stem to the front.

5. Hold the eyes out to the sides and wind plenty of tight thread-turns both ways.

Binding on the Eyes

Smash down the barb on a size-6, heavy (or standard) wire, 3X or 4X long hook; the hook should have either a down- or ring-eye (an up-eye will result in a fly that doesn't tend to properly invert in water). The hook's shank can be straight or the lightly arched French-curve style. (The hook shown in the photos is a Daichii 1260.) Mount the hook in your vise. Start the thread 1/8-inch back from the hook's eye, as a narrow band. Build a little ball of thread all in one place, as in the photo. The ball should now be about 1/8-inch back from the hook's eye. Cut off the tag-end of the thread.

This thread-ball and the next one will cradle the barbell-eyes, so it may seem to you that the eyes will be awfully far back and that the thread-head will be overlong—don't worry about it. You need the eyes well back to tie a decent Clouser, and a long and large head here is required to secure the slippery buck tail and—please, trust me—will look good on the finished fly.

Spiral the thread back at least 1/16-inch; then build a second thread-ball about the same size as the first one.

Hold a pair of 5/32-inch-diameter barbell eyes atop the shank; their stem should lie in the depression between the two thread-balls, crossways to the shank. Wind five moderate-tension thread-turns over the eye-stem, from the rear of the stem, over the top, and down in front of the stem. Wind the thread in the normal direction—the bobbin going away over the hook; towards you under the hook. Pressure from the thread-turns will turn the near eye forward and the far eye back. No problem.

Force the eyes straight out to the sides now, so that the eye-stem lies at a right angle to the hook's shank. Wind five thread-turns over the stem from the other angle—from the *front* of the stem, over the top, and down the rear of the stem. Again, wind the thread in the normal direction. The eyes should now stay more or less at a right angle to the shank.

It's time to *really* lock the eyes in place. Wind three to five more thread-turns—*tight* thread-turns—from the back to the front of the eyes' stem. This will kick the far eye back and the near eye forward. Wind the same number of tight turns the other way, from front to back, as the eyes shift angle again. Keep winding turns and switching directions until the eyes are solidly locked in place and are straight out to the sides. (You can always twist them around the shank with enough pressure, but you want the eyes as secure as reasonably possible.)

Sight down the front of the shank to see if the stem of the barbell-eyes is level. Twist it firmly to level if need be.

Binding on the Eyes—
Problems, Solutions, and Suggestions

1. This bears repeating: when building the thread-balls, and mounting the eyes, be sure you leave the full 1/8-inch behind the hook's eye I recommended. It's okay for a minnow imitation like the Clouser to have a long head, but you'll wind up struggling to bind in the hair and create a neat head if you don't leave enough room for it on this fly.

2. Guidelines for making the balls of thread by thread-size: 8/0, about 25 thread-turns; 6/0, 16 to 20 turns; 3/0, 10 to 15 turns. These may vary with different brands of thread, but they should be close.

3. I used to struggle to keep barbell eyes straight out to the sides as I bound them on—a waste of energy and time. They don't have to start out perpendicular to the shank; they only have to *end up* that way. So, don't make my mistake. Let the eyes angle as they will; then work them straight out to the sides with lots of tight crisscrossing turns of thread, as described above.

Creating the Belly

Wind the thread to just behind the stem of the barbell eyes. Snip a thin bunch of white buck tail off the hide—don't take much. Use the photos as a guide. Do not even the hair in a hair-stacking tool; instead, hold the bunch of hair in your left hand, and then grasp about the last 1/2-inch of the hair's tips with your right-hand thumb and first finger. Draw out these longest hairs from the main bunch. Return these hairs to the main bunch with their tips about even with the tips of the longest remaining hairs—this is called hand stacking. But stack the hair only a little, two to four times. The Clouser Minnow is best tied with only roughly stacked hair.

Measure the hair along the hook. Note the point where the hair is about two times the full length of the hook.

Using the pinch, bind the hair at its measured point atop the shank just behind the stem of the barbell eyes with ten *tight* thread-turns. Try to keep the turns all in about the same place, as a thread collar. The butts of the hair should now be pushed up against the stem of the eyes and should be angling up, as in the photograph.

Wind the thread forward *under* the shank and eyes to just ahead of the eye-stem. Grasp the butts of the hair with your right-hand thumb and fingers and pull the butts down. Hold the butts horizontal under light tension (this step will be more difficult if they tip up or down). Work three turns of thread over the butts by repeatedly draping the bobbin down the far side of the hook and then raising it up the near side. Hold the hair-butts firmly in place as you pull the thread-turns tight. Grasp the hook behind the barbell eyes with your left hand now and add five more tight turns to really secure the butts.

Grasp the butts and raise them firmly. Slip in the tips of your scissors and trim off the butts. Trim the butts some more, at an angle, to taper them down towards the eye (unless they already happen to taper). Bind the butts at least partly with tight thread-turns.

Creating the Belly—
Problems, Solutions, and Suggestions

1. Generally, a sparse Clouser Minnow is the most lively and quickest to sink, and fishes best overall. Most tiers use too much hair (in fact, *way* too much hair) for both the belly and the wing. For some species, a little extra fullness is best (Lefty has told me that a thin, but-thicker-than-usual Clouser is best for largemouth bass). Still, go thin, and when in doubt, thinner, on the hair. In his book *Advanced Fly Fishing Techniques*, Lefty says that "on a size 2, the total wing, when compressed, should have a diameter no larger than a barn-burner wooden match." Size-2—that's a big Clouser—and a wing only as thick as a wooden match. Get it?

6.

6. Snip a thin bunch of white hair off a buck tail. You can hand-stack the hair a little—but not much.

7.

7. Bind the hair atop the shank directly behind the stem of the barbell-eyes.

8.

8. Advance the thread to just ahead of the eye-stem. Bind the hair-butts there.

9.

9. Trim off the butts of the hair and trim them to a taper. Bind the butts.

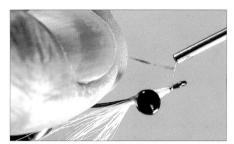

10. Invert the hook. Loop two Flashabou strands over the thread and slide them down to the hook.

11. Hold the strands back and bind them back atop the shank.

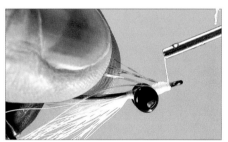

12. Loop two strands of *Krystal Flash* over the thread and bind them as you did the Flashabou.

13. Bind a slim bunch of chartreuse buck tail atop the hook. Bind it ahead of the eye-stem only.

14. Trim the butts of the hair to a taper. Bind all the butts and build a thread-head.

2. Make the forward bindings of the belly-hair back *close* to the eye-stem—this will leave you plenty of room for binding the hair-butts and, later, building the thread-head.

3. At first, you may want to trim the hair-butts to a taper with several careful snips—insurance that the job is done well. In time, though, a single well-planned snip may be just right.

Adding the Under-Wing and Wing

Remove the hook from your vise, invert the hook, and then mount it again in the vise's jaws. (Or just flip the jaws upside down, if you have the sort of rotary vise that keeps the hook's shank horizontal.) The bend of the hook should now be up and the barbell eyes should lie below the shank. Wind the thread to halfway between the hook's eye and the stem of the barbell eyes, double two strands of pearl Flashabou over the thread. Hold the bobbin directly above the fly with the thread under moderate-tension. Slide the strands down the thread to the top of the hook. Swing the bobbin down the far side of the hook to secure the loops of Flashabou atop it.

Hold the thread down firmly, pull the strands back and down over the shank, and then wind four tight turns of thread back to secure all the strands. Because the strands are doubled, you now have four ends streaming back. Do not yet trim the strands.

Put all the ends of the Flashabou strands back in the materials clip. Double two strands of pearl Krystal Flash over the thread and then bind them exactly as you bound the Flashabou.

Wind the thread to just ahead of the stem of the barbell eyes. Snip a sparse bunch of dyed-chartreuse hair from a buck tail. Hold the hair near the tips and pull out the shortest fibers, as you did with the belly hair. *Hand* stack the bunch a little as described for the belly hair, if you wish, but as before, you don't want the tips *too* even. Measure the hair along the hook. Find the point on the hair where it equals two full hook-lengths.

Bind the hair-bunch at it's measured point atop the hook, in front of the barbell eyes. (The eyes make the standard pinch impractical, so use a reverse pinch, the hair in your right hand, left hand draping and working the bobbin.) The hair should be bound just ahead of the stem of the eyes. Add seven to ten tight thread-turns as a narrow collar, to really secure the hair.

Trim the butts of the hair to taper from the thread-collar down to just short of the hook's eye. Bind all the cut butts with lots of tight thread-turns. Whip finish the thread and cut its end.

Draw the Flashabou and Krystal Flash back off the hook's bend. Trim all the strands about 1/4-inch past the tips of the longest hairs. The Flashabou strands will probably droop from the wing. Trim the Flashabou and Krystal Flash strands to various lengths from about half the length of the wing out to the two to four strands you'll leave extending roughly 1/4-inch beyond the wing. Add head cement to the thread-head, to complete the Clouser Minnow.

Adding the Under-Wing and Wing— Problems, Solutions, and Suggestions

1. When you invert the hook, don't mount the hook so deep in the vise-jaws that your tying access is impaired.

2. If you draw all the hair upwards, well away from the shank, before mounting the now-inverted hook in your vise, the jaws cannot crush and break off any of the buck-tail hairs.

3. A good way to remove strands of Krystal Flash and Flashabou from the package is to cut off one corner of the plastic bag (at the end of the bag where the strands are doubled), tease out a few strands with your bodkin, and then tease the strands out of the bag with a bodkin or closed scissor blades.

4. Remember what I said earlier under the heading, "Creating the Belly—Problems, Solutions, and Suggestions"—a sparse wing is nearly always best on a Clouser Minnow.

15. Whip finish and cut the thread. Trim the ends of the Mylar strands to various lengths, some slightly longer than the wing.

MORRIS MINNOW, BROWN

New Techniques: building a fly-body in sections, trimming a minnow-fly body, making and painting an epoxy-coated thread-head and a Mylar-tubing head

I've expected great things of fly designs that fish soundly rejected, and I've judged as hopeless others that proved themselves to be killers and then sailed to popularity—this has taught me that it's unwise to guess at a fly pattern's effectiveness. So I'm glad I'd learned to keep an open mind by the time I stood on a stream-bank considering the first version of my Morris Minnow. The fly had a fish-shape and sparkled like a little trout's sequin-scales—*like* the scales, but at a noticeably higher intensity. I considered declaring the pattern a too-detectable impostor on the spot and relegating it to the Nice Try category of failed fly-designs without ever putting it in the water. But experience told me to tie it on and toss it out there anyway. So I did, now and then, and caught most of my biggest river trout on it, in one of its evolutionary stages or another, over the next few years.

Teased along the cut bank of a winding Colorado river it took me a four-pound cutthroat, intensely yellow along its flanks, slashes of deep-crimson nearly covering its cheeks. In Oregon's Williamson River it accounted for the best fish of the day, a thick five-pound rainbow. Guide Lynn Hescock told me to work the fly down into a deep slot between two high, gnarled lava-rock walls whose tops lay just below the swirling surface of the water. I did, and felt the fly stop with a living thump. September before last, a great silver-white deep-bodied rainbow trout as furious and as strong per pound as any I've hooked grabbed a current version of my Morris Minnow in a wide Alaska river and exploded up out of fast water with the fly. It then charged downstream stripping out most of my ample backing so rapidly that I could

think only to run in pursuit. I kept a little backing, worked the fish in, lost nearly all the backing again in another wild run, and after more of this eventually drew the fish over the lip of guide Patricia Edel's broad net, a quarter mile downstream from where the trout struck. We watched the fly drop from the upper jaw of the twelve-pound fish—the hook's point had broken off, leaving barely enough of the bend to hold anything, much less a crazy huge trout with iron flanks.

Clearly, this somewhat overly shiny fly is fine with trout, especially *big* trout.

That's reasonable when you consider that the real juvenile trout this fly imitates are, if not quite so brilliant as the fly, certainly metallic bright. And the rest of the fly is perfectly plausible: a dark back graduating down to a properly pale underside, a tapered head with lots of detail (inspired by Hal Janssen's Janssen's Minnow), well-defined eyes, and an overall fish-shape. And all that waving Mylar.

The big secret with this fly is to tie it on with a loop knot and retrieve it with twitches—then it waggles and swims with such natural ease that you're tempted to believe it's a fish yourself.

Lots of flies, especially saltwater flies, have epoxy-coated heads, some of which are painted, and you'll learn to both paint flies and coat them with clear epoxy here.

I tend to tie my Minnow small, sizes 10 and 8, when the trout are mostly 12 to 16 inches long. When I'm specifically hunting big trout and I know they're there, I go to size 6 and up. These sizes apply not only to the brown-trout version we'll tie here but to all the Morris Minnows that imitate trout.

MORRIS MINNOW, BROWN

HOOK: Heavy wire, standard length to 3X long, straight eye, sizes 10 to 2 (a bass-bug hook is optional).

THREAD: Light-tan or cream (or yellow) 6/0 or 3/0.

WEIGHT: Lead or lead-substitute wire.

BODY: Fine medium-brown Mylar strands (Angel Hair, Lite Brite...) on top, tan or light-brown Mylar along the sides, and yellow or dark-yellow Mylar for the belly.

HEAD: The working thread, or copper (or bronze or gold) Mylar tubing, painted with kids' acrylic paints, poster paints, or such, and coated with epoxy. (Option: plastic or Mylar eyes.)

Adding the Lead

Smash down the barb on a size 4, 1X or 2X long, heavy wire hook—with a *straight eye*. A down-turned eye will tend to make the fly flip upside down. (The hook shown here is a Daiichi 2141.) Because the head will block a little of the gape, and because that blockage won't be much different on small hooks than on big ones, longer-shank hooks are really for the largest Morris Minnows. So you could probably use a 3X long shank for this size-4 hook if you wanted. Conversely, shorter-shank hooks with their big bites are best for smaller Minnows. Another option is to use a stout bass-bug hook with its exceptionally wide gape.

Anyway, once you've chosen a hook, smash down it's barb and mount the hook in your vise. Start the thread 1/16-inch back from the eye, and break off the tag-end of the thread. Spiral the thread halfway down the shank to the bend.

Wind 0.025-inch lead or lead-substitute wire from the center of the shank forward to 1/8-inch short of the eye. The turns of wire should abut one another, gathered together rather than spread over the shank. Break off the ends of the wire.

Breaking off the ends of the lead wire should have pulled them down against the shank. But if the ends of the wire stick out at all, press the ends of the wire in, to lie close to the shank, using your thumbnail or the flats of your scissors. It's important the ends of the wire lie close to the shank.

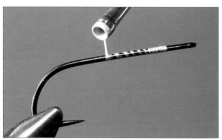

1. Start the thread back from the eye. Spiral the thread tightly back to the center of the shank.

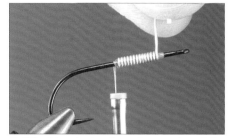

2. Wind lead-wire from the center of the shank forward to 1/8-inch behind the eye. Break off the ends of the wire.

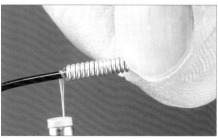

3. If the ends of the wire stick out, press them down against the shank.

Adding the Lead— Problems, Solutions, and Suggestions

1. You can make the lead-windings shorter or longer if you like (although they should always end well back from the eye). The only snag is that the lead helps build the head, so if you shorten the lead-windings you must also make a shorter head. If you lengthen the lead-windings, you'll probably have to make the second section of Mylar strands *on* the lead rather than behind the lead on the shank—this probably doesn't make sense now, but it will soon.

Building the First Mylar-Section

Cut a bunch of fine tannish or light-brown Mylar strands (I used Angel Hair in "Light Brown" here). The strands should be at least five inches long. How much Mylar? If you bunch the strands together in the center, then pinch them firmly, the bunch should be about 1/16-inch to 3/32-inch wide right at your pinching fingertips; also, study the photos. Using a sort of side-pinch, bind the Mylar bunch at about its center on the *far* side of the shank, 1/8-inch ahead of the bend. Hold the strands back along the far side of the shank and bind them back to the bend. Now one end of the strands should project back down the shank and off the bend and the other end forward off the eye, and about the same distance in each direction from the point at which they're bound on at the bend. Wind the thread forward to 1/8-inch ahead of the bend.

Draw the forward end of the Mylar strands over the shank and towards you, then back along the *near* side of the shank. Bind the strands back to the bend.

4. Bind a small bunch of fine tannish Mylar strands along 1/8-inch of the far side of the shank, at the bend.

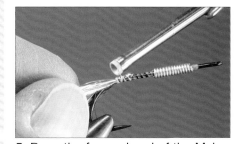

5. Draw the forward end of the Mylar-bunch over the shank to the near side of the shank and bind them back.

6. Spiral the thread forward to 1/8-inch up from the bend.

7. Use the pinch to bind fine brown Mylar strands atop the shank.

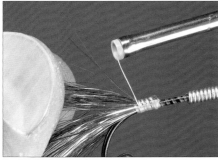

8. Spiral the thread forward 1/8-inch up from the bend. Draw the front ends of the brown Mylar back and bind them back to the bend.

9. Use a modified right-hand pinch to bind some fine yellow Mylar strands under the shank. Draw the front of the Mylar bunch back under the shank and bind it to the bend.

6. Spiral the thread forward up the shank 1/8-inch.

7. Use the pinch to bind a five-inch-long bunch of fine medium-brown Mylar (I used Angel Hair in "copper" here) *atop* the shank, 1/8-inch ahead of the bend. Bind the Mylar back to the bend.

8. Spiral the thread forward 1/8-inch (to where you bound on this bunch of Mylar). Draw the forward end of the strands up and tightly back, and bind them back to the bend. Now the brown Mylar on top is doubled back and bound, so that all of it projects back off the bend, over the tannish Mylar.

9. Use a sort of modified reverse pinch (making the pinch with your right hand) to bind a five-inch bunch of fine yellow Mylar strands (I used Angel Hair in "yellow" here) *under* the shank as you bound the medium-brown Mylar on top—bound on and then doubled back and bound over 1/8-inch of the shank.

Now you have lots of fine Mylar strands streaming back off the bend in brown-trout colors: brown on the back, tan along the sides, and yellow for the belly. That's one Mylar-section completed. You'll make two more.

Building the First Mylar-Section— Problems, Solutions, and Suggestions

1. Fine Mylar can come out of the package messy. To align the strands and even their ends, stroke a hank of them and keep putting the strands that come out back with and in line with the main bunch until the strands are all roughly aligned with their ends fairly even.

2. A little water from a bowl on your tying bench can really help you tame the Mylar, help you keep it back out of your way. Just stroke the water through the strands and they'll stay put.

The trick is to use just *a tiny amount* of water, and to keep the water away from the head-area. Thing is, you don't want the head at all wet when you later coat it with epoxy glue. Water seems to spoil the cure of epoxy, making it set up gummy, appear cloudy, or both. (Once the epoxy is hard, though, water won't bother it, and neither will much else.)

3. You can make the Mylar-section thicker if you like. The resulting body will be more substantial, but it will move less freely in the water than the thinner body in the photos. This rule applies not only to this Mylar section, but to the other two as well. (The completed fly shown on page 46 is dense, tied with lots of Mylar, so you can see the difference.)

4. A quick and efficient way to bind the Mylar strands for the back and underside each time is to loop the strands over the thread, slide the looped end down the thread to the shank, lower the bobbin (and thread), wind a turn of thread to secure the Mylar, hold the thread down firmly as you hold the ends of the strand-loop lightly back, and then bind back over the Mylar. This won't work for the tannish side-strands, of course, since the two ends of the strands must be bound along different sides of the shank.

5. As you hold the strands back so that you can bind them down the shank, hold them back firmly, so they stay where you want them, but not with so much tension that they stretch and deform or break.

6. You can hold the strands out from the shank a bit as you bind back over them; this may help you control their position.

Building the Second Mylar-Section

Spiral the thread up to the lead-windings and bind the wire (as you did in the chapter titled "Prince Nymph." Of course, you could have bound the wire as soon as you wound it on if you'd wanted). With the thread just 1/32 inch short of the rear of the lead-windings (in other words, just *barely* short of the lead) use the pinch to bind another section of the tannish Mylar strands against the far side of the hook there. Bind the section at its center. This bunch should be about 3 1/2-inches long. Bind the strands back along the far side of the shank 1/8-inch. Wind the thread forward to 1/32 inch behind the lead.

Pull the front ends of the strands over the top of the shank and back along the near side of the shank. Bind back over the strands 1/8-inch.

Bind another section of brown Mylar strands atop the shank just behind the lead, a section about 3 1/2-inches long. Double the forward end of the Mylar bunch back and bind it back 1/8-inch.

Bind a 3 1/2-inch bunch of yellow Mylar strands under the shank, doubled back along 1/8-inch of the shank.

Now you've completed the second of the three Mylar-strand sections. This section, like the last one, should have brown Mylar on top, tan along the sides, and yellow underneath.

10.

11.

12.
13.

14.

10. Bind the lead wire.
Bind a section of tannish Mylar strands along the far side of the hook, from the rear of the lead to about 1/8-inch back.

11. Draw the front end of the Mylar bunch over the shank and back along the shank's near side. Bind it back 1/8-inch.

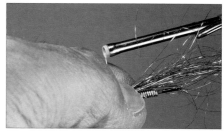

12. Bind a bunch of the brown Mylar atop the shank from the lead back about 1/8-inch.

13. Double the front of the brown Mylar back over the shank and bind it back 1/8-inch.

14. Bind a doubled section of yellow Mylar strands along the underside of the shank, back 1/8-inch.

Building the Second Mylar-Section— Problems, Solutions, and Suggestions

1. Stroking back all the strands from the first Mylar-section, especially the yellow belly-strands, really clears the way for making the second section close behind the lead.

2. You don't want the rear of the second Mylar-section back too close to the front of the first Mylar-section—if it is too close, the bulk of the first section will push against the strands of the second section and angle them out. The fly will look better if the strands from the second section lie back close to the shank. So make sure there's some space between the sections. Here are three solutions if your problem is that the strands from the second Mylar-section are up against the bindings for the first section:

*Make sure you bind all the strands for the second section up close to the lead.

*Make the bindings for the second Mylar-section slightly shorter than 1/8-inch (but not much shorter, or the thread may slip off the Mylar allowing the fly to loosen and come apart).

*Start the the lead-windings *slightly* forward of the center of the shank. You'll wind up making a shorter thread-head this way, but that's no big deal.

Building the Last Mylar-Section

You'll build this final Mylar-section a little differently than the others.

15. Spin dubbing onto a few inches of the thread.

16. Dub over the lead, end to end, but do not dub past either its front or rear ends.

17. Bind some tannish Mylar against the far side of the shank, in front of the lead.

18. Hold the rear end of the Mylar strands back along the dubbing. Press the strands down against the dubbing. Spiral the thread back over the Mylar strands and dubbing to the rear end of the lead-windings.

15. Begin with the thread hanging from the rear of the lead-windings. Spin some dubbing onto the thread. Any tannish dubbing will do, natural or synthetic—rabbit, Antron dubbing... The point of the dubbing is simply to fill out the head-area (although there's an advantage to using *tan* dubbing: should any of it peek through the Mylar strands, it will blend in.

16. Dub forward over the lead. Build the dubbing thick from the rear to the center of the lead, and then taper it down a bit to the front of the lead. Stop dubbing at the front of the lead; do not dub *in front* of the lead. Make the dubbing fairly full, to provide a foundation for an appropriately large head (and remember that the dubbing will compress down noticeably as you build the Mylar-section back over it).

17. Wind the thread forward to right in front of the lead-windings. Use the pinch to bind a 3 1/2-inch-long bunch of the tannish Mylar strands there, on the far side of the shank. Bind the bunch at its center. Add a few tight thread-turns to really secure the Mylar; try to keep the thread-turns all close up against the front of the lead.

18. Draw the Mylar strands back along the far side of the lead and shank and pinch them down flat against the lead. Spiral the thread back over the strands and dubbing to the rear of the lead-windings—but be sure you don't wind the thread back *beyond* the lead.

19. Spiral the thread forward to the front of the lead (but no further). Draw the forward end of the tan Mylar back along the near side of the dubbed lead. Pinch the Mylar to hold it back and to spread the strands. Spiral the thread back down the Mylar and shank to the rear of the lead (but no further).

20. Spiral the thread forward to right in front of the lead-windings.

21. Use the pinch to bind a 3 1/2-inch bunch of the brown Mylar strands right in front of the lead, on top of the shank. Bind the Mylar bunch at about its center. Add a few tight thread-turns close to the lead to really secure the Mylar.

19. Press the front of the Mylar bunch back along the near side of the dubbing. Bind it back to the rear of the lead.

20. Spiral the thread to right in front of the lead-windings.

21. Use the pinch to bind brown Mylar strands atop the shank in front of the lead.

Hold the rear end of the brown Mylar bunch down atop the dubbing. Press the strands down flat against the dubbing, so the strands spread a bit, to help them cover the dubbing and shank behind the lead.

Spiral the thread back over the brown Mylar and dubbed lead to the rear of the lead. Add a couple of tight thread-turns at the rear of the lead, and then spiral the thread forward over the lead most of the way to its front end.

Draw the front end of the brown Mylar up and back atop the lead and atop the other end of the brown Mylar. Press the Mylar down flat again and spiral the thread back to the rear of the lead.

Spiral the thread forward to just in front of the lead-windings.

Using a sort of modified pinch, bind a 3 1/2-inch section of the yellow Mylar fibers up under the shank right in front of the lead. Add a few tight thread-turns to really secure the Mylar. Try to keep the turns gathered and back close to the front of the lead.

Press the rear end of the yellow Mylar, the end that projects back, up against the underside of the dubbing-covered lead-windings. Spiral the thread back over the Mylar and dubbed lead to the rear of the lead (but not *beyond* the rear of the lead-windings). Add a couple of tight thread-turns there. Spiral the thread forward most of the way up the lead.

Draw the front end of the yellow Mylar back up against the other end of the yellow Mylar that is already projecting back. Spiral the thread down the dubbed lead again, and the Mylar, to the rear of the lead, and add a couple of tight thread-turns there.

Cover the entire head-area (from the eye back to, but not beyond, the rear of the dubbing-covered lead-windings) with tight thread-turns. Leave no dubbing or bound Mylar exposed—cover it all with thread. Whip finish the thread and trim it.

Now the final Mylar-section is completed.

Building the Last Mylar-Section— Problems, Solutions, and Suggestions

1. Make sure the dubbed lead is larger in diameter than the bindings holding the second Mylar-section—if the second section's bindings stick out beyond the dubbing, the Mylar for the last section will angle out from the body rather than lying neatly down against it.

2. If your Mylar strands aren't covering the rear of the head and hiding the shank, bind them lightly, tug them apart (that is, spread them), and then add some tight thread-turns.

3. You can use more Mylar than in the photos if you like, which will result in a Mylar body that is fuller and more substantial than it would be with less Mylar, but also less lively (like the finished fly on page 46).

4. Getting the thread to spiral back from the front of the lead up onto the dubbed lead can be tricky. The solution: angle the thread steeply back and apply constant tension. The thread should ride easily up and back.

5. If the thread keeps slipping down the front of the head-area as you cover it with thread, try building a bunch of really *tight* turns from the eye back to the front of the lead—these thread-turns will act as an anchor so that you can build back over the head-taper with turns of *modest*-tension.

6. After you've covered the head-area with thread, check it top, bottom, and sides for gaps where dubbing or Mylar show through, and then cover those gaps with thread-turns.

22. Spiral the thread down the rear end of the Mylar back to the rear of the lead.

23. Draw back the front end of the brown Mylar and spiral the thread down it to the rear of the lead-windings.

24. Bind yellow Mylar strands under the shank, right in front of the lead. Bind both ends of the strands back under the dubbed lead to the rear of the lead.

25. Cover the entire head-area, from the eye to the rear of the lead, with thread-turns. Whip finish, then trim the thread.

26. Hold the hook and trim the Mylar straight up at the rear, two shank-lengths back from the rear end of the shank.

27. Trim the top of the Mylar to taper back with a fish-shape.

28. Trim the underside of the Mylar to a fish-shape.

29. Tug the Mylar out along the sides. Trim the side-Mylar to a slim fish-body shape.

30. Coat the thread-covered head-area lightly and evenly with epoxy glue.

Trimming the Body

26.

It's time to give all that shiny Mylar a fish-shape. Remove the hook from your vise and hold the hook by its bend or head in either hand. Measure the hook's shank with the tips of your open scissors. Now measure to find the point where the Mylar extends two shank's lengths past the bend (where the bend meets the shank). Make a vertical cut at this measured point.

27.

Trim the top of the Mylar back from the head to the trimmed ends of the strands. A generally horizontal cut, curving slowly, in line with the shank. The top of the Mylar should bow slightly up, like a real fish's back.

28.

Trim along the underside of the Mylar to make a similar line to the one you cut along the top. Leave a little blunt end at the rear of the Mylar, to suggest a tail.

Turn the hook so that you're looking down on top of it. Tug the Mylar out along one side of the shank.

Trim the tugged-out Mylar fairly close to the hook, tapering in slightly towards the rear.

29.

Tug out and then trim the other side of the Mylar. Your hook with Mylar strands should now resemble a slim fish, a fish with a peculiar head...if you'd call it a head. The next steps will make the head the most convincing part of this fly.

Trimming the Body— Problems, Solutions, and Suggestions

1. If you're concerned about trout grabbing the tail of your Minnow and missing the hook's point, trim the fly shorter, up to 1/2-inch shorter.

2. I always find it easiest to trim the Mylar working forward, from the rear end towards the head.

3. When you tug out the Mylar along the sides of the shank, try not to tug out much of the Mylar from the first bunch that's bound back to the bend—this bunch creates much of the rear half of the body, so you don't want to trim too much of it away.

Painting and Completing the Head

Thoroughly mix some two-part epoxy glue. (Information on selecting epoxy glue and working with it safely are on page 32, in the chapter titled "Copper John.")

Hold the hook and coat the fly's thread-head thinly with the epoxy glue. Try to keep the glue *barely* short of the eye in front and *barely* short of the Mylar in back. The best way I know to control the glue is to build

30.

a small rim of epoxy around the rear of the thread-covered head-area, and then tease the epoxy forward, adding more as needed. When the whole head-area is coated, I wipe off much of the glue using the same toothpick I used to mix and apply the epoxy, cleaning off the toothpick on a piece of paper as needed. Again—keep this first coating fairly thin.

Put the hook into an electric fly-drying wheel or push the fly into a board and keep flipping the board as the epoxy cures.

When the epoxy is nearly cured (fairly firm but still tacky), mount the hook in your vise (or just hold it by its bend). Paint the epoxy-coated head with almost any paint. Kid's non-toxic paints are the cheapest and easiest to find—poster paints, acrylics, even watercolors. Epoxy contains no water, so the second coating won't make these paints run. I use toothpicks to paint the head, a different toothpick for each color. Keep the paint fairly thin.

Paint the top of the head medium-brown, a sort of wide stripe stretching from the hook's eye almost to the Mylar; leave the sides unpainted tannish thread; and paint the belly as a yellow stripe. When these paints are dry, make red or black gill slits, and yellow or white eyes with black pupils (I used white here, yellow for the finished fly at the start of the chapter). Add dots, mostly black and a few red, over the back and down the sides. (See the illustration on the right.) Mix the paints if necessary to get the colors about right. Let all this paint dry thoroughly.

Mix another batch of epoxy. Coat the head as before—a fairly thin coating—and turn the fly in an electric rotating wheel or in a board you flip regularly. When the epoxy is set, the fly is completed.

Painting and Completing the Head— Problems, Solutions, and Suggestions

1. If the thread-foundation for the head is lumpy, the head will probably be lumpy too. You can *lightly* press down any lumps with smooth-jaw pliers, round nose or flat nose. (Serrated jaws may cut the thread.)

2. Ideally, the head should extend back far enough to cover the lead, but no further. To check this you can press down the Mylar to feel for the lead, or pull the strands up to see the lead's end.

Making the Alternate Mylar-Tubing Head

An epoxy-coated thread-head is easier to make than a Mylar-tubing head, and the trout probably won't care which one you choose—but the Mylar-tubing head just looks *so* sharp! Okay, I confess: this is really about pleasing you rather than about convincing the fish. So...welcome to fly tying.

The Mylar-tubing head tends to extend down and block the gape. The cure is to use tubing that's not overlarge in diameter and to use a really wide-gape hook—the Daiichi 2141 will work fine if you control the Mylar-head well, but now, especially, consider using a wide-mouth bass-bug hook like the Tiemco 8089 in the photos with captions 33 through 41.

To make the Mylar-tubing head, tie the fly up to the point that the body is built and trimmed to shape (up through caption and photo #29), although you needn't cover the head-area thoroughly with thread as before, since the tubing will hide all that. The thread should be hanging just back from the eye. Cut off about a 7/8-inch section of the tubing. Carefully slide out the soft core (tweezers help) trying not to unravel the ends of the tubing.

Bind one end of the tubing just behind the hook's eye. The bulk of the tubing should extend to your right, away from the rest of the hook. Bind the tubing by about 1/8-inch of its cut edge. You'll probably need to hold the tubing in your right hand while you drape the bobbin over the tubing with your left hand (although it's possible to hold the edge of the tubing with your left hand and work the bobbin and thread with your right).

31.

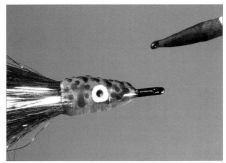

31. When the epoxy is nearly cured, paint the head.

PAINTING THE HEAD

32.

Black Spots, Some Red, over top and sides

Medium Brown

Eyes, Yellow (or White) with Black Pupils

Tan Thread

Red or Black Gills   Yellow

32. When the paint is dry, coat the head thinly again with epoxy.

33.

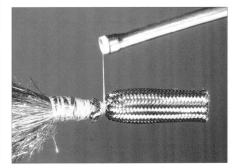

33. To make a Mylar-tubing head, bind a short section of tubing by its edge just behind the hook's eye.

34. Bind back the unravelled ends of the tubing, whip finish the thread and cut it.

35. Push the Mylar back over the head-area, turning the tubing inside out.

36. Coat the tubing with epoxy. When the epoxy is nearly hard, trim the rear edge of the tubing.

34. Once you've got a couple of tight thread-turns over the tubing, hold the edge of the Mylar behind the eye and wind on more tight turns of thread. Bind back over the Mylar ends, whip finish and then cut the thread.

35. Push the tubing back over the head-area, turning the tubing inside-out. Try not to unravel the tubing as you do this.

36. Coat the tubing with epoxy as before, back to about the center of the shank. When the epoxy is mostly cured but still slightly soft, trim its rear edge, neatly, at about mid-shank, cutting either just short of the epoxy or slightly into it. Push the Mylar-tubing head firmly up, from its underside, with the flats of your closed scissor blades or something similar (best not to handle the epoxy until it's fully cured). The nearly hard epoxy should hold the head up in its new higher position.

37. Paint the head now, as previously described. If you want to use Mylar or plastic adhesive-backed eyes, press them onto the sides of the head now (I used Mylar eyes in the photos). Leave some of the Mylar tubing unpainted, especially where it's color blends with the body's color. Coat the head with epoxy again, but stay just short of the rear edge of the tubing and keep the coating thin. Turn the fly until the epoxy hardens, as described earlier.

Making the Alternate Mylar-Tubing Head—Problems, Solutions, and Suggestions

1. To bind the tubing, you may need to unravel its end slightly to get the thread over its strands, but that normally happens on its own—the challenge is typically to keep the tubing from unravelling *too much.*

2. If the tubing rotates around the shank as you tighten the thread, let it rotate. This may help you tighten the thread and secure the tubing.

3. Turning the tubing inside out without unravelling it is tricky. So, be patient (that really helps), and stroke the tubing a few times to coax it gradually down the shank and inside out. Trying to complete the operation in one hard push can make a mess of things.

37. Paint the head. Coat the head thinly with epoxy. Turn the fly until the epoxy is fully cured.

38. To make a Morris Minnow with a metal cone, mount the cone and tie the fly behind it. Lead-windings are optional.

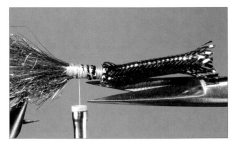

39. Bind the tubing on right behind the cone. Whip finish and cut the thread.

40. Push the Mylar tubing back, inside out.

41. Complete the tubing-head as before, but paint the cone too. I used plastic adhesive-backed eyes here.

MARABOU MUDDLER, BROWN

New Techniques: making a hair-tip collar, flaring hair, spinning hair, shaping hair, tying the basic Muddler-style fly

The Muddler Minnow is probably tied and fished even more often today than when it became a hit clear back in the early 50s. However, with a nod of respect to the beloved original version, I chose to demonstrate a variation: the *Marabou Muddler*. The original—good as it is—has always struck me as stiff. I prefer streamer and bucktail flies that wave or billow or undulate in a river's current or at the angler's direction, flies that suggest *life*. And the Marabou Muddler does suggest life; it's a billower. All marabou-winged and marabou-tailed flies are billowers.

Once you've learned the Marabou Muddler—which covers all the tricky stuff, like flaring deer hair and making a hair-tip collar—you'll have little difficulty with the standard Muddler Minnow; just make the same wet-fly wings you'll soon learn in tying the Cowdung, but cup them around a small bunch of hair, and form the tail by mounting a single section of mottled turkey primary upright on its edge, using the pinch. The pattern and photo for the Conehead Muddler Minnow in the chapter titled "Additional Streamers" will give you everything you need—just skip the cone and you have the original dressing.

Both the original and marabou versions of the Muddler are usually considered imitations of "sculpin," dark little bottom-hugging fish with tadpole bodies, magnificent pectoral fins, and broad heads so wondrously ugly you ponder how they can stand to share the same riffle, let alone mate. But I suppose sculpin don't find carnivorous trout and heron and the anglers who stomp around in wading shoes all that attractive either. In any case, sculpin clearly do mate—lots of rivers carry loads of them.

Both the standard and marabou-winged Muddlers are well-established for bass. For largemouth bass they are generally fished on sinking lines, well down, around shoreline lily pads and fallen trees or out around deep structure. Most largemouth never see a real sculpin, so it's illogical to show them a Muddler, but if the fly works, well... The Muddlers make perfect sense in smallmouth-bass streams—that's sculpin water, and smallmouth relish sculpin.

But most of all, the Muddlers are trout flies, to be teased along over the beds of rivers, and they've accounted for a great many trout, including lots of lunkers, for two generations of fly fishers.

The Marabou Muddler includes an optional under-wing of calf or squirrel-tail, but I've never seen any purpose in it and chose the option of omitting it here.

All Muddler designs are mostly tied and fished for trout in sizes 8 to 4, though larger and smaller sizes have their place.

MARABOU MUDDLER, BROWN

HOOK: Heavy wire, 3X or 4X long, sizes 12 to 2.

THREAD: Red 3/0 or 6/0 for the body, white or gray size-A rod-thread for the head and collar.

WEIGHT (OPTIONAL): Lead or lead-substitute wire.

TAIL (OPTIONAL): Red hackle-fibers.

ABDOMEN: Gold Diamond Braid (or flat or round tinsel or woven Mylar tubing slipped off its core).

WING: One brown marabou plume. (An under-wing of brown calf tail or red fox squirrel tail is optional.) Atop the wing, several peacock herls. Other wing-colors include white, black, olive, and yellow.

HEAD: Natural gray-brown deer hair.

1. Start the thread two thirds up the shank, and then spiral it to the bend.

2. Wind a layer of lead from 1/8-inch ahead of the bend to two thirds up the shank.

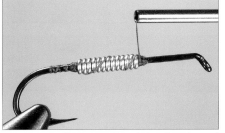

3. Break off the ends of the lead, and then bind it. Build a thread-dam at each end.

4. Use the pinch to bind a bunch of red hackle-fibers behind the lead. Trim off the butts of the fibers.

Adding the Lead and Making the Tail and Body

1. Smash down the barb on a size-6, 3X or 4X long, heavy wire hook, and then mount the hook in your vise. (The hook in the photos is a Mustad 9674.) Start some red 3/0 thread two thirds up the hook's shank. Cut off the tag-end of the thread. Spiral the thread back to the bend.

2. Wind a layer of 0.025-inch lead from 1/8-inch ahead of the hook's bend up two thirds of the shank. (That's two thirds up the *entire* shank, not just from the rear end of the lead-wrappings.)

3. Break or cut off the ends of the lead. Build a small tight thread-dam against the rear of the lead. Spiral the thread forward to the front of the lead and build a narrow thread-dam there.

4. Spiral the thread back to the bend. Stroke out a section of fibers—about 1/2- to 3/4-inch of stem, along a large red hackle (typically, a rooster "streamer" type saddle hackle)—to whatever angle evens the tips of the fibers (usually a right angle to the stem). Strip off the fibers. Measure them against the hook's gape. Use the pinch to bind on the fibers as a tail, projecting about a gapes' length off the bend. Strip off a second bunch of fibers in the same manner and bind them atop the first bunch, same length, to finish the tail.

Push down the butts of the fibers with your left hand as you wind the thread—under moderate tension—up the butts to the rear of the lead. Just behind the lead, add a few tight thread-turns. Trim off the fibers' butts right at the lead—so that they abut the lead but do not extend past it.

5. Using the pinch, bind the end of a length of gold braided tinsel up close behind the lead. Hold the tinsel back angling just above the shank under light tension as you spiral the thread down tinsel and shank to the bend. At the bend, add a few tight thread-turns.

6. Trim off the stub-end of the tinsel. Bind the cut end of the braided tinsel just behind the lead. Spiral the thread forward to two-thirds up the shank, to the front of the lead. Wind the braided tinsel up the shank in touching turns to the hanging thread. Use firm tension, but not so much that the tail rotates off the top of the shank.

7. Bind the front tag-end of the tinsel with several tight thread-turns. Trim off the end of the tinsel closely.

5. Bind the end of some braided tinsel against the rear of the lead and back to the bend.

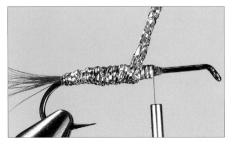

6. Trim off the front stub-end of the tinsel. Spiral the thread two thirds up the shank. Wind the tinsel up the shank.

7. Bind the end of the braided tinsel two thirds up the shank. Trim off its front tag-end.

Adding Lead and Making the Tail and Body— Problems, Solutions, and Suggestions

1. As you work the thread and make the body, make sure to keep the one third of the shank in front bare, for making the hair-head. The front of the body and the base of the wing tend to creep out over this bare shank, unless you watch them. Flaring and compressing the hair for the head will later be much easier if you have bare shank to work on.

2. A tail that looks more like a real sculpin's tail makes more sense to me than a red hackle-fiber tail. (Never seen a red-tail sculpin, hope I never do.) So you could use the turkey-feather tail of the original Muddler (like the conehead version on page 143) or make a tail of a short wing-colored bunch of marabou. Or you could skip the tail altogether and let the wing suggest both body and tail.

Making the Wing

Hold a medium-brown (or dark-brown) marabou plume by the butt of its stem, dip the fingers of your free hand in tap water and stroke your wet fingers down the plume. (I keep a small bowl on my bench with just a half-inch of water for this purpose.) The marabou shouldn't be dripping with water, only damp. Damp marabou is much easier to manage than dry marabou.

Measure the plume against the hook. Find the point at which the plume equals about two shank-lengths.

Using the pinch, bind the plume, at this measured point, atop the hook at the front of the body. Use plenty of tight thread-turns, and make sure you bind the plume *only atop* the front of the body, not *in front* of the body (in other words, not on the front section of shank we're leaving bare for the head). Bind the plume with a thread-collar that is a bit narrow, about 1/8-inch wide, or slightly slimmer—the collar must be wide enough to really secure the marabou, but not so wide that it covers more of the body than necessary.

Gently stroke five to eight peacock herls out to an angle to the stem that evens their tips. Draw the tips together, trying to keep them fairly even. Trim off the herls at their butts, close to the stem. Hold the herls directly atop the marabou so that the tips of both the herls and marabou are even. Use the pinch to bind the herls atop the thread-collar holding the marabou. Add a few tight turns in another narrow thread-collar that really secures the herls.

Trim off the butts of the herls and plume closely (though the butts of the marabou are so soft that it won't be a problem if they project forward a little). Wind the thread out in front of the body in five close turns. Whip finish, then cut, the thread.

8.

9.

10.

11.

12.

13.

8. Wet a marabou plume and then measure it against the hook.

9. Find where the tip-end of the plume equals twice the shank's length. Use the pinch to bind the plume atop the front of the body.

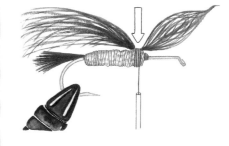

10. The plume should be bound *atop* the end of the body, *not* in front of it.

11. Use the pinch to bind a few peacock herls atop the marabou.

12. Trim off the butts of the marabou and herl.

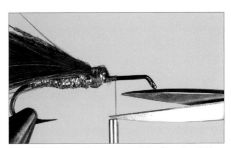

13. Wind the thread out in front of the body a few close turns. Whip finish and trim the thread.

14. Start some size-A rod-thread over the whip finish in the 3/0.

15. Cut off a bunch of spongy deer hair. Comb out the hair. Drop the hair, tips-first, into the stacker.

16. Tap the stacker on a hard surface about 30 times.

17. Hold the stacker level (or with the cap slightly raised), remove the cap, pull out the hair by its evened tips.

Making the Wing—
Problems, Solutions, and Suggestions

1. A point worth repeating: So that you don't cover much of the body, the thread-collar holding the marabou-and-herl wing must be narrow. If you're concerned that the wing might later pull out, add head cement (or the epoxy glue I use) to the thread-collar.

2. When you wind the thread out in front of the body, you want to do so in a way that makes the thread-windings secure. So, do not wind the thread forward from the collar at a steep angle, but instead at a mild angle; and wind the thread forward to the shank *under* the lead—by winding under you only have to work the thread from the lead to the shank, but if you wind it forward *over* the top of the lead the thread will have to drop from the added height of the bound butts of the marabou and herl.

Flaring the Hair

"You're traveling through another dimension, a dimension not only of *sss*ight and *sss*ound, but of *hair,*" Rod Serling, host of "The Twilight Zone" TV show, might have said with his signature bared-teeth, hissing articulation, if he were a fly tier. And he'd be right— flared and shaped hair really is a world unto itself, a unique aspect of tying that includes trout flies, tropical flies, Atlantic Salmon and steelhead flies, and so many flies for largemouth and smallmouth bass. So enter this new world, and remember that what you learn here will serve you through the tying of a wide assortment of fascinating fly patterns.

You need a stout thread in order to flare hair, so mount a spool of size-A rod-winding thread (the standard for flaring deer hair) in a bobbin, just as you would mount any tying thread. Start the size-A thread tightly over the whip finish in the 3/0 thread, up close against the front of the body. Use only four turns forward and five back to start the size-A—when you start a thread for flaring hair, you usually want to start it with just enough turns to really secure it but no more. Trim off the tag end of the thread.

Snip off a thick bunch of undyed gray-brown deer hair close to the hide, a bunch, when lightly compressed, of about 3/8-inch diameter. This should be the spongy sort of hair that is often marketed as "bass-bug" or "spinning" or "Muddler" hair. (You'll need hair that is at least 1 1/2-inches long, but if your hair is shorter than this, it is probably some other kind of deer hair—coastal deer, deer-hock...—and won't flare properly anyway.) Hold the hair-bunch by its tips, about 3/4 of an inch down from its very tips, and stroke a comb down through the hair and off its butts. Almost any comb will do; a plastic hair-comb is fine. After a few strokes the comb should contain short hairs and soft fuzz; throw the short hairs and fuzz away.

Stack the hair in a hair-stacking tool. (We covered hair-stacking thoroughly in the original *Fly Tying Made Clear and Simple*, but...drop the hair bunch, tips-first, into the stacker, tap the stacker on a hard surface 20 to 40 times, remove the stacker's cap, and then remove the hair while taking care not to lose the evenness of the tips.) Handle the stacked hair with purpose, and as little as possible, so that the hair-tips stay even.

14.

15.

16.

17.

Hold the hair bunch in your right hand atop the hook, the hair's cut butts projecting off the *eye* and its tips pointing back at the *tail*. The tips of the hair should project back about halfway to two thirds down the tinsel body.

Work the bobbin over the hair to make two light-tension turns of the size-A thread around both the hair and shank. (Remember: we left the thread hanging at the front of the body? That's where you should make these two turns.) Rock the hair slightly from side to side as you work it down around the shank a bit—but not too far. You want the hair over the shank only a third to no more than halfway down, so at least half the hair is above the shank.

You can hold the hair with either your left or right for the next step, just make sure you hold the hair close to the two thread-turns. (Or grasp the hair *over* the thread-turns, for added control.) Pull gradually down on the bobbin. As you pull the thread ever tighter, swing the bobbin off to the far side, then near side, then the far side of the hook, repeatedly, so the hair will stay centered.

Once the thread is down truly tight (size-A is *strong*, so you can really lean on it), hold the bobbin straight down firmly in your right hand, keeping full tension on the thread—do not let up on the tension through the next few steps. Stroke back the hair-butts repeatedly with the thumb, first, and second fingers of your left hand (a sort of exaggerated triangle technique). Try to keep the butts on their appropriate sides—those bound on the far side back along on the far side, those bound on top on top...

When you've got all the hair pulled back, continue to hold it there with your left hand as you pull the thread down tight one last time, pull it forward, and then wind it forward in one turn ahead of the butts. Maintaining tension on the thread, add five tight thread-turns at the front of the hair. *Now* you can let the bobbin hang.

This first bunch of hair, and the hair-tip collar, is now flared and secured. The way we handled this hair is the best way to make a hair-collar and an excellent way to flare hair in general. But once you look into hair-flies you'll read and hear a lot about *spinning* hair, so let's explore that next. Then you can decide whether to spin or just hold and flare your deer hair. However, to flare hair *and* make a hair-collar, never spin the hair; instead flare the hair as I just described.

Wind the thread forward over the bare shank in three slightly open spirals in preparation for spinning the next bunch of hair.

Snip another bunch of hair from the hide. This bunch should be slightly slimmer than the first bunch; when lightly compressed its diameter should about equal that of a common lead pencil (about 1/4-inch, or slightly more). Comb out the hair as before, but don't stack it in a hair-stacker. Snip off the *tips* of the hair-bunch, the last 3/4-inch or so.

18.

18. Hold the hair-bunch atop the hook in your right hand; the tips halfway down the body.

19.

19. Work two turns of thread around the hair. Hold the hair firmly as you pull the thread really tight.

20.

20. Hold the thread down tight as you stroke the hair-butts back.

21.

21. Pull the thread forward and wind it in five turns around the shank.

22.

23.

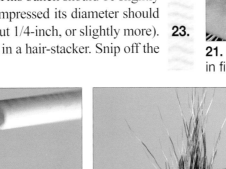

22. Wind the thread forward over the shank in three open spirals.

23. Snip off and comb out another bunch of hair, a bit thinner than the first bunch. Don't stack this bunch. Snip off the pointed tips of the hair.

24. Hold the hair against the side of the shank. Wind three turns of thread around the shank and the hair. (I used yellow hair and a bare shank here for clarity.)

25. Tighten the thread slowly and release a few hair-ends as the front ends of the hair begin to flare.

26. Keep letting hair-ends spring free of your grip as the thread tightens.

27. When about half the hair-ends are free, let go and pull the thread down hard—and watch the hair *spin.*

28. When the thread is tight, draw back the front hairs, pull the thread forward, wind five tight turns on the shank.

24.

25.

26.

27.

28.

In your left hand, hold the hair-bunch up against the shank just in front of the first bunch, on your side of the hook. Tip the rear end (the end towards the bend) of this second bunch back slightly, so the hair is angled at around 45 degrees. In the middle of the bunch make three *light*-tension turns of thread. You are about to spin your first bunch of deer hair.

It will really help you spin the hair effectively if you understand the process beforehand. So read through this paragraph and the one that follows it before trying to spin the hair. Hold the bunch by its upper end, the one tipping back. Tighten the thread *slowly.* As the thread tightens a little, you'll see the blunt hair-ends on the bottom of the bunch start to flare out. Release a few of the upper blunt hair-ends from your left hand, about 14 to 18 ends. Release them *completely*—it does no good to just loosen your grip on them; they must spring free altogether. Now tighten just a little more and release some more hair-tips. Keep tightening the thread and releasing hair-tips until at least half the tips are free of your grasp.

Now—give a hard pull straight down on the bobbin and let go of the hair altogether. The hair should spin around the shank and flare out into a rough ball. The hair will stop spinning when the thread-turns are fully tightened. As with the first bunch, maintain constant heavy thread-tension until the thread is secured in a few tight turns in front of the flared hair.

Now that you've read the instructions for flaring hair and understand the results you're seeking, do it—spin the hair!

As with the first bunch, draw back the hair in front, pull the thread tightly forward, and add five tight thread-turns in front of the hair.

Congratulations—you've spun deer hair! Now all you need to do is compress the bunches of hair back together. I'll show you how next.

Flaring the Hair— Problems, Solutions, and Suggestions

1. You can really lock the hair to the shank, and make the finished hair-head resistant to slipping, by smearing just a dab of low-odor epoxy glue on the shank before binding on each bunch of hair. You can even add a little epoxy to the whip finish in the 3/0 before starting the size-A over it—this will really lock both threads onto the shank.

2. Here's another way to make a thick hair-collar, and insure that it's even on both sides. Stack a fair-size bunch of hair and bind it lightly against the far side of the shank with two turns of thread; then stack a second bunch the same thickness as the first and bind it against the *near* side with two more light-tension turns—then pull the thread tight.

3. Most hair-spinning instructions will tell you to make just two thread-turns around the hair, but two is too few for me—I've watched hair bound with only two turns whirl around and then fly off the shank. But this has *never* happened to me with three thread-turns.

4. Do make the thread-turns around the hair-bunch you intend to *spin* in the *center* of the hair, halfway between the cut butts and the trimmed tips. If you are off center by much, half the spun hair-tips may be too short.

5. When you bind the hair-bunch against the side of the shank for *spinning,* make sure you hold the bunch not just *close* to the shank but right up *against* it.

6. Instead of adding the five tight thread-turns to lock the thread after the hair is flared, you can make just a couple of turns and then half-hitch the thread if you prefer.

7. The butts of the first hair-bunch, the bunch that includes the hair-collar, may tend to get in your way as you prepare the second bunch for spinning. The best solutions I've found: stroke back the butts of the first bunch repeatedly and *firmly,* until they stay pretty much back, and out of your way, on their own.

8. This bears repeating—as you tighten the thread and release the hair little by little, truly *release* the hair. Don't just loosen your grasp on the hair—let hair-tips spring free altogether.

9. To work the flared hairs out away from the shank, in order to draw them back, I sometimes push my first finger straight into the hair from the front. I just hold my finger in line with the shank and push the fingertip straight into the eye, which pushes the hair-ends out to their respective sides.

10. Though normally you tighten the thread and secure it in front of a bunch of hair *before* compressing the hair back, it is always permissible to tighten the thread and then compress the hair back *before* pulling the thread forward and securing it—this is especially useful on the last hair-bunch, close to the eye. If you do decide to compress the hair back before securing the thread, you'll need to compress the hair again after the thread is secured in front of it.

29. Compress the hair back with thumb and fingers or a tool.

Compressing the Hair (and flaring a last bunch)

"Compressing hair" (also known as "packing hair") means pushing flared hair bunches tightly back so the hair is dense. Dense hair, once trimmed, looks barely like hair at all, more like clean-cut wood. Flared hair that isn't compressed, spread thinly along the shank, still *looks* like hair even after its trimmed, failing to suggest something solid like, with a Muddler, the bony head of a sculpin. (Though, to be fair, thin-headed Marabou Muddlers and Muddler Minnows have caught tons of trout, so this is really more a matter of a tier's pride than a fly's effectiveness.)

There are various tool-designs for compressing hair. Some have a few small holes, the right hole barely passing the hook's eye so that the flat of the tool can press back the hair; others, like the Brassie, have scalloped jaws that clamp together to form a single tiny hole over the hook's shank, allowing the jaws to slide back against the hair. The cheapest and handiest tool is your thumb and finger, but packing hair is awfully hard on this particular muscle-and-bone apparatus.

The key to effectively compressing hair is to push the *bases* of the hair-bunches together, the thread-bindings, really—compress only the outer parts of the hair and it will just spread back out, but compress the bunches at their thread-bases, and the hair *must* remain packed.

So, you need to compress the second flared bunch of hair (the bunch that was *spun* on) back into the first bunch. Begin by reaching up inside the stacked tips of the first hair-bunch and grasping the body right behind the hair. (Or you can instead hold those first *hair-tips* down against the body, but do not hold the *butts* of the first hair-bunch, the butts that are in front of the thread-windings holding the hair.) Hold the hook firmly; this **29.** will support the hook and keep the body from slipping as you compress the hair back. If you're using a Brassie, as I usually do, clamp the Brassie's jaws over the shank just ahead of the thread. Make sure the scallops in the jaws lie around the shank. Pinch the jaws firmly together, and then push the tool back against the hair. Apply force straight in line with the shank.

30. If enough bare shank remains (as here), cut, comb, and trim off the tips of another modest hair-bunch.

31. Work the bunch down around the shank a little. Take two light-tension thread-turns around hair and shank. Hold the hair firmly and pull the thread down tight.

32. Draw the hair back, again, draw the thread forward, add a few tight thread-turns. Compress the hair back, again.

29. (cont.) Twist the Brassie from side to side a little as you push. Don't get violent about this! If you use extreme force the hook may collapse and you may stab yourself on its point. Use *some* force, but patiently accept that in time you'll learn to pack the hair ever better and more efficiently, and to use force more effectively.

With that, the compressing of this hair is complete.

Typically, you'll compress back each bunch of flared hair before adding the next, regardless of the fly pattern.

30. If a significant amount of shank remains bare after you've compressed the hair, then you'll need to add a third bunch of hair. You could spin this next bunch, as you did the second bunch, or you could just bind and flare it as I generally prefer. We'll do this one my way.

Cut from the hide and comb another bunch of hair about 1/4-inch in diameter. Do *not* stack the hairs' tips. Trim off the tips of the hair as you did with the previous bunch.

31. Hold the bunch atop the shank up against the front of the last, compressed, bunch. Hold the hair in your right hand. Wind two light-tension turns of thread around the hair, in about the center of the bunch.

Work the bunch down around the shank a bit, as before.

Pull the thread tight (pulling from one side, then the other, as before).

32. Draw back the ends of the hair as before. Pull the thread forward and wind it in a few tight turns in front of the hair, as before.

Compress the hair back into the previous bunches.

33. Now you need to add a few half hitches in the thread (a whip finish is nearly impossible, and unnecessary). Getting half hitches past all those hair-ends is a real challenge with only two hands (it takes one to

34. hold back the hair and two more to make the hitches). But the half hitch tool can slip in easily past those hairs. Such tools usually come in sets, each tool with a different hole size at each end.

35. Find the particular tool whose hole just fits over the hook's eye. Wind one turn of thread around the end of the tool, slip that end over the eye, and then slip the thread down around the hook in a half hitch. Pull the hitch tight.

Add five more half hitches with the tool.

33. To get a few half hitches in past the hair-tips, use a half-hitch tool. Such tools usually come in sets.

34. Find the tool whose hole just slips over the eye. Wind the thread around the tapered end of the tool once.

35. Slip the tool over the eye; pull the thread down onto the shank. Add five more half hitches in this manner.

Trim off the thread closely. Add head cement to the half hitches and let it set up. (Or you can add cement after trimming the hair and otherwise completing the fly; but, just hope the half hitches hold...)

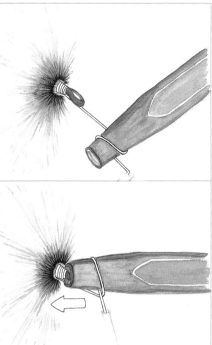

Compressing the Hair (and flaring a last bunch)— Problems, Solutions, and Suggestions

1. Packing hair tightly is more a matter of esthetics than effectiveness with a Marabou Muddler or Muddler Minnow. In dry flies, however, the tighter the pack, the longer and more stubbornly the fly will float. So, you may as well learn how to pack hair tightly.

2. As I said, it is the compressing together of the *bases* of the hair-bunches that really packs the hair, and this is a point worth exploring further. At the base of each hair-bunch is a thread-collar composed of two or three tight thread-turns. You need to slide each thread-collar back; then the hair *has* to compress and *stay* packed. You can push the hair back as much as you want, but if the bases of the bunches are separated, the hair will eventually spread. That's why I lock a hair-packing tool (or, years ago, the tips of my thumb and first finger, before I wised up) right down onto the shank against the *thread,* not the hair, to compress flared hair.

3. If you have trouble getting the hair-packing tool down onto the shank in front of this third, final, bunch of hair, you can push back the hair a little with the half-hitch tool, or your thumb and finger.

4. If there is too little room for a third hair-bunch—skip it. Without enough shank for a hair-bunch, you'll end up with an uncontrollable mess. Besides, a little bare shank in front of the hair head won't discourage any fish from taking the fly.

5. You can vary the size of the last bunch of hair as appropriate. If there's just enough room for a little more hair, use a small hair-bunch, perhaps only 1/8-inch wide. Hair-bunches of around 1/4-inch in diameter or a bit wider seem the most efficient to manage for me. But hair-bunches can run quite a range of size and, with the exception of extremely thick or skimpy ones, are generally easy enough to flare.

6. It's worth repeating, and emphasizing—a half-hitch tool will make the infuriating job of finishing off a line of flared hair a cinch, and such tools cost little.

36. Cut the thread. Add head cement now and let it set up.

Trimming the Hair-Head

It is the Marabou Muddler's (and the original Muddler Minnow's) broad deer-hair head that gives this pattern both the appearance of a sculpin and its unique character. Therefore, a tapered and somewhat flattened head is what you want to produce. Bear this in mind as you trim the hair.

The easiest and neatest way to trim flared hair is with a double-edge razor blade. (Don't bother with safety razors, the one-edge type—too safe; they won't cut the hair). It is also the riskiest—one overzealous swipe will slice the thread to let the hair burst off the hook; one careless touch and fresh blood will drip from a clean, new nick in the flesh. Here are some suggestions for safe and effective razor-trimming:

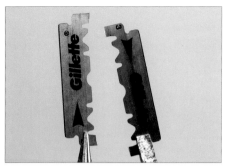

37. A razor blade will cut the cleanest hair-head. I break a double-edge blade into two halves using two pairs of pliers. *Handle all razor blades with extreme caution.*

38. Mount the hook in a hand-vise, old vise-head, or such.

39. Look straight down the hook and cut down the underside—not too close...yet.

40. Looking at the underside of the fly, cut the sides tapering back. Stop just before the hair-collar.

37.

*Break the blade in half along its length by holding firmly one side in the jaws of pliers (flat-nose, round-nose, household pliers...) and the other side of the blade in another pair of pliers, and then bending the blade until it breaks into, essentially, two single-edge blades. A single-edge blade is a bit safer to handle than a double-edge—but still, handle either with great care.

*If you do not break the blade into halves, you can *carefully* wrap a heavy tape, such as masking tape (more than one layer if in doubt) over one sharp edge of the blade. Make sure you cover the entire edge. Now you have only one sharp side to avoid touching.

*It really does help to mount your hook in an old tying-vise head, a "midge-head" (a little vise-head with tiny jaws that mounts in the jaws of your standard vise), a "hand-vise" (a small vice designed to be held in the hand)—whatever will hold the hook securely, give you plenty of access for trimming, and will keep at least one hand away from that deadly-sharp blade. Mount the hook firmly in any of these devices just as you'd mount the hook in your tying vise.

*The safest way to trim the head is with scissors. If you choose to do so, just follow the razor-blade instructions but cut with modest snips rather than long strokes of the blade. Even with scissors, though, some sort of hook-mount will make the process easier and reduce the odds of you sticking or snipping yourself with the scissors' blades.

38.

Back to tying. Mount the hook securely in an old vise-head, a hand-vise, midge-vise, or such.

Hold the hook so you are looking at its eye and sighting straight down the length of its shank—you won't see the shank, of course, behind all the hair and beneath the body, but nevertheless, sight down the shank as though you *can* see it. The hook's bend (and, therefore, the vise-head) should be vertical, rather than on its side. Make your first cut with the blade horizontal, and saw it back lightly along the underside of the hair. Use the hook's eye as a guide. *And keep your fingers away from the sharp edges of the blade.*

39.

This deserves it's own paragraph—don't cut close to the shank yet! In other words, cut about 1/8-inch down from the shank. You can't really see what you're doing at this point and you're likely to cut the thread if you try to cut close. If you cut the thread, you have to start all over with the deer-hair head, which is frustrating, not fun.

Continue this flat, horizontal cut back to the hair-tips you stacked—they're at the very rear of the hair, and sweep back. From here, you have two choices: (1.) trim off the hair-tips below, leaving the body exposed underneath or (2.) stop just short of the hair-tips, leaving them intact. Either way is acceptable. My personal preference is to trim off most or all of the tips below to show a bit more of the body and to get the fly closest to a sculpin shape.

If you trim the flared hair over a waste basket, you won't leave a pile of trimmed hair on your bench or floor. However you trim, make sure you have good light pouring down on the fly.

Now turn the fly so its shank is vertical, and so that you are looking straight at its trimmed underside. Make a cut from one side of the hook's eye

40. back to just short of the stacked hair-tips—an angled cut that is close to the hook in front and further out as it nears the hair-tips (as in the photo).

Make another cut just like this last one along the other side.

Turn the fly upright, so that the shank is horizontal and you are viewing it directly from the side. Make a cut from about 1/16-inch (at least 1/32-inch) above the shank tapering up and stopping just short of the stacked hair-tips. In other words, this cut starts close above the shank, at the hook's eye, and angles up away from the hook near the stacked hair-tips. This top-cut is the final rough, preliminary cut.

Time to clean up the underside of the hair, now that you have a clear view. Sight straight down the shank from the front and cut closer to the shank—but don't push your luck. You'll lose the whole hair head and have to start over if you cut the thread.

You now have an angular, sort of geometric Muddler head with a few long cut-end hairs back against the collar. Trout, however, don't eat geometric sculpin, so...

Make long shallow strokes of the blade along the edges of the head, from the front back. You want to take off very little with each stroke. Press the blade against the hair only lightly and gradually round out the top of the head. You can leave the underside flat, as here, or you can round those edges too, if you prefer.

This next step is best performed after the half-hitches in the size-A thread are safely coated with head cement (or epoxy glue), although with great care it can be performed without trouble on bare thread. But you need to know that this step is optional—you can skip it or just trim with scissors. Still, the method that follows makes the cleanest front on a hair-head. Holding the fly horizontal and the blade vertical, cut straight in from the side just *slightly* behind the hook's eye. Saw the blade a little while applying very little pressure. The blade should cut straight into the hair and then stop lightly against the size-A thread. That's the key—stopping the blade *lightly*. If the blade comes up against the thread with *any* real pressure...well, how much do you want to start all over flaring the hair head? Cut lightly in this manner all around the front of the head to make a neat front on the hair.

Store the razor blade safely, and pick up your scissors. (I usually store my razor blades in clear plastic film canisters—just make sure the blade is stored safely, and that children or pets can't get to it, in something soft enough not to dull the sharp edges.) Hold the fly horizontal so you are viewing it from the side. Hold the open blades of your scissors vertical. Slip the blades of the scissors up so they catch the last blunt-cut hairs in front of the hair-tip collar. Press the flat of the blades down against the trimmed hair-head. Snip off the cut butt-ends of the hairs to leave a neat transition from the head to the hair-tip collar. Keep reaching in with the scissors as you work them around the sides and top of the head (and the underside, if you left the collar uncut there) until the whole rear of the head is trimmed. That's it—Marabou Muddler completed.

Flaring and shaping deer hair really is a big deal in fly tying. You can't escape it; some of the best and most popular flies require it. And now you can do it. Congratulations.

41.

41. Taper the top of the hair back and up to just short of the hair-collar.

42.

42. Now that you can see, trim the underside of the hair closer—but don't cut the thread!

43.

43. Round out and even the top and sides of the hair.

44.

44. Trim off the hair around the eye.

45.

45. Push the tips of the hair-collar back with your scissor-tips and snip off the last head-hairs.

Trimming the Hair-Head—
Problems, Solutions, and Suggestions

1. It is possible to trim with the razor blade right back against the hair-collar. You'll lose a few stacked collar-tips, but if you used plenty of hair to start with there will be no problem—providing you cut very carefully when the blade nears the tips. One overzealous swipe and you'll have a bare spot in the collar—the fly will still catch fish, but it'll be a fly you hide from your friends.

2. Razor blades aren't expensive—switch to a new blade any time you feel the one you're using isn't cutting as it used to. But dispose of old blades safely, so they won't cut anyone rummaging through the trash for a lost bill or carrying out the trash bag.

3. Trimming flared hair is fun, perhaps a bit too much fun for some personalities—keep merrily shaving the head down to perfection and you may wind up with a precisely symmetrical head just right for a hook four sizes smaller than the one your fly is tied on. Simply put: learn when to stop trimming, and use willpower as required.

HEAD SHAPES FOR MUDDLERS

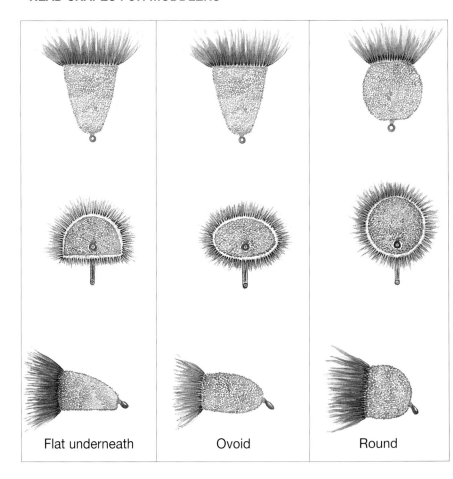

| Flat underneath | Ovoid | Round |

COWDUNG

New Techniques: breaking thread, making a tag, making a floss body and a folded hackle and wet-fly wings, tying the classic wet fly

There are plenty of good reasons for learning to tie the classic wet fly. Among the best: (1.) the wet fly can still be effective today when fished with the same passive, swinging retrieve Englishman Alfred Ronalds recommends in his *Fly Fisher's Entomology,* published clear back in 1836, (2.) contemporary fly patterns—including subsurface, emerger, and dry-fly designs—keep turning up with standard or only slightly altered traditional wet-fly wings, making the techniques for creating such wings important still, and (3.) wet flies can serve as perfectly plausible imitations of adult insects that wind up under water, such as caddis adults that swim down to deposit their eggs and alderflies that fall onto and sink into lakes.

One final reason to learn the wet fly: few patterns can match the simple elegance of such dressings as the Leadwing Coachman, Hare's Ear, and Light Cahill. And the Cowdung.

The Cowdung, despite its name, *is* elegant: powdery-looking tan-brown turkey quill, golden tinsel, softly shining olive floss. It would almost be difficult to create an *in*elegant fly with these materials. Really, though, to the eye its the gracefully cupped wings that put everything else right. Wet flies are mainly about their wings.

These are not, however, the only materials used in tying the Cowdung. In his thick classic, *Trout,* published in 1952, Ray Bergman lists the Cowdung with an olive-green wool body, brown hackle, no tag, and "cinnamon (Orpington Cock)" wings. (*Orpington Cock*—wh*aaat?*) But Eric Leiser describes quite a different Cowdung in his volume *The Book of Fly Patterns,* published in 1987: gold tag, green floss body, brown hackle, and wings of cinnamon turkey which he says can be

replaced with mottled turkey quill. Other pattern and tying books by authors I consider reliable call for tinsel ribs, dubbed bodies, gray duck primary wings, even ginger hackle. The version we'll tie here, then, is something of a composite from these sources, but closest to Leiser's dressing.

The Cowdung resembles a number of green- and olive-bodied caddisfly and mayfly adults, making it a sound choice for imitating them. However, the Cowdung always was and probably still is fished most often as an attractor pattern, suggesting a sort of swimming (on a wet-fly swing) or helpless (fished dead-drift) insect of some perfectly edible yet undefinable sort. Fact is, for whatever reason, attractor flies can sometimes work magic.

Perfectly adequate wet-fly wings are easy enough to make, but they are one of those fly-tying Quests For The Holy Grail—serious devotees of the wet fly tie hundreds, perhaps thousands of flies in pursuit of perfectly matched, evenly and gracefully arched, symmetrically cupped wet-fly wings. I'll teach you the principles; you can take the thing as far as you like. Remember, though, that trout don't care about grails, holy or otherwise—a passable pair of wings will convince them as well as any.

The middle hook sizes, 14 and 12, are the most useful in my experience, but 16 and 10 are worth tying and carrying. Seems a hook of standard length is the standard for wet flies, but that a 1X long nymph hook has long been an accepted alternative.

Learn to tie the Cowdung and you learn the basics of tying nearly all wet-fly patterns, along with a wing-style you'll run across in all sorts of fly patterns, old and new.

COWDUNG

HOOK: Heavy wire, standard length (standard wet-fly hook; a 1X long nymph hook is fine), size 16 to 10.
THREAD: Olive 6/0 or 8/0.
TAG: Flat gold tinsel.
BODY: Olive floss.
HACKLE: Brown hen-neck.
WINGS: Mottled turkey quill.

1. Strip the long, soft fibers from the the base of a brown hen-neck hackle. Set the hackle aside for now.

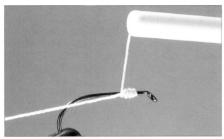

2. Start the thread about 1/16-inch back from the eye. Wind eight tight turns of thread in one place. (I used heavy white thread here, for clarity.)

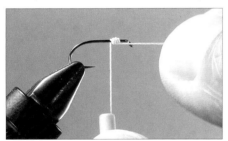

3. Hold the bobbin firmly straight down as you jerk the thread-end sharply to your right.

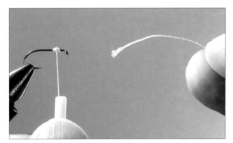

4. Thread broken!

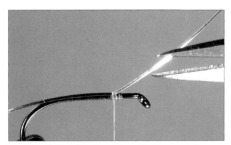

5. Bind flat Mylar tinsel silver-side-up atop the shank, just behind the eye, and then trim off its tag-end.

Selecting and Preparing the Hackle

Using your hackle gauge, select a natural-brown hen-neck hackle for a size-12 hook. Pluck the hackle from the skin; then strip the overlong and soft fibers from both sides of the stem. This will normally leave bare stem from about the middle of the stem down to the nub-end at its base. Set the hackle aside for now.

Making the Tag (and breaking the thread)

Smash down the barb on a size-12, heavy wire, standard-length hook. (This is, essentially, a typical nymph-hook but with the shank a little shorter, and is simply called a "wet-fly hook." The hook shown is a Daiichi 1550.) Mount the hook in your vise. Start the thread 1/16-inch back from the hook's eye, and then cut the end of the thread...or break it off. What do I mean by "break it off?" Read on.

Breaking off the end of tying thread is a time-saver used by every professional tier I've met, and I've met more than a few. It's easy. After starting the thread (by winding it forward and then back over itself), wind eight tight thread-turns all in one place on the shank, hold the bobbin firmly straight down, get a good grip on the tag-end of the thread and jerk it quickly forward. You want to snap the thread off to your right, in line with the shank, and really follow through. If all goes well, the thread should part so closely to the thread-collar that the broken end is invisible.

Any time you break thread, you can eliminate the remaining thread-bump by quickly backing off a few of the eight turns you made in one spot.

Before you make the tag, let's have a strategy session so you understand the tying principles at work here and can do good work with ease. The thread-windings that lock the thread on the shank and secure both ends of the tinsel for the tag will create some bulk—it's unavoidable. You can cover this bulk with the floss body, but the larger you make this bulk, the greater the challenge of covering it and the fatter the resulting floss-body will be. Point is, if you want an appropriately slim and tapered floss-body on this fly and you want to make it with the least trouble, use only enough thread-turns to do the job right—and no more—as you make the tag.

Use the light turn to bind the end of about four inches of flat tinsel atop the shank 1/16th-inch short of the eye. The tinsel should now lie silver-side-up, bound atop the shank. (Flat Mylar tinsel normally has a silver side and a gold side.) Add four tight thread-turns, and then trim off the tag-end of the tinsel in front.

Hold the rear end of the tinsel under light tension just above the shank. Spiral the thread tightly down tinsel and shank to just a couple of close thread-turns short of the bend (to be precise, 1/32-inch short). The bulk of the tinsel should project back straight off the bend. Slim tinsel, around 1/32-inch wide ("small," some manufacturers call it), makes the neatest tag on the full size-range of hooks for the Cowdung.

Add four tight thread-turns where the thread stopped, just ahead of the bend, to really secure the end of the tinsel.

Raise the tinsel under light tension until it is straight up. Begin winding it back, down the bend. The tinsel should fold over itself sideways, which turns the gold side up.

Wind the tinsel down the bend in four (or five) turns with their edges touching; then wind the tinsel forward in the same number of touching turns back up to the thread. Bind the end of the tinsel with five tight thread-turns. Trim off this tag-end of the tinsel.

That's it—you just made a tag. I've always wondered what a tag, which many wet-fly patterns include, could possibly suggest to a trout, and consequently have long considered it optional. Sure looks sharp, though.

Making the Tag (and breaking the thread)— Problems, Solutions, and Suggestions

1. If breaking off the end of the thread fails—which usually means that the thread on the hook breaks and slowly unwinds—then you probably made one or more of the following mistakes: (1.) you spread the last thread-turns over the shank rather than winding them all in one place, (2.) you didn't pull *firmly* down on the bobbin, (3.) you didn't pull the thread *straight* off the eye, or (4.) you didn't pull the end of the thread with enough speed and force.

2. When you tug the end of the thread to break it—follow through! Don't make a short tug of only an inch; instead sweep your hand in a quick snap well off to the right.

3. You may have to play with the tinsel a little to get it to fold over. Try moving it back and forth. If the silver side comes up, start over with the first turn of tinsel at another angle. Do whatever it takes to get the tinsel to fold over and expose the gold side. Normally this is pretty easy.

6.
7.
8.
9.

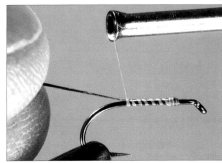

6. Raise the tinsel, and then spiral the thread down it and the shank to just short of the bend.

MAKING A TAG

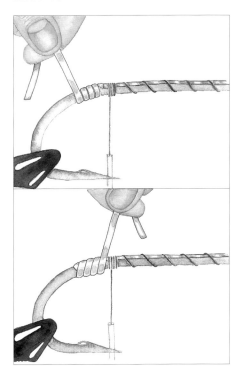

7. Add a few tight turns of thread. Raise the tinsel straight up; then wind it down the bend. (The gold side of the tinsel should now be out.)

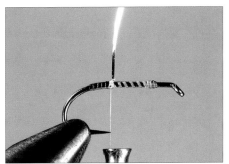

8. Wind the tinsel back up to the thread and bind it there.

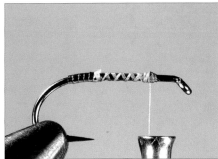

9. Trim off the tag-end of the tinsel. Spiral the thread up to near the eye.

10. Cut off a length of floss and bind a single strand just back from the eye.

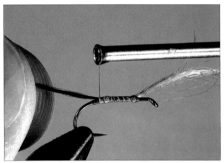

11. Raise the floss and bind it back to the bend. Add a few tight thread-turns. Cut off the short front end of the floss.

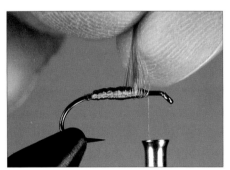

12. Spiral the thread forward to near the eye. Wind the floss forward in overlapping turns to near the eye.

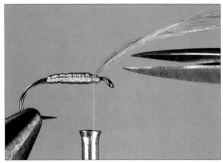

13. Bind the end of the floss near the eye. Trim off the tag-end of the floss.

4. As you wind the tinsel both down the bend and back up it, try swinging it from side-to-side a little. The flat tinsel will make a faint click as it drops neatly off the edge of each previous wrap and lies neatly against it. (You may not hear the click, just feel it; in any case, it's there.)

5. Everything you're doing to make the tag is near the point of the hook—watch that point constantly, or you'll cut your tinsel. Even a shallow nick may start a tear that runs clear across the strand.

Building the Floss-Body

Spiral the thread tightly forward to about 1/16-inch short of the hook's eye. There, bind the end of a length of olive single-strand floss atop the shank using the pinch. (One foot three inches of floss should do it.) Add a few tight turns of thread as a collar.

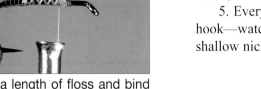

Floss normally comes in spools designated as single-strand, two-strand, or four-strand. A variation of single-strand floss is flat waxed nylon. Any of these will do, but with two- or four-strand floss you'll want to separate out and use only one strand.

Hold the floss up just above the shank as you spiral the thread down floss and shank to the bend. Bind the floss back *just far enough* to cover the fold in the tinsel. Add four tight thread-turns over the thread-turns securing the tag. Trim off the front tag-end of the floss.

Spiral the thread forward to about 1/16-inch short of the eye. Wind the floss up the shank to about 1/16-inch short of the eye. Make sure you cover the fold in the tinsel with the floss.

You want to make each turn of floss slightly overlap the previous turn, so that the turns blend together into an even surface. Floss tends to spread, and when it does, it becomes difficult to control. You can keep the floss from spreading by twisting it slightly; even a little bit of twist makes a difference. What you don't want is to twist the floss tightly, so that it goes on with a segmented look (although the trout won't care if you do).

Try to keep the body thinner at the rear end, by letting the floss splay a little and overlap only slightly. Make the body thicker as you work up the shank by twisting the floss a little more and overlapping its turns slightly further. Near the front of the body, begin spreading the floss and overlapping it less to narrow it again.

Bind the floss about 1/16-inch short of the eye. Trim off the tag-end of the floss

That's it; you should now have a fairly slim, even floss-body that tapers from narrower at the bend to thicker towards the front, and then tapers quickly down to the shank in front. The rear end of the body should cover the fold in the tinsel so that only two or three turns of tinsel are exposed in a neat row, as a tag.

Building the Floss-Body—
Problems, Solutions, and Suggestions

1. It really helps to work floss with smooth hands. Rough skin or nails will snag tying floss, fray it. So rub lotion on your hands and use a file on your fingernails if you're having trouble. (Some tiers smooth their fingertips with fine sandpaper).

2. Floss is really just a bundle of such slender filaments, and you'll get the cleanest results if you can even the tension on them all. Do this by stroking your grasp down the floss occasionally as you wind it.

3. Really watch the hook's point as you wind the floss—if you think rough hands can fray floss, wait until you see what a chemically sharpened hook-point can do.

Making the Folded Hackle

You can certainly make your hackle-collar as you did on the Prince Nymph, simply winding the feather back and then spiraling the thread forward through it. This makes a quick and durable collar.

But although the folded hackle takes longer to make and is not quite as tough as a thread-reinforced hackle collar, it looks so even, so good—what tier can resist a method that makes his or her flies look consistently cleaner, and a shade more elegant? There is more to tying than mere function, at least for most of us.

So tie a Cowdung or two with a folded hackle; then decide if this approach justifies the added time it requires. But do remember: this is not about the fish. Trout don't care about debates concerning folded versus reinforced hackles.

The thread should hang at the front of the body, about 1/16th-inch back from the eye. Hold the hackle (that you prepared earlier) by its tip with one hand (or your hackle pliers) and grasp the stem between the thumb and finger of your other hand. Gently stroke your grasp down the stem and fibers to force the fibers out to the sides. You'll be stroking against the cant of the fibers. Quit when the fibers all stand out at about a right angle to the stem. Ideally, you want to stroke only the fibers from the tip-end of the sweet spot down. (Typically, this would mean holding the hackle by the last 1/4- to 3/8-inch of its tip.)

Use the light turn to bind the hackle by its tip, at the front of the body. The hackle should be bound on top of the hook. The tip of the hackle should project forward off the eye, and the body of the hackle should lie back over the body. Try to bind the hackle so that its concave, cupped, side faces down, towards the hook. Add a few tight thread-turns to really secure the hackle's tip. Trim off the hackle's tip and all its bound fibers closely.

Hold the butt of the hackle straight up in your right hand, the stem under light tension. Reach around the hackle with your left hand as though you were going to grasp it, but close the tips of your thumb and first finger together to the right of the hackle, just past it. Now your left-hand thumb and first finger encircle the hackle. Draw your left hand to your left as your thumb and finger pinch and stroke the fibers back. Don't pinch too hard or you'll break the stem. Keep stroking the fibers off to the left in this fashion until all the fibers sweep to your left.

14. Stroke the fibers straight out from the stem of the hackle.

14.

15. Bind the hackle by its tip at the front of the body. The cupped side of the hackle should be down, facing the body. Trim off the hackle's tip.

15.

16.

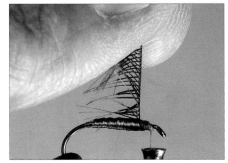
16. Hold the hackle up by its butt and pinch back all the fibers.

17. Wind the folded hackle forward in two to four touching turns.

16.
(cont.)
Now, to really fold the fibers, pinch them down hard. You want the stem in the center of your pinch. When you've done this to all the fibers they should sweep sharply to your left.

Wind the thread forward 1/32-inch, to halfway between the front of the body and the eye.

17. Lock the butt of the hackle in the jaws of your hackle pliers. Wind the hackle forward up the shank. Make each turn of the stem up close to the last. Stroke back the fibers of each turn as you add it—this will provide the neatest results, keeping the fibers back where they belong. Wind on two to four turns of hackle.

18. Work the thread down between the fibers to the stem of the hackle. A few fibers will be bound; just try to keep them to a minimum. Add five tight thread-turns over the first turn, to really secure the stem.

Trim off the hackle's stem closely. This is the thick end of the stem, so a close trimming will keep it from poking out and interfering with the mounting of the wings.

19. Pinch the hackles down firmly, at the stem. Pinch them top and bottom, then at the sides.

18. Bind and then closely trim off the butt of the hackle.

Making the Folded Hackle—
Problems, Solutions, and Suggestions

1. When you bind the tip of the hackle, bind it with enough tight turns of thread so that it won't pull free under the tension of wrapping. If the tip *does* pull out, just unwind the last turns of thread and bind it back on, but this time, bind it to *stay.*

2. You must stroke the hackle's fibers until they stand straight out from the stem before folding the hackle. If you skip the stroking, the folding just won't work.

3. If the hackle fibers resist folding, try stroking the needle of a bodkin or the outside edge of your closed scissor blades down the stem along the line of the fibers. Mostly stroke from the hackle's tip out towards its butt. A few strokes will often crease the fibers right over.

4. As I said earlier, you need to trim the thick butt of the hackle closely. The best way I've found is to trim the stem closely at a longish angle with a double-edge razor blade—but if you do, handle that blade with *extreme care.* You can find more detail on working with a razor blade in the chapter titled "Marabou Muddler, Brown."

19. Pinch down the fibers at the stem.

Adding the Wings

Start with two matched mottled tan-brown turkey quills (primary feathers); "matched" means they come from the opposite wings of one bird, one a sort of flipped-over image of the other. These quill feathers will each have one broad side of thick well-marked fibers with a fine neat edge, and another side that is thinner and whose edge is more ragged. Normally, the good side will run along the *outside* edge of the quill's graceful curve. (Save the ragged-edge fibers along the inside of the curve for wing cases on nymphs and such.)

Cut a section from about the same spot on each of the two quills. Each section should be about one-half to no more than two thirds as wide as the hook's gape. (Measure the wing-section about three-quarters up the fibers from the quill.)

The best way I know to separate out a section on a primary feather (such as a turkey quill) is to work the point of a bodkin's needle straight into the fibers and then draw the needle along the line of the fibers and out. Then I measure the width and use the bodkin-needle to separate out the other side of the wing-section.

Cup the sections together, tips even, aligned.

You have a choice: you can mount the sections with their short edges up, or down. Both ways are common, both make an effective fly. We'll mount them here with their short edges down.

Teasing a curve into the quill-sections helps the completed wings lie down atop the body; the technique for this is called "humping." To hump the wings, start by setting them cupped together, their tips even, and their short edges down. Stroke a finger down the top edges of the sections while pushing down lightly—too much pressure will split up the quills. Keep stroking the sections down, from their bases out towards their tips, until the sections curve downward. This may take a little while, but not long. Be patient, stroke lightly.

Now it's time to use a a variation of the pinch: the *wing* pinch. Hold the wings atop the hook so that their tips terminate *slightly* past the far edge of the bend. The wings should be down truly horizontal, not tipping upwards (though they will tip upwards slightly when they're completed). Take a turn of thread over the quills just as you would for a normal pinch. But there will be differences from the normal pinch, and here they are:

1. As you tighten the thread-loop, you will lower your thumb-tip and fingertip slightly, to compress the wings down a little beneath the thread-loop.

2. You'll want to pull the thread not only down, but slightly towards you—this will keep the thread tight against the lower edge of the far wing.

3. You'll press your fingertip firmly against the far side of the wing and body as you pull closed the pinch-loop. This keeps the lower edge of the far wing from slipping down the body.

Once the loop is closed and tight, keep constant tension on the thread as you hold the wing and add six more tight thread-turns over the first; all these subsequent turns must be either atop or just in front of the pinch-turn of thread—even one turn back will probably throw the wings off.

20.

20. Cut a section from each of two matching turkey quills.

21.

22.

21. The sections can be mounted with their short edges up (as on the top, above) or short edges down (as on the bottom) for wet-fly wings. We'll mount them with the short edges down.

23.

22. Hold the sections cupped together and stroke their top edges to bend down—"humping" the wings.

23. Use a wing pinch to bind the sections just ahead of the hackle—leave room for a thread-head.

24. Trim the butts of the wings closely and neatly to a short taper—trimming the butts closely will control the size of the thread-head.

25. You *can* trim the wings with a razor blade, but if you do, handle the blade with extreme care. Cut at an angle up from the eye. Be careful not to cut the thread.

26. Bind the butts of the turkey sections to build a tapered thread-head. Whip finish and trim the thread; add head cement.

24.
25.
26.

Release the bobbin and trim the butts of the wings closely.

Build a tapered head. Whip finish the thread and trim it. Add head cement to the head.

Adding the Wings—
Problems, Solutions, and Suggestions

1. It's better to make the wings a little too wide rather than too slim—if they're too wide, you can just strip off a couple of fibers before you mount them. But if the wings are too slim, the solution is more complicated. You can add fibers to a section of turkey quill by holding a slimmer section up against the main section and working the two gently back and forth against each other until the fine hairs on the edges of the fibers lock together. (Fly tiers call this "marrying" quill-fibers.) Still, too wide is best, because making a section slimmer is much easier than making it wider.

2. The size and neatness of the thread-head will be largely determined by how you trim the butts of the wings—trim them roughly and leave a lot of bulk and the head will be big and ugly, trim them closely and neatly and...you know. To trim the butts closely, work the very tips of your scissors in and take all the snips you need, or cut very carefully with a razor blade as described for trimming deer hair in the section titled "Marabou Muddler, Brown" on pages 63 and 64. Work the blade with great care so as not to cut yourself, or the thread.

3. You *can* lift the butts of the wings to get a good angle for trimming them closely. Then you work a razor blade in just over the eye and cut, angling up just over the thread-turns holding the wing. Use the razor with extreme care so as not to cut yourself (see pages 63 and 64 in the chapter titled "The Marabou Muddler, Brown."). If you do raise the butts, raise them slowly and as little as possible—raising them can collapse the wings or set them at odd angles or create some other mischief.

4. Because you'll be binding the butts of two fairly wide quill sections to make the thread-head, expect that thread-head to be on the large side. No problem—just make it a *neat* large thread-head.

5. The wings will tend to lie lower to the body if you use a "beard-hackle," hackle-fibers bound as a bunch to the underside of the shank, or if you wind the hackle on *in front* of the wings. But I think the folded hackle *behind* the wings looks best; and if we'd used a beard-hackle you wouldn't have learned to make an elegant folded hackle that looks so good and fits so neatly with not only wet flies but with steelhead, Atlantic salmon, and even some nymph patterns.

KLINKHAMER SPECIAL

New Techniques: making a parachute hackle with a poly-yarn wing, building a peacock-herl thorax around a parachute wing, tying a parachute-emerger-style fly

I suspect the Klinkhamer Special is a hit fly mainly for the obvious reason—it catches trout—but partly because it represents to fly tiers a straightforward sort of entryway into emerger patterns with parachute hackles. There are plenty of other parachute-emerger patterns, and one of them might have become the standard-bearer for flies of this style, but the Klinkhamer had the advantage of appearing fairly early in the game, and just looks so manageable at the tying vise and so plausible as an imitation—and it contains peacock herl, which few tiers can resist.

Hans van Klinken created the Klinkhamer and considers it an imitation for both mayflies and caddisflies when tied in various sizes and colors. This supports my own perspective on the pattern: that it is imitative, but in a general way. (I suspect that larger midges, too, could be successfully imitated with Klinkhamers.) Though fly fishers may fret about whether a fly pattern has tails like a mayfly's or a wing suggesting a caddisfly's freshly unfolded pairs, trout aren't generally sticklers about such details. Sure, specific, realistic imitations may sometimes have an edge—the Anatomical Green Drake presented earlier in this book, for example, imitates not just any mayfly nymph but a *green drake* mayfly nymph, and, if the fly fisher is confidant the trout are focused on nymphs of this family, is a wise choice of fly. But if the

fly fisher *isn't* sure what the trout want, a broad-purpose imitation may improve his or her odds by casting a wider imitative net, that is, by suggesting more than one insect. Besides, there are more important requirements for convincing a trout than offering it a detailed imitation—a proper drift of the fly, appropriate movement of the fly (which is often no movement at all), the right size and shape and posture of the fly, among others. And no experienced fly fisher would deny that broad-purpose imitations, like the Klinkhamer, catch lots of persnickety trout, even ones that are locked onto a specific hatch. Don't discount the multipurpose imitative fly.

The Klinkhamer is designed to rest on its hackle, with its abdomen submerged—the suggestion of an insect in an early stage of emergence, wings up and legs free of the split top of a shuck that still contains most of its body.

Because the emerging insects the Klinkhamer imitates are struggling to escape their shucks rather than swimming or fluttering, a dead-drift presentation is the standard for this fly. Although an occasional light twitch may sometimes move an otherwise reluctant trout.

I like the Klinkhamer most in sizes 18 to 14, the size-range of so many insects that emerge in open water. Of course, each hook-size throughout the full range given in the pattern below has its place.

KLINKHAMER SPECIAL

HOOK: Light wire, humped shank (pupa/emerger hook or slow-curve 2X long), sizes 18 to 8.

THREAD: Originally, gray or tan 8/0 or 6/0, but dark-olive, to match the thorax, makes sense as an alternate.

WING: White poly yarn. (Or use whatever color you see most easily—red, yellow, orange...)

HACKLE: Hans prefers light to dark blue dun and chestnut hackles, but says any color is fair game. (I like grizzly.)

ABDOMEN: Tan (or any imitative color) synthetic dubbing.

THORAX: Peacock herl.

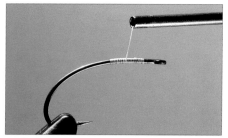

1. Select and prepare a neck hackle. Start the thread just behind the eye. Wind the thread halfway down the shank, then halfway back to the eye.

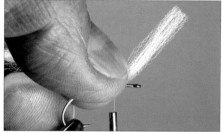

2. Bind a section of white Poly yarn atop the hook where the thread hangs. Add a few tight thread-turns.

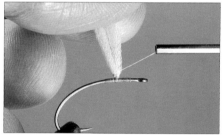

3. Raise the yarn and wind the thread tightly around its base.

4. Release the ends of the yarn. Wind a *light* layer of thread up the yarn.

5. Wind the thread back down the wing, under slightly more tension.

Making the Wing

Use your hackle gauge to find a dry-fly neck or saddle hackle to fit a size-12 hook. (That's the right hackle-size if you're tying on a standard size-12 humped-shank pupa/emerger hook. In the photos, I'm tying on a size-12 Partridge Grey Shadow GRS15ST, also called the "Klinkhamer Special hook." This good-looking and cleanly machined hook appears to be 1X long, but is about a size larger for its designation than most American and Japanese hooks. So select a hackle for a size-10 hook on your hackle-gauge if you choose this hook. Also, use a size-10 hackle if you decide to tie on a slow-curve *2X long* hook, such as the Daiichi 1260.) We'll use grizzly hackle, my favorite for the Klinkhamer, here, but I used Hans's preferred blue dun for the completed fly on the previous page. Prepare the hackle by stripping the longer softer fibers from both sides of its base. (See the next chapter titled "PMD Quigley Cripple" on page 82, or the original *Fly Tying Made Clear and Simple,* for more information on preparing a hackle for a dry fly.) Set the hackle aside.

Smash down the barb on a size-12, light wire, humped-shank, 1X long pupa-emerger hook. Mount the hook in your vise, and then start some gray thread just back from the hook's eye. Break off or trim off the thread's end. Wind the thread back tightly about halfway down the hook's shank. (True, there's no easily identified straight shank, but just imagine the shank *is* straight and then guess how far back it reaches—that's the shank, for our purposes. And use the photos as a guide.) Wind the thread forward again to about halfway up this first layer of thread. Now the thread should be hanging about three fourths up the shank.

Split some white poly yarn up its length into three sections of about equal thickness. You can simply tug the yarn apart, or push the point of your bodkin in from the side and draw it up and out of the fibers to divide them. Snip off one section about two inches long. Using the pinch, bind the section at about its center atop the hook (about three quarters up the shank, remember?). Add eight more tight thread-turns all in one place, as a slim collar, to really secure the yarn.

Raise both ends of the yarn and hold them straight up firmly together, in your right hand. Work the bobbin around the *base* of *all* the yarn in two turns. I do this by bringing the bobbin around with my left hand, and then laying the thread over the extended little finger of my right hand temporarily as I reach around with my left hand to regrasp the bobbin and continue winding the thread. So, essentially, I'm doing the winding with my left hand and using my right hand-little finger as a rest when I have to release the bobbin. When looking straight down on the wing, you should see the thread-turns going on counterclockwise. Still holding the wing up firmly, pull the bobbin until the thread-turns are tight.

Release the yarn; it should remain upright and gathered. During these following steps *you should not have to hold the wing again;* controlling thread-tension makes this possible. Wind the thread in close *light-tension* turns up the base of the yarn. Wind it far enough to accept five to eight turns of hackle (just imagine how much *shank* the hackle would require and wind the thread that same distance up the yarn. With this size-12 hook, I'd wind up the yarn about 3/32-inch.)

Now wind the thread back down the base in *moderately* tight turns to the shank.

Making the Wing—
Problems, Solutions, and Suggestions

1. When you first bind on the yarn—really nail it down tightly. If you don't, the resulting wing will slip around the shank and drive you mad—*mad* I tell you! Making the base of thread-turns, the ones beneath the yarn, truly tight helps, as does winding a tight thread-turn around the shank after each of the first few turns around the base of the wing.

2. Keep the turns of thread holding the yarn to the shank gathered, as a narrow band. If the turns are spread, the wing will be difficult to form.

3. The fastest way to wind the thread up and down the base of the poly yarn is to hold the bobbin pointing straight down and then just circle the tip of the bobbin's tube around the wing. But if you're more comfortable passing the bobbin from hand to hand, it's much slower, but, pass away...

Mounting the Hackle

Hold the hackle that you prepared earlier in your left hand, with the stem against the base of the poly-yarn wing and your hand below the hook. Hold it vertical (which would make it parallel to the wing). The stripped base of the stem should extend up along the thread-windings on the wing's base. A little of the stripped hackle stem (no more than 1/16-inch) should extend up above the thread-windings on the yarn-wing.

Wind the thread *counterclockwise* (when viewed from the top) around both the base of the yarn and the hackle's stem. You want the thread-turns to work up the yarn and stem to the top of the previous two layers of thread. Use *fairly firm* thread-tension—the previous thread-turns and, now, the hackle's stem, have made the yarn's base quite stiff, stiff enough to handle it.

Take a couple of turns of thread right at the top of the thread-layers, to really secure the hackle stem, and then wind the thread back down the yarn's base to the shank, in truly *tight* turns. But use only as much tension on the thread as the wing-base will take without significant bending.

Draw the hackle's stem back along the shank (on top or on one side). Bind the stem back along approximately one third of the shank (that is, one third from the wing back, about 1/8-inch, in this case). Trim off the stem closely.

Mounting the Hackle—
Problems, Solutions, and Suggestions

1. Whether the dull, concave side of the hackle ends up facing up or down in the finished hackle-collar is a minor point—either way the fly will be perfectly effective. But...I prefer a parachute hackle-collar with it's concave side down. The best way to accomplish this is to mount the hackle so that its concave side faces *away* from the wing (which, of course, means the convex, shiny, side lies against the wing's base).

2. How much thread-tension do you apply as you wind the thread up and then back down the base of the wing and the stem of the hackle? Answer: as much as you can get away with. Simply put, if the base of the wing bends around much as you wind, you're using too much tension. So, back off a little, but no more than required, so the hackle and wing will be firmly set.

6. Hold the stripped stem of the hackle to the base of the wing and wind the thread somewhat tightly up both.

7. Wind the thread back down the wing—use tight turns now.

6.

7.

8.

8. Draw the hackle's stem back along the shank, bind it, and then trim off its end.

9. Dub a tapered abdomen from just down the bend forward to just short of the wing.

10. Snip the tips off a few peacock herls, bind the herls on behind the wing. Trim off the ends of the herls.

11. Spin the herls and thread together to form a fuzzy rope.

12. Wind the herl-rope up the thorax-area to just short of the eye. Separate out, bind, and then trim the herls.

Dubbing the Abdomen

9. Spiral the thread well down the curved shank and the bend—in other words, if that shank were straight you'd wind the thread to the bend and then just a little ways down it (use the photos as a guide). Spin tan dubbing onto the thread (Hans prefers Extra Fine Poly made by the Fly Rite company for hooks size-14 and larger, and Super Fine Dry Fly dubbing for size-16 and smaller, but feel free to use whatever synthetic dubbing you prefer.) Wind the dubbing up the shank to create a slim body that tapers to somewhat thicker the nearer it gets to the wing (or a body of constant thickness). Stop dubbing about 1/32-inch (1/16-inch at most) short of the rear of the wing.

Dubbing the Abdomen—
Problems, Solutions, and Suggestions

1. Since the rear half of a Klinkhamer Special is supposed to hang below the water's surface (essentially, to sink) consider a natural dubbing for the abdomen, such as rabbit, since most natural dubbings absorb water. Another option: a natural dubbing blended with a shiny synthetic, such as Hare-Tron or Arizona Sparkle Nymph Dubbing.

2. If you have a particular insect in mind to imitate with that Klinkhamer Special under construction in your vise, hold the image of the insect in mind as you dub the abdomen. Caddisflies have plump abdomens; mayflies have abdomens slender and tapered; midges have abdomens of slow taper even slimmer than a mayfly's. Of course if you don't know what insect your Klinkhamer will be made to suggest, go with a tapered abdomen of middling thickness, as in the photo of the finished fly at the start of this chapter.

Building the Thorax

10. Snip the very tips off four to six long, full peacock herls. The thread should now hang at the front of the abdomen, about 1/32- to (at most) 1/16th-inch short of the rear of the wing. Using a light turn (or a modified pinch), bind the herls by their cut tips on the top or near side of the shank. Bind the herls with plenty of thread-turns. Try to bind the herls close to their cut tips, to preserve most of their length. The herls should now project back, off the bend.

There shouldn't be much to trim off the cut front-ends of the herls, but if there is, trim it closely.

11. Wind the thread back to where the herls are bound on. Spin the herls and thread together (as you did with the Prince Nymph).

12. Wind the resulting herl-thread rope up the thorax-area in consecutive turns to just back from the eye. Separate out the thread and herls. Bind the ends of the herls with a few tight thread-turns. Trim off the ends of the herls closely.

Building the Thorax—
Problems, Solutions, and Suggestions

1. There is some small advantage to binding the herls on the *underside* of the shank—then when you hold the thread and herls straight towards you, they'll both come from exactly the same place. (This is true for any herl fly, including the Prince Nymph you tied at the beginning of this book.) The disadvantage is that binding herls onto the underside of a shank is trickier than binding them to the side or top.

2. If you need more instruction for handling peacock herl, refer back to pages 10 and 11 in the chapter titled "Prince Nymph."

3. Make sure you cover everything around the base of the wing with the herl. The sides of the shank just below the wing's base tend to escape covering, so check them and wind the thread-herl rope around them if needed. Keep adding herl until the thorax-area is fully covered, but don't go nuts—you don't want an overstuffed, outsized thorax in the finished fly.

4. You can treat twisted thread-and-herl just as you would dubbing— crisscross it, double it back on itself, whatever works.

Winding the Parachute Hackle

Clamp the tip of the hackle in the jaws of your hackle pliers. Hold the pliers so the hackle aims straight towards you. Begin winding the hackle around the base of the wing—*counter clockwise* when you stand and look straight down on the fly. Pass the hackle pliers from hand to hand, working the hackle down the base of the wing in close turns of the feather's stem. Wind at least five turns of hackle, and no more than ten turns.

When the hackle is down into the herl-thorax, let the pliers, and the hackle's tip, hang over the shank in front of the wing and just behind the eye. The pliers should hang on the *far side* of the shank.

Reach your left-hand thumb and fingers down under the front hackle fibers (the ones over the eye), and raise the fibers up and clear of the eye. Still holding the fibers, work a few thread-turns over the hackle's tip, to secure it.

Still holding the fibers, pick up the scissors in your right hand and trim off the hackle's tip. Build a small, tapered thread-head.

Release the hackle-fibers. The fibers should remain somewhat tipped up, which frees both hands for making a whip finish. Make a whip finish, trim the thread closely, and add head cement to the head. (You can draw the hackle-fibers up and back, as in the photo, if that helps you with adding the head cement.)

You can tug the hackle (and the wing, which was probably forced back when you tugged the hackle-fibers up) back into position after the head cement is set.

13.

14.

15.

16.

17.

18.

13. Wind the hackle down the base of the wing in close turns to the thorax.

14. Let the hackle-tip and pliers hang on the far side of the shank.

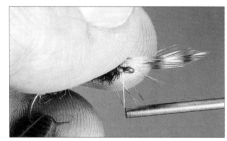

15. Reach in and raise the front hackle fibers up clear of the eye. Wind a few turns of thread over the hackle-tip.

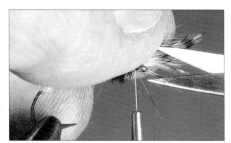

16. Continue holding the fibers as you trim off the hackle-tip, and then build a tapered thread-head.

17. Whip finish the thread, cut it, and add head cement to the thread-head.

18. Once the head-cement is set, tug the wing straight upright. Tug the hackle-fibers back into position.

19. Draw up the wing-yarn and cut it straight across.

19.

After the head cement is set and the wing and hackles are tugged back into position, measure the yarn to find where it extends up a distance equal to the distance from the tip of the hook's eye to the center of its bend. (As with all curved-shank hooks you'll have to estimate where the bend would be if the shank were straight. Also, this measurement needn't be perfect.) Draw the yarn up firmly and then snip it straight across at it's measured point—a squared cut. (Note: some tiers like a *slightly* short wing on parachute flies, about shank-length; they feel it helps the fly to land upright. But the slim, tail-less, down-turned abdomen of the Klinkhamer, acting as ballast, probably eliminates any advantage of a shortened wing.)

Winding the Parachute Hackle— Problems, Solutions, and Suggestions

1. When you trim off the tip of the hackle, you can insure you don't also cut the thread by either raising the hackle and letting the thread hang or holding the tip down and the thread up—if the thread and hackle-tip are on opposite sides of the shank, it is nearly impossible to cut both with a scissor-snip.

2. You can make the hackle a little tougher, and possibly the fly a little neater, by winding only a little herl in front of the wing, winding the hackle, binding it close in front of the wing, trimming off the tip, binding on a couple of new herls, and then building the remainder of the herl-thorax to the eye. This way, the stem of the hackle isn't extending from the wing to the hook's eye and asking to be cut by a trout's tooth. (Although I've never had a problem with trout teeth and parachute hackles whose tips are bound at the hook's eye, so it's not a big deal.)

3. Han's uses a unique method for finishing off his parachute hackles: he completes the fly with the hackle unwound and cuts the thread, then remounts the hook so its shank is vertical, the eye pointing straight down. He then starts a very fine thread on the base of the wing (he uses a thread called Spiderweb), winds the hackle, and then binds and trims the hackle-tip at the base of the wing. He completes the hackle by working a whip finish in around the base of the wing, trimming the thread, and finally adding a little head cement over the whip finish.

PMD QUIGLEY CRIPPLE

New Techniques: making an emerger-shuck, making the Quigley Cripple wing-shuck

Fly-fishing guide Bob Quigley got tired of watching suspicious trout in California's smooth, clear Fall River drift up to inspect his dry flies during the pale morning dun mayfly hatch, then drift down leaving the flies untouched. So he started studying those trout and insects in earnest, trying to find an angle, a clue, anything that might improve his odds in the game. His break came when he realized that the fish were ignoring fully emerged mayfly duns to take insects that were still in the process of struggling from their shucks. That discovery sparked his development of a truly new fly design: the Quigley Cripple.

All this happened in the 1980s. Today, the Quigley Cripple has many believers. You'll hear a lot about the fly if you hang around spring creeks, tailwaters, any sort of river known for strong hatches and difficult trout.

The rear half of a Quigley Cripple suggests a nymph, the front half suggests a dun drying its freshly unfurled wings. That's why the fly is half dark like a real pale morning dun (or PMD) nymph and half pale like the dun. The nymph-half's tail is replaced with yarn or marabou to represent a tinted, translucent shuck, partially shed. To fly fishers, "cripple" (as in Quigley Cripple) refers to either an insect that is fouled with its shuck and unable to complete its hatching or a fly that

imitates such an insect. The Quigley Cripple probably does suggest a mayfly cripple, but it probably also imitates a mayfly emerging successfully as well; both are pretty helpless and, consequently, attractive to trout.

The Quigley's hackle-legs tend to position the fly upright in the water, with its abdomen down, its blunt-cut elk-hair butts suggesting the burst wing case while helping to buoy the fly, and the tips of the hair creating an illusion of wings while making the fly easy for the angler to spot.

Fish any Quigley Cripple—the PMD version we'll tie here, the Olive Marabou Quigley Cripple (detailed in the "Additional Emergers" section), and the rest of the series— dead drift. That is, drifting naturally, with no drag. Although an occasional light twitch of an emerger-fly is sometimes just the right tactic.

The PMD mayflies I encounter normally match size-18 and -16 hooks, so I tie most of my imitations—nymph, emerger, dun, spinner—in these sizes, including the PMD Quigley Cripple. PMDs can run a size larger and a size smaller, however.

Bob has created quite a few innovative and effective fly patterns. If you want to explore them, watch his DVD: "Tying Bob Quigley's Signature Flies."

PMD QUIGLEY CRIPPLE

HOOK: Light wire, standard length to 1X long (standard dry-fly hook; Bob prefers the Daiichi 1180 or Tiemco 100), sizes 20 to 14.
THREAD: Olive or yellow 8/0 or 6/0.
TAIL (SHUCK): Brown Z-lon, Antron, or marabou.
RIB: Fine natural or red copper wire. (I prefer fine gold wire, but not so fine that it's fragile.)
ABDOMEN: Pheasant tail.
THORAX: Pale yellow synthetic dubbing (Superfine Dry Fly, poly, Antron...).
WING AND WING CASE: Light natural elk hair.
HACKLE: Ginger or cream.

1. Select a size-16 dry-fly hackle using your hackle gauge.

2. Strip the long, webby fibers from the base of the stem.

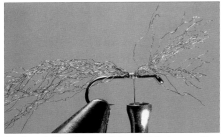

3. Materials for the shuck, left to right: marabou, Antron, fuzzy Antron, and fuzzy Antron combed out.

4. Start the thread two thirds up the shank. Bind a small bunch of Antron or Z-lon or marabou there.

Selecting the Hackle, Binding on the Yarn and Wire

1. Use your hackle gauge to select a ginger or cream neck or saddle dry-fly hackle for a size-16 hook.

Strip the softer and longer hackles from both sides of the feather's stem, down its base.

2. (Preparing a dry-fly hackle is covered in detail in the original *Clear and Simple*, but here is the process in a nutshell: strip all the overlong and soft fibers from the base of the hackle—with a neck hackle, this will normally mean stripping the fibers from the center of the feather down to the base of the stem, though with smaller hackles you may have to strip only a third. With a long saddle hackle, just strip all the softer, webbier fibers from the base of the stem, leaving only stiff, bright fibers all of one length.)

3. Smash down the barb on a size-16 standard dry-fly hook. (The hook shown in the photos is a Tiemco 100.) Start the thread about two thirds up the shank from the bend. Separate out a small section of brown Z-Lon or Antron fibers from the main bunch, about one quarter of the thickness of the yarn. (Use the photos as a guide to get the thickness of the section right.) These fibers will form the shuck-tail. Snip off a 1 1/2-inch section of this small bunch of yarn. (Note: there are currently two common forms of Antron yarn—the unwoven kind with thicker, hair-like filaments and the loosely woven kind that's fine and fuzzy. If you use the fuzzy kind, comb out the end of the yarn with any comb. Both kinds will do the job. If you choose marabou fibers for the shuck, strip the fibers from the side of the plume. Do not use the stiffer tip-fibers.)

4. Use the pinch to bind one end of the section of yarn atop the hook's shank, two thirds up the shank.

5. Hold the yarn back and slightly raised under light tension, over the shank, as you spiral the thread tightly down shank and yarn to the hook's bend. When you reach the bend, add a few tight thread-turns, release the yarn, and spiral the thread forward to its starting point (two thirds up the shank).

6. Raise the front stub-end of the yarn and trim it off closely. (Do not trim off the *rear* of the yarn yet.)

7. Use the light turn to bind the end of some fine copper wire atop the shank (two thirds up the shank, of course). You can work with either about a four-inch section of wire cut from the spool or you can set the spool to your left on your tying bench, to hold the wire out of your way, and then cut the wire later when you're ready to wind it as ribs. Add a few tight thread-turns to fully secure the wire.

5. Bind the shuck-material down the shank to the bend.

6. Trim off the front end of the shuck-material closely.

7. Bind the end of some fine copper wire two thirds up the shank.

Hold the wire above the shank under light tension as you spiral the thread tightly down shank and wire to the bend. Add a few tight thread-turns at the bend, and then spiral the thread forward again to the two thirds point. Closely trim off the front, stub-end, of the wire.

8.

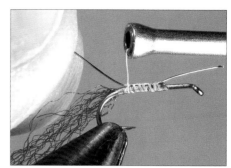

8. Bind the copper wire back to the bend. Trim off the front of the wire.

Selecting the Hackle, Binding on the Yarn and Wire— Problems, Solutions, and Suggestions

1. A real mayfly shuck is slim, supple, and translucent. So regardless of whether you use Antron filaments that come in a loose bundle, fuzzy Antron yarn, or marabou, keep the shuck truly spare on your Quigley Cripple.

2. Even fine copper wire adds slight but significant weight to the Quigley Cripple. That weight can help submerge the rear half of the fly, which is right. But it can also sink the entire fly in choppy currents, and that's just wrong. So for the rib I like to substitute fine gold wire in place of the copper. You could take this a step further and use fine tippet or heavy thread or something else lighter than water for a rib—but do use a rib of some kind to toughen the fragile pheasant-tail abdomen you'll create next.

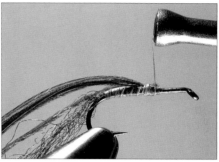

9. Trim off the very tips of a few pheasant-tail fibers. Bind the fibers two thirds up the shank, atop the hook.

Making the Abdomen and Winding the Rib

Stroke five to seven pheasant-tail fibers out to a right angle to the stem, to even their tips. Cut the fibers off down close to the stem—the longer the fibers, the easier they'll be to manage. Hold the fibers, bunched together, near their tips. Snip off the very points of the fibers, only about the last 1/8-inch.

9.

Using the pinch, bind the fibers atop the hook two thirds (*at least* halfway) up the shank. Bind the fibers close enough to their cut-off tips that you won't have to trim later. (Though it's no big deal if you do have to trim them.) Add a few tight thread-turns to really secure the fibers.

Hold the fibers slightly up and back over the shank under truly *light* tension—pheasant tail is fairly fragile (though we'll fix that with a rib). Spiral the thread back over shank and pheasant-fibers to the bend. At the bend, add four tight turns of thread.

Spiral the thread two thirds up the shank.

10.

Stroke the pheasant-fibers lightly towards you, to even out the tension on the fibers. Wind the pheasant-fibers up the shank, each turn neatly in front of and abutting the last, to the hanging thread—the result should be a slim, neat abdomen. Remember: the pheasant-tail fibers will break if you put much tension on them. Bind the ends of the fibers with five to seven tight thread-turns two-thirds up the shank. Trim off the butts of the fibers closely.

11.

10. Spiral the thread down the shank and fibers to the bend.

11. Spiral the thread two thirds up the shank. Wind the pheasant to the thread; bind and trim it there. Trim off the cut tips of the fibers.

12. Wind the wire up the pheasant as ribs—opposite the normal direction.

12. Wind the copper wire up the pheasant in four to six evenly spaced ribs—but wind the wire *opposite* the normal direction. That is, wind it away from you *under* the shank and towards you *over* it. This will make the body tougher, with the rib and pheasant forming a helix. Keep firm tension on the wire (though it needn't be extreme) so that the ribs are tight and secure.

13. Bind the wire two-thirds up the shank, at the front of the abdomen, with a few tight thread-turns. Trim off the end of the wire closely.

13. Bind the end of the wire at the front of the abdomen; then trim it.

Making the Abdomen and Winding the Rib— Problems, Solutions, and Suggestions

1. Because you want to get all the length you can out of pheasant-tail fibers, make sure you even the tips of the fibers well, cut them off right up against the quill, and cut only the very fragile points off the tips of the fibers.

2. An excellent way to wind pheasant-tail fibers, because they are short, is to wrap the fibers to just the top of the shank, stop, and then press a fingertip from your other hand down on top of the fibers to hold them as you reach around to regrasp them. Keep stopping, pressing down, and regrasping for every wrap. This way is a little slow, but it's efficient and really doesn't take long. And you practically *can't* lose the fibers because you never have to pass them from hand to hand, which is when they normally slip free.

3. To keep the fiber together as you wind them, you can twist them a little: but don't twist them much—that would weaken them and build too thick an abdomen.

4. Though pheasant-tail fibers are fairly consistent in length, there is enough variation to make saving the longest fibers for the larger hooks a wise strategy.

5. Keep constant tension on the wire as you wind it as ribs—an instant of slack will loosen *all* the ribs, and the ribs must be firm to protect the pheasant-fibers.

14. Dub a full thorax from about the center of the shank to at least 1/16-inch back from the eye.

Dubbing the Thorax

14. This is easy. Just spin some pale-yellow synthetic dubbing onto your thread, and then dub a thorax. This thorax should be full—even round— really swelling out from the abdomen. The thorax should start halfway up the shank. The front of the dubbed thorax should end at least 1/16-inch, up to 3/32-inch, short of the hook's eye, to leave room for the wing and hackle.

Don't hesitate to dub back over the pheasant-abdomen while building the thorax, if that's what it takes to make the dubbed thorax start at the center of the shank.

Making the Wing and Burst Wing Case

Wind a tight layer of thread from the front of the abdomen forward to about an eye's length short of the eye (or even right up to the eye, if you don't mind having a slightly larger head in the finished fly). Wind the thread tightly back to the front of the thorax—these two thread-layers will provide something for the wing-shuck hair to grip.

Cut a small bunch of pale elk hair from the hide. Hold the tips of the hair and comb out the short hairs and fuzz with any comb. Even the tips of the hair in a hair-stacking tool. (For more detail on combing and stacking hair, go back to page 58 in the chapter titled "Marabou Muddler, Brown.") The correct thickness for this bunch is difficult to describe, but I'll try: it should be of enough hair to make a wing neither skimpy nor bushy. Imagine a thin wing with too few hairs to really fill it out, and then imagine a bristling explosion of hairs; then use an amount of hair that will make a wing somewhere between these two extremes. If that's not enough, study the photos.

Measure the hair against the hook to find the point where the hair-tips extend the full length of the shank. Hold the hair down *atop* the hook with this measured point over the hanging thread, at the very front of the dubbed abdomen. The hair's tips should now extend forward, off the eye, a distance equal to the length of the shank. Use the pinch to bind the hair; then continue holding it firmly as you add 12 to 15 *tight* turns of thread all in one place as a slim collar. Really try to keep all the hair up on top of the shank; truly tight turns of thread will help keep the hair on top. One way to get the thread tight is to stop after each turn is added, give the bobbin a firm pull down, and then try to maintain that tension as you add the next turn; then stop, pull the bobbin down firmly... Just keep following this sequence until all the turns are tight. Securing this wing all *atop* the shank *tightly* will make your tying easiest from here on, and the finished wing the best it can be.

Still holding the butts of the hair-bunch, raise them to about a 45-degree angle, slip in the open blades of your scissors from the side, and make one crisp snip to leave all the hair-butts as a squared stub of hair. This stub represents the burst wing case, and should extend back to the rear edge of the dubbed thorax—the hair-stub can be shorter than this, but no longer. All the hairs of the stub should be bunched atop the abdomen, but if some angle downward, you can just snip them off.

15.

15. Wind a tight layer of thread to just short of the eye, then back again.

16.

16. Cut, comb, and stack a small bunch of pale elk hair.

17.

17. Bind the hair, tips forward, atop the hook in front of the thorax.

18.

18. Raise the hair-butts and trim them straight across over the rear of the dubbed thorax.

Making the Wing and Burst Wing Case— Problems, Solutions, and Suggestions

1. It's easy to let the thorax and wing creep right up to the eye—then you've got no room for turns of hackle in front of the wing, perhaps not even room for a thread-head. So keep *your* eye on that 1/16th-inch of shank behind the hook's eye (*at least* 1/16th-inch), and make sure the thorax covers none of that 1/16th-inch and that the wing covers only the rear part of it.

2. This is worth repeating: get the wing-hair *tightly bound with at least a dozen turns of thread.* Unlike most hair-wings that are bound along the shank, the Quigley's wing is bound only with a narrow thread-collar—so make sure that collar is tight and secure.

19. Bind the hackle by its bare stem against the near side of the thread-collar holding the hair.

20. Bind the hackle's stem thoroughly, up along the shank, to a little way in front of the wing. Trim off the stem.

21. Wind two to four turns of hackle over the thread-collar holding the hair.

22. Raise the hair-tips and wind one to three turns of hackle in front of them.

3. It's good insurance to stand up and look straight down on the top of the wing-hair after you bind it on—you may find that the butts of the hair were cut at an angle, or cut too long, and need trimming.

Mounting and Winding the Hackle

Hold the hackle—the one you sized and prepared earlier—up to the hook. The stem should lie against the near side of the thread-collar. The stripped stem should project forward (off the eye), and the fibered tip-end of the hackle back (over the abdomen). It's best if you hold the hackle so that its concave (dull) flat faces down, towards the body. (The convex, shiny side should therefore face up.) But which flat of the hackle faces up or down is a minor point, and either way is fine.

Using a light turn, bind the hackle against the near side of the thread-collar, and then add five more tight turns of thread right away.

Draw the stripped butt of the stem forward under or along the shank. Raise the wing a little with your left hand and wind the thread forward over the shank and stem to just short of the eye (leaving enough room for a thread-head). Trim off the end of the stem closely. Now *that*'s a hackle that won't pull out.

Mount the tip of the hackle in the jaws of your hackle pliers. Wind the hackle forward, each turn abutting the last. You'll probably reach the hair-tip wing in two to four turns.

When you reach the wing, grasp the tips of the hair with your left hand and pull the hair up and back—but don't force the hair aggressively, because in the finished fly it should project forward. Just pull it back firmly, take up the pliers again with your right hand and wind one to three more turns of the hackle up from the front of the wing to the thread-head space.

Bind the end of the hackle, and then trim off its tip closely.

Draw the hackle-fibers and hair-tips back from the eye using the triangle. Build a small, tapered thread head, whip finish the thread, trim the thread closely, and then add head cement to the head.

Trim the Antron yarn (projecting off the bend). The resulting yarn-shuck should equal two thirds to the full length of the shank. You can trim the yarn straight across, square on the end—the usual approach—or, if you're picky, you can taper it out like a real shuck. Trout are rarely as picky as fly tiers—any trout sophisticated enough to analyze the shape of a collapsed insect shuck will probably notice that tippet sticking out of that faux-insect's face.

Mounting and Winding the Hackle—
Problems, Solutions, and Suggestions

1. If you find yourself short on hackle-room with the 1/16-inch of shank you left in front of the dubbed thorax, try leaving slightly more space next time.

2. If you have trouble winding the hackle in front of the wing, the problem is usually the wing itself getting in the way. Making sure you catch all the wing-hairs when you draw the hair up out of the way is important. Just taking a little extra time and care can also make a big difference. And magnification is always an option.

3. Having trouble getting the whip finish in past those leaning wing-hairs? Try working in a few half hitches with a half-hitch tool instead.

4. The hackle will wind on easiest and neatest if it is mounted on its edge. You can use thread-torque to mount the hackle this way—just angle the flat of the hackle so that it rotates onto its edge as you tighten the thread.

23.

23. Bind the hackle's tip just behind the eye. Trim off the tip closely.

24.

24. Build and complete a tapered thread-head. Add head-cement.

Trim off the shuck-material, leaving a shank-length shuck.

25. Here's the Quigley wing from the front—a long triangle of hair within a disk of hackle-fibers.

WD 40

(and a refresher on tying tiny flies)

New Techniques: making a combination tail-wing case, dubbing on a tiny hook

If you prefer your fishing in miniature, refined and precise, then the *Baetis* mayfly and the midge will provide all you seek. Fishing the hatches of both insects requires tiny flies presented accurately on fine tippets and quiet casts—about as sophisticated as fly fishing gets.

I offer these two insects as a set because midges and *Baetis* have a lot in common. Both are tiny—flies for *Baetis* require hooks of size-16 to -22; midge imitations run from size-18 to as small as fly-hooks go. Both live in soft currents (though slower for midges than for *Baetis*). Both hatch best in poor weather (*Baetis* especially loves chilly days and wind-swept rain). And more: both generally come off around midday (though mostly in morning and evening during hot summer months), both swim up in open water to hatch (providing excellent opportunity for both trout and anglers), and both can emerge in abundance. Perhaps best of all, both range across North America—if you live near a trout stream anywhere in the United States, odds are you can fish midge and *Baetis* hatches.

But the main reason I group these insects together is that you can imitate them both with the fly you're about to tie: the WD40.

Mark Engler, creator of the WD 40, guides on New Mexico's San Juan, a river known for big trout that feed conscientiously on tiny insects. On the San Juan, Mark told me, size-26 flies are common and 28s are for when the trout get picky. I've fished plenty of 22s and 24s, even the occasional 26—but *28?* Good Lord!

Generally, the WD 40 is fished emerger style, drifting freely like a dry fly, but resting low on the water like an insect in transition. Fished in this way it can suggest either a midge or *Baetis* struggling free, with the tail representing the remaining shuck. But Mark fishes it sometimes as a tiny nymph, suspended a few inches below a dry fly or right along the bottom below a strike indicator. Then it suggests the *Baetis* nymph and the fly's tail then actually *is* a tail.

All this talk of diminutive flies can intimidate even a really good fly fisher, especially if he or she has never fished anything so small. But size-10, -18, -26, it's all pretty much the same—you try to put the fly, drag-free, before a rising fish; set the hook when he takes; play him lightly enough to suit the tippet. Casting? Line control? Not much different with a small fly than a large one. But the tiny dry fly is harder to see than larger trout flies, so you learn to sense, or guess, where the fly is and strike when a rise appears in that area (or you trail your size-24 on some tippet from an obvious size-14 dry fly). Sure, fishing 26s is different than fishing 12s, but it's neither as different nor as *difficult* as you might suppose. Don't be intimidated by the fishing of tiny flies.

And don't be intimidated by the tying of them either. I'll provide guidelines for tying tiny, and the WD40, like most fly patterns for hooks size-18 or smaller, is a simple affair at the vise. (If you tied the Griffith's Gnat in the original *Clear and Simple,* you'll find the following chapter both a refresher and a step further into the world of tying tiny.)

I find the WD 40 most useful in sizes 20 to 24 for midges and 18 to 22 for *Baetis* hatches. But if I'm ever tying up a bunch for a trip to New Mexico's San Juan, well, some will be...smaller.

WD 40

HOOK: Light wire (heavy wire for a sinking version), short shank or standard length (straight shank or humped pupa/emerger type shank), sizes 28 to 16.
THREAD: Olive-brown 8/0 or finer.
TAIL AND WING CASE: Natural-light bronze mallard.
ABDOMEN: The working thread.
THORAX: Muskrat fur.
NOTES: Lots of color variations around now—brown, olive, black, gray or dark-gray thread with similar colors of rabbit for the thorax. Natural-dark mallard is another option.

Tying Tiny

Although I ran through strategies for efficiently tying neat and well-proportioned tiny flies in the original *Fly Tying Made Clear and Simple*, you may not have seen that chapter ("Griffith's Gnat") for some time (or ever). So here is a refresher on the subject, along with a few new ideas.

Bulk is the enemy of the tier of tiny flies. So start with fine thread. (I do well with 8/0 down even to my smallest flies, but there are finer threads, and they can be a blessing.) Cut *way* down on materials—only six or eight hackle-fibers for a dry-fly tail; two to four turns of hackle for a dry-fly collar; the fewest thread-turns required for each step; and so little dubbing, just a hazy pinch of fibers, you'll wonder if it'll show up at all when the fly is completed. (But trust me, it will.)

Magnification is many tiny fly tiers' best asset—a necessity for those over 40, an advantage for even the best young eyes. Reading glasses (3X power), a binocular magnifier (a jeweler's tool), or a lens on a flexible arm (fly shops carry them), are among the magnifying tools tiers use—each has its fans, each is effective (though I've only used the first two myself).

Proportions are as important for tiny flies as for any, though trickier to control in miniature. To get the tails on your tiny nymph truly one half to two thirds the shank's length, or the wings on your midge dry fly to stretch just above the hackle-collar tips, use magnification, and measure with a little extra care and patience.

Tools for tying tiny flies needn't be tiny themselves, but most must be fine at their working ends. Any vise will do, for example, just so long as its jaws, or one set of interchangeable jaws, are slim and fairly small at their tips. Your hackle pliers must have smallish jaws (which many do). And your scissors should have fine tips. (I file down the sides of my scissors's tips to about a 45-degree taper with a mill bastard file, but I always leave just a little thickness at the ends so they're not fragile.)

However, not every tool for tying minuscule flies must taper to a fine end. A hair-stacker, for example, is a hair-stacker—if it works for a lot of hair it will work for the small amount you might use for a size-20 Quigley Cripple. (Though for a small amount of hair you'll probably need to tip the stacker slightly, to keep the hair grouped.) And don't worry about finding a bobbin with a fine tube—large tubes, the kind on floss bobbins, are easiest to thread, and you'll never get the tube so close to the fly that its diameter will matter. Additionally, bodkins are bodkins, whip-finish tools are whip-finish tools (if you use them), and dubbing whirls and dubbing twisters are...well, you know.

Fortunately for the fly tier, tiny fly patterns are generally simple designs, offsetting considerably the challenge of tying on minuscule hooks. Trout, even really difficult trout, are generally unimpressed with ribs and gills and wings that curve gracefully apart on flies of size-20, -22, or smaller. So tiny fly patterns are simple not for the tier's sake, but because they catch fish (though this works out fine for the tier). The venerable Adams dry fly (which you learned to tie in the original *Clear and Simple*) is a perfect example—its tiny version, the Adams Midge, eliminates the striped hackle-tip wings to leave an elemental effect of just tail, body, and hackle. There *are* complicated tiny-fly patterns, and though they may occasionally have an edge, they are the exception. Most anglers never feel the need of them.

1. Tying threads, left to right: 3/0, 12/0, 10/0, and 8/0—any of the last three is right for tiny flies.

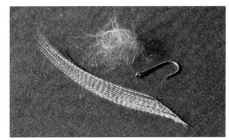

2. Here is just the right amount of the materials for a size-18 WD40. Not much there, eh?

3. Two magnifiers for tying tiny: reading glasses and a binocular magnifier. There are other good options.

4. Left: my HMH tying vise with its "micro jaw." Right: a "midge head," that locks into the jaws of a tying vise.

5. The sides of your scissors' tips can be tapered down finer with a file.

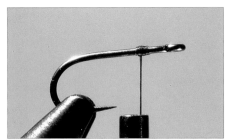

6. Start the thread three quarters up the shank, and break off the tag-end.

7. Strip the soft, fluffy fibers from the base of a bronze-mallard feather, as on the right. Cut a slim section of fibers from the feather.

8. Measure the fibers; then bind them atop the hook. The tips should extend off the bend a full hook's length.

9. Hold the fibers back and slightly elevated as you wind the thread down fibers and shank to the bend.

10. Wind the thread forward to the center of the shank.

Making the Tail and Abdomen

6. Smash down the barb of a light-wire standard or short-shank hook of gargantuan proportions for a WD 40—a *size-18*. (The hook shown is a Daiichi 1110.) Mount the hook in your vise. Start the thread three quarters up the shank and break off its end. (Even though this is a tiny fly, you can take all the turns you need to lock the thread firmly, since they will all be covered with the stout dubbed thorax. If the turns that lock the thread on the shank spread back a bit from the three-quarters point, they may even help taper the thread-abdomen.)

7. Strip the soft, fluffy fibers from the base of a bronze-mallard feather. Typically such feathers have a longer dark side and a shorter light side. Throw away these fluffy base-fibers.

Stroke a section of fibers out along the *light* side of the feather to whatever angle puts a squared end on the tips, evens them. The flat fiber-section should be 3/16-inch wide. Cut the section from the stem. When this section is finally built into the fly, it will stretch from tail-tips to the front of the wing-case, uncut.

8. Measure the section against the hook. Find the point where the tips of the fibers equal the full length of the hook, from the tip of the eye to the far edge of the bend. Using the pinch, bind the section atop the hook three quarters up the shank, with this measured point atop the *bend*. The fibers should therefore extend off the bend a full hook's-length. Add a few tight thread-turns immediately to really secure the fibers. (The "bend," of course, means where the shank *meets* the bend; which you'll have to guess at if you chose a curved-shank hook.)

9. Hold the section back just above the shank under light tension as you wind the thread in *abutting turns,* a smooth layer, clear back to the bend.

10. Wind the thread back up the shank in abutting turns. Stop winding at the center of the shank. These two layers of thread create the abdomen. Yes, just two layers—doesn't take much to make a mayfly- or midge-slim abdomen on a size-18 hook (much less a size-*26*). The tails should project straight back in line with the shank if you chose a straight-shank hook; they'll angle downward if you chose a hook with a humped shank.

Making the Tail and Abdomen—
Problems, Solutions, and Suggestions

1. You may find it easier on fine, flexible, tiny hooks to cut off the thread-end rather than break it off.

2. The tail on a WD 40 functions as either the true tail of a hatching mayfly or the shuck of a hatching midge (midges have no tails). In either case, a little is plenty when it comes to the tails. So measure the width of the section of mallard fibers carefully, and refer back to the photos often—I made sure the tail in the photographs is of appropriate fullness.

3. On curved hooks, it can be tough to judge the location of the bend, from which the tail should project. Try to imagine the shank being straight, conventional. Then you may be better able to approximate where it meets the bend.

4. If you want a thick wing-case for your WD40 but not an over-thick tail (or shuck), no problem—just bind on plenty of fibers, then trim some off at an angle, so that the cut ends taper back to the tail. Stroke the cut ends back repeatedly as you wind the thread down them to the bend. Wetting the cut fibers a little (with tap water, not saliva) can help you control them. This way, the tail will be spare, the wing-case full, and the abdomen thick in front while tapering to fine at the tail.

5. For a clean abdomen, be sure you make the thread-turns even, each new one up against the last, but not overlapping it.

Dubbing the Thorax

Because you first bound the mallard-section three quarters up the shank, then built the abdomen up only to the center of the shank, you should have room remaining on the shank to double the butts of the mallard back and bind them atop the center of the shank. So, do it—pull back the butts of the mallard and bind them atop the center of the shank, with a few tight thread-turns.

Snip off a little muskrat fur, close to the hide. Once you've cut off this tiny amount of fur, *do not* pull out the longer, stiffer guard hairs—they'll look spiky, like legs. Spin the fur onto your thread.

Dub a full thorax. Leave a little bare shank behind the eye for a thread-head. End with the thread hanging at the very front of the dubbed thorax.

Dubbing the Thorax—
Problems, Solutions, and Suggestions

1. If you have trouble doubling back the mallard-section, it's probably because (1.) you didn't first bind the mallard a full three quarters up the shank or (2.) you didn't stop the thread-abdomen at halfway up the shank and continued it up too far.

You have three simple solutions: (1.) if you didn't bind the butts fully three quarters up the shank, you can work the thread forward a few turns over the butts of the mallard, to provide more space for doubling back the butts, (2.) just bind the mallard-butts back further over the abdomen than the center of the shank (which may make the thorax over-long, but no big deal), or (3.) just complete this fly as best you can and concern yourself mainly with measuring more carefully next time.

2. On this size-18 WD40 you will want to make a head smaller than one you'd make on a size-10 or even a size-14 hook. Despite this, fly-heads will naturally be larger proportionately on tiny hooks than on larger ones—consequently, the head on your size-18 WD 40 won't require all that much less shank than if you tied the fly on a size-12. Bottom line: leave at least a modest amount of shank for a thread-head, tiny fly or not.

3. Anything that helps make tying easier on tiny hooks is worth considering. So with your WD 40, wax the thread for dubbing the thorax, if that helps; experiment with different thicknesses and even brands of thread; vary the techniques I've described if the varying makes them fit your style of tying better; and, if your eyes have changed through middle-age, as mine have, consider reading glasses, binocular magnifiers, or other magnification.

11. With the thread hanging at the center of the shank, draw the butts of the fibers up and firmly back.

11.
12.
13.
14.

12. Bind the butts at mid-shank.

13. Snip a small bunch of muskrat fur from the hide. Spin a little of the fur onto the thread.

14. Dub from mid-shank to just short of the eye.

15. Draw the butts of the fibers up, forward, and down.

16. Hold the fibers as you work the bobbin over them to make a thread-turn. Add three more turns.

17. Trim off the fibers closely; then build and complete a thread-head.

18. You can pick out some fibers at the sides of the dubbed thorax, though this is optional. Add head cement to the thread-head.

Completing the WD 40

15. With the thread still hanging at the front of the thorax, grasp the butts of the mallard near their cut ends in your right hand and pull them up, forward, and down under *light* tension. The butts should now be down over the dubbed abdomen and about horizontal.

16. Continue holding the butts down as you take up the bobbin with your left hand. Wind one half-turn of thread over the top of the mallard-fibers, and then let the bobbin hang on the far side of the hook. Reach back under the hook with your left hand and regrasp the bobbin—pull the bobbin firmly down and slightly towards you. Release the butts. Add three tight thread-turns as a little collar to secure the mallard. Look at the wing-case fibers; they should spread neatly over the thorax and then gather down evenly in front to the thread-collar you just built. Holding the fibers down and then draping the bobbin over them in this way has consistently made the cleanest wing cases for me.

17. Trim off the butts of the mallard closely. Work the scissor-tips in carefully and use several snips if that helps. If you want a clean head proportionate to the hook with this tiny fly—and you do!—you'll need to trim the wing-case fibers down very close. Really fine-pointed scissors will help (as I mentioned earlier, you can carefully file down the sides of the points). You can also raise the butts under light tension and then—with great care—work the fine edge of a double-edge razor blade in barely past the thread-wrappings to slice the mallard neatly away in a few strokes. But be warned: a double-edge blade is so sharp you could cut the thread—or your finger—with a thought. Careful, careful, careful...

Add just enough turns of thread to cover the cut ends of the mallard and then build a tiny, tapered thread-head. Whip finish and then trim the thread.

You can tease out the fur and guard hairs at the sides of the thorax with a bodkin or dubbing teaser, to suggest insect-legs. Or you can get the same effect by tying the fly on your tippet and making a few casts.

18. Add head-cement *sparingly* to the head. If you *ever* check and then, if necessary, clear an eye after adding head cement—do it on tiny flies. It's difficult enough to get 7X tippet through that diminutive ring as it is, triply frustrating if cement even slightly clogs the opening.

Completing the WD 40— Problems, Solutions, and Suggestions

1. Making a head small enough to suit a size-18 hook (or smaller) will require some extra care, and some strategy. I've described how to trim the wing-case fibers closely, but how you build the head will also make a difference. Use the fewest turns of thread possible to cover the trimmed ends of the mallard—and you may find that you can accomplish most of the covering of the butts and the building of the head simply by working three turns of a whip finish from the front of the thorax (that is, from the rear of the thread-head area) forward to the eye.

2. I've told you to make the head tiny, to suit your tiny WD 40. But... mallard is a bit slippery, so don't make that tiny thread-head *too* tiny, or the wing case might later pop free. A sufficient amount of strong head cement (I use a low-vapor epoxy glue) counts for a lot here.

YELLOW STIMULATOR

New Techniques: counterwinding a hackle with a rib (as with the Elk Hair Caddis in the original *Clear and Simple*), making a hair downwing, and tying a popular Stimulator-style fly

Randall Kaufmann's Stimulator has become the standard big dry fly for trout in North America. As an imitation, it is used mostly for hatches of stoneflies and caddisflies.

But I see the Stimulator employed most often as an attractor fly, imitating nothing in particular and simply suggesting something alive, meaty, and, in particular, edible. It works as an attractor, of course, so anglers just keep tossing Stimulators, hatch or no hatch.

The main feature of the Stimulator that sets it apart from a number of similar patterns (such as the Improved Sofa Pillow and Dark Caddis) is the way the body-hackle is secured with a wire rib in the style of a fly called the Elk Hair Caddis. This is a modest difference, but a smart one—the rib repeatedly crosses and, consequently, toughens the stem, and the hackle spiraling back leans its fibers towards the hook's bend, which helps the fly skate, not sink, when twitched.

And a Stimulator should be twitched, if a dead drift isn't working or the natural it's imitating is lively. Still, letting a Stimulator drift freely on river currents is the standard approach, and often the right one.

Big hooks, size-8 and -10, are the most common for the Stimulator, though the fly is equally good on smaller hooks. The Yellow Stimulator we'll tie is one among several standard color combinations, and perhaps the most popular of the bunch. Randall ties it in smaller sizes for imitating the yellow Sally stonefly complex. In larger sizes it's a fair match for the enormous golden stonefly of the West (though the Golden Stimulator was designed especially for this purpose). In any size it can pass, in a pinch, for a grasshopper (a more reliable choice, however, is the Dave's Hopper in the chapter titled "Dave's Hopper"). All this aside, I still consider this yellow version, as I consider any Stimulator, primarily an attractor pattern.

YELLOW STIMULATOR

HOOK: Light (or standard) wire, 2X or 3X long (slow-curve or straight shank), sizes 18 to 6.

THREAD: Orange (or fluorescent orange, or yellow) 8/0, 6/0, or 3/0.

TAIL: Natural-light elk hair.

RIB: Fine gold wire.

ABDOMEN: Bright-yellow synthetic dubbing (Antron, Poly, Superfine Dry Fly...).

ABDOMEN HACKLE: Badger or ginger.

WING: Natural-light elk hair.

HACKLE: Grizzly.

THORAX: Amber goat or synthetic dubbing (Antron, Poly, Superfine Dry Fly...).

1. Using your hackle gauge, find a saddle hackle to suit a size-12 hook.

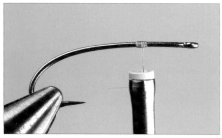

2. Again using your gauge, find a neck hackle for a size-8 hook.

3. Start some 3/0 thread two-thirds up the hook's shank.

4. Wind the thread tightly down the shank to the bend, then back up two thirds of the shank.

Selecting Hackles, Binding on the Tail and Rib

1. Using a hackle gauge, find a badger or ginger dry-fly saddle hackle suited to a size-12 hook—this is two sizes smaller than the size-8 hook we'll be using, and this two-size difference is standard for the abdomen-hackle on a Stimulator. You can use a neck hackle rather than saddle, but you probably won't be able to make the usual number of ribs. And I used a ginger hackle (grizzly ginger, actually, which ends up looking like plain ginger) because it's far more common than badger hackle these days.

2. With your hackle gauge, find a grizzly hackle, neck or saddle, matching a size-8 hook. This will be the hackle for the thorax. Set aside both hackles for now. (Because the hook is 2X or 3X long, this hackle is theoretically one size too small, but it looks right to me.)

3. Smash down the barb on a size-8, 3X long (or 2X long), light wire hook (or a hook with standard wire—for *big* trout). The hook can have a straight shank, or a slow-curve shank like the Tiemco 200, Randall's favorite Stimulator hook (and the one shown here). Mount the hook in your vise. Start some orange 3/0 thread about two thirds (or *slightly* short of two thirds) up the hook's shank. (Use 8/0 or 6/0 if you prefer, but remember that 3/0 is stronger, and that this is a big, stout fly in which thread-bulk won't be an issue.) Break off the end of the thread.

4. Spiral the thread tightly down the shank to the bend. (I know—where's the bend on a curved-shank hook like the one in the photos? Trust your instincts, and use the photos as a guide.) Maintaining firm tension on the thread, wind it back up to barely short of its starting point, almost two thirds up the shank. You just added a little diameter and texture for the tail and body to grip—this will help keep them from later slipping around the shank.

5. Cut close to the hide, comb, and stack a modestly thick bunch of natural-light elk hair. Measure the stacked hair against the hook—find the point where the hair-tips extend a distance equal to about one and a half times the hook's gape.

6. Hold the hair down atop the hook, with the tips of the hair extending a gape's length past the bend. Using the pinch, bind the hair about 1/16-inch (1/8-inch at most) short of two thirds up the shank. Add a few tight thread-turns.

7. Slide your left-hand grasp down the hair until you are holding it near its tips (just *comfortably* near). Raise the hair to a *slight* angle above the shank. Still holding the hair firmly back with your left hand, take up the bobbin in your right and spiral the thread tightly down hair and shank to the bend. Add a few tight thread-turns at the bend, to really secure the hair.

5. Cut a small bunch of elk hair and comb out its butts. Even the tips of the hair in a hair-stacker.

6. Measure the hair, and then use the pinch to bind it just short of two thirds up and atop the shank.

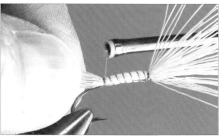

7. Hold the hair back and slightly elevated as you spiral the thread tightly down it to the bend.

Spiral the thread back up the hair and shank to where you first bound the hair on.

Trim off the butts of the elk hair. Cut the hair so that it tapers down to the shank at about a 45-degree angle.

Use the light turn to bind the end of a few inches of fine gold wire atop the shank, about two thirds up the shank. (Or pull some wire off the spool, and then set the spool on your tying bench, to your left, to hold the uncut wire out of your way.) Add a few tight thread-turns to really lock the wire on.

Hold the wire back and just over the shank under light tension. Keep holding the wire as you spiral the thread down it and the shank to the bend. Add a few tight thread-turns at the bend. Trim off the forward stub-end of the wire if necessary.

Selecting Hackles, Binding on the Tail and Rib— Problems, Solutions, and Suggestions

1. I find it fastest and easiest to cut the butts of the tail-hair *before* binding the hair to the shank. I cut the butts at an angle, and then hold the hair to the shank and bind it close to its cut ends using the pinch (or the light turn).

2. Elk hair is fairly soft, so if you bind it at the bend with tight thread-turns you'll get a widely flared tail. If you want the tail-hairs to stay more gathered, use thread-turns of only *firm* tension at the bend— neither tight nor loose.

3. I've noticed that gold wire of various brands runs from very fine—and fragile—to moderately fine and, consequently, fairly tough. The Stimulator is designed such that if the wire breaks, the hackle over the abdomen comes loose. So, I suggest you avoid wire that looks like golden spider web and prefer something more stout.

Dubbing the Abdomen and Adding the Hackle

Spin buoyant bright-yellow synthetic dubbing onto a few inches of the thread, and then dub a modestly thick, fuzzy body swelling gradually from the tail to a little thicker at the front end (or the body can be constant in thickness). The body should stretch no more than two thirds up the shank.

8.
9.
10.
11.
12.

8. Add a few thread-turns at the bend, spiral the thread back up the shank.

9. Trim off the butts of the hair, at an angle.

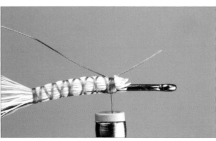

10. Use a light turn to bind some gold wire on top, two thirds up the shank.

11. Raise the wire; spiral the thread down wire and shank to the bend. Cut off the stub-end of the wire.

12. Add a few thread-turns; then spin dubbing onto the thread. Dub a full body up two thirds of the shank.

13. Strip the fluff and overlong fibers from the base of the saddle hackle.

14. Bind the hackle atop the shank at the front of the dubbed abdomen.

15. Angle the stem forward and bind it partway to the eye. Cut off the butt of the stem.

16. Spiral the hackle down the abdomen to the bend.

13. Strip the fluff and overlong fibers from the base of the short-fibered hackle you selected earlier.

14. Use the light turn to bind the hackle by its stem immediately in front of the dubbed body. Add ten tight turns of thread, to really secure the hackle. The hackle should project back over the top of the body. A little of its bare stem below the remaining fibers should show where it is bound on. If the bound hackle lies on its side, with its flat surface vertical, it will tend to wind best. I like the shiny convex side of the feather facing forward, towards the hook's eye.

15. Bind tightly forward a little along the hackle's stem; then trim off the butt-end of the stem.

16. Clamp the tip of the hackle in hackle pliers; then wind the hackle *back* over the abdomen in two *close* turns. Continue winding the hackle in five to ten open spirals to the bend.

17. Hold the hackle pliers in your left hand so the hackle angles slightly back off the bend. With your right hand, take up the gold wire and wind it in one firm turn over the shank and hackle. Now the hackle is temporarily secured. Squeeze the hackle pliers to open their jaws and release the hackle's tip. Continue winding the wire forward in five to ten firm, spiraled turns up the abdomen and through the turns of the hackle. When the wire reaches the front of the abdomen, hold it angling up and slightly forward over the hook's eye.

18. Continue holding the wire as you work the bobbin with your left hand to add a few turns of thread around the hook and over the wire. With the wire now lightly secured, take up the bobbin in your right hand and add more tight turns of thread as a collar over the end of the wire, just in front of the hackles and abdomen.

Trim off the tag end of the wire closely. Let the bobbin hang. Bind thoroughly the end of the wire you just cut.

19. Trim off the tip of the hackle closely.

Dubbing the Abdomen and Adding the Hackle— Problems, Solutions, and Suggestions

1. There is some advantage to mounting the hackle not so that it projects straight back over the abdomen but so that it projects out to the far side of the hook, at about a 45-degree angle. This angled-out hackle will tend to wind more easily and more neatly than one in line with the shank.

To mount the hackle angling out, hold it *straight* out to the side and bind the stem tightly. When you release the hackle it will tip back in, but only partway. Bend the stem (the butt) of the hackle forward and bind it.

17. Wind the wire over the hackle's tip, release the hackle pliers, spiral the wire forward through the hackle.

18. Bind the wire at the front of the hackle. Trim off the end of the wire.

19. Trim off the tip of the hackle.

2. If you wind the wire in the same number of turns as you wound turns of hackle, you'll get a neater body than if the number of turns of wire and hackle differ. Better yet, for a really clean body, make each turn of wire cross the hackle's stem at the same point, so that the pattern of wire and stem is consistent.

3. Just winding the wire forward over and through the hackle will probably hold the hackle through casting, fish-chewings, and the teeth of forceps. But for insurance you can wind two firm turns of wire over the hackle at the rear of the body, two turns right up against one another.

4. A safe way to cut off the tip of the hackle without cutting off any of the wound-on fibers is to *saw* a finely serrated scissor blade against the stem. Just hold the hackle tip out firmly as you stroke the blade back and forth across the stem.

20. Snip a modest-size bunch of elk from close to the hide. Comb and stack the hair.

Adding the Wing

Cut from close to the hide a modestly thick bunch of natural-light elk hair. (Use the photos as a guide for how much hair to cut.) Comb out the hair, and then even its tips in a hair-stacker.

20.

Use the pinch to bind the hair atop the hook about two thirds up the shank (directly in front of the abdomen). The evened tips of the hair should terminate right above the far edge of the hook's bend. Add a few more tight thread-turns to firmly secure the hair.

21.

Trim the butts of the hair to a taper, ending about 1/16-inch short of the eye. Stroke the trimmed hair-butts down against the shank. Wind the thread *lightly* up the trimmed hair-butts in a few turns to just short of the eye. These light-tension turns will gather the hair-butts. Now bind the butts tightly.

22.
23.

Adding the Wing— Problems, Solutions, and Suggestions

1. Rather than trimming the butts of the wing-hair *after* binding it on the shank, you can trim the butts of the hair to a long taper *before* you bind it. Try both methods, and see which you prefer.

2. To even the taper of the bound wing-hair, you can press it *lightly* with smooth-jaw pliers. A bumpy foundation can make the dubbing and hackle slide around where you don't want it later.

21. Bind the hair atop the shank in front of the abdomen. The tips of the hair should lie directly over the far edge of the bend.

22. Trim the hair-butts to a taper ending just short of the eye.

23. Bind the tapered hair-butts.

24. Strip the fluff and overlong fibers from the second, larger, hackle.

25. Bind the hackle atop the shank at the front of the abdomen.

26. Bind the stripped stem forward partway to the eye. Trim off the stem.

3. Getting the taper-cut hair-butts bound up the shank can be tricky. This may help: pinch the tapered hair-butts down just behind each turn of thread as you add it—holding the hairs close to the thread forces them to stay down.

4. As with the tail, the wing-hair will flare widely if the last thread-turns at the front of the abdomen are tight. So if you want the wing to lie gathered, bind the wing a little ahead of the abdomen with tight thread-turns, and then work the thread back with only *moderately* tight turns.

5. Here's a good way to keep the wing-hairs from working down the sides of the hook, rather than staying gathered neatly on top. Bind on the hair *slightly ahead* of the front of the body. Wind one modest-tension turn of thread around the *hair only,* and not around the shank—this one turn will really gather the hair into a bunch and keep in gathered. (But too much thread-tension will create problems, so, again, keep the tension only moderate.) Now hold the wing-hair back and bind it back to the front of the body—the thread-turn around the wing will keep the hairs from slipping down the sides.

6. There's plenty of range for the thickness of a Stimulator wing. The point is, it needs to be thick enough to truly represent a wing rather than a wisp, but not so full that it overwhelms the rest of the fly. Use the photos as a guide—the completed Stimulator on the first page and the one tied step-by-step both have wings of moderate thickness, so you can go up or down from there.

However, a modest amount of hair goes a long way in a deer-hair wing. So you'll probably find that you can use less hair than you thought and still get a proper wing. And it's really much easier to tie a Stimulator with a thin wing than with a thick one—a thick wing creates a steep taper for the thorax, and dubbing and turns of hackle tend to slide down such a taper.

7. If you want a thick wing, whose butts tend to create a taper over which it is difficult to make a thorax, or if you're just having trouble making the thorax, try making a *longer* thorax. The shorter the thorax, the steeper must be the taper of the wing-butts; the longer the thorax, the lower the taper and the easier it is to dub and wind hackle since they'll have less of a tendency to slip forward. Also, the lower the taper, the more durable the thorax. I've seen Stimulators whose thoraxes were only just short of half the shank. They looked fine to me.

Completing the Thorax

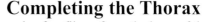
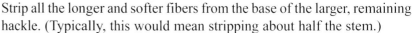

24.

25.

26.

Strip all the longer and softer fibers from the base of the larger, remaining hackle. (Typically, this would mean stripping about half the stem.)

Hold the hackle's stripped stem atop the bindings that hold the base of the wing. The stem should lie at the very rear of those bindings (which is also the front of the abdomen). The tip of the hackle should project back off the bend, and the butt should project forward off the eye. I prefer the concave (dull) side of the hackle facing me and the convex (shiny) side facing away from me. I want the hackle to lie up on its edge. And I want a little bare stem, about 1/16-inch, showing beyond the thread-windings.

So, use the light turn to bind the hackle as I've described; then add a few tight thread-turns to really secure the stem. Bind the stem forward, towards the eye, with tight turns of thread. At least 1/16-inch short of the eye, trim off the butt of the stem.

Dub, a bit roughly and heavily, from the rear of the wing-bindings to just short of the eye. You want the thorax to be at least as thick as the abdomen, and preferably a bit thicker. If you use the goat (rather than a synthetic dubbing), wax your thread and spend a little more time spinning the fibers onto the thread. Generally, longer, stiffer fibers like goat will look rough on the thread but will wind onto the hook without much difficulty and look good. With goat, the rough effect I described will probably create itself.

Clamp the tip of the hackle in the jaws of hackle pliers. Wind the hackle forward in three to five open spirals to the eye.

Bind the tip of the hackle at the eye, and then trim off the tip. Build a smallish, tapered thread head; whip finish the thread; trim the thread; and add head cement to the thread-head.

Completing the Thorax—
Problems, Solutions, and Suggestions

1. You can mount the hackle so that it angles out from the far side of the hook, rather than lying back over the shank, if you prefer. You'll find instructions in this chapter on page 96 under "Dubbing the Abdomen and Adding the Hackle—Problems, Solutions, and Suggestions."

2. When you dub the thorax-area—from the rearmost bindings on the wing to just short of the eye—make certain you cover all the thread-turns with dubbing. Just after you start dubbing the thorax, pause to take a quick look on both sides of the thorax (and the top and underside if you like), and then cover any exposed thread before working forward towards the eye.

To make *sure* the dubbing over the rearmost thread-turns covers them and *continues* to cover them after a trout or two, spin the dubbing *tightly* and not too heavily onto the thread for the first few turns, and apply those turns with care. Waxing the thread can also help you get the dubbing packed down to last. Okay—a few turns of thread showing around the thorax matters little, if at all, to a trout. But it may matter to you.

3. The thorax-dubbing will compress down considerably under the spiraled hackle-stem, so spin plenty of dubbing roughly onto the thread and build a thick, bristly thorax.

4. An alternate to just spiraling the hackle over the thorax: try making one full turn, or even two close turns, in one place, then spiral the hackle over the dubbed thorax, and then add another unspiraled turn or two just back from the eye.This gives a fuller and more defined effect than a hackle that's only spiraled over the thorax.

27.

27. Dub from the abdomen to just short of the eye.

28.

28. Spiral the hackle over the dubbed thorax in a few turns to the eye.

29.

29. Bind the tip of the hackle, and then trim it off. Build a small, tapered thread-head, whip finish the thread and trim it. Add head cement.

CDC *CALLIBAETIS* SPINNER

New Techniques: making splayed tails, split tails, a biot abdomen, and CDC spinner-wings

At first glance you'd never guess that a CDC feather would be a popular fly-material. Two sparish rows of fibers, covered with a glistening fuzz, like frost, lining the sides of a stout stem; a tier would think, Interesting...but nothing useful here. What that tier doesn't know, however, is that this mildly curious feather contains an oil that makes the fibers remarkably buoyant.

European fly fishers were the first to recognized the value of CDC (an acronym for "cul de canard"), and it was the book *French Fishing Flies* by Jean-Paul Pequegnot, published in 1984, that provided the American introduction. Today, all the big fly-fishing catalogs display CDC patterns on their pages.

I gave CDC a go-around back when it first started catching on in the West. I tied an all-CDC sort of Compara-dun—I used the fibers for the tail and wing and dubbed them for a body. At first, I was impressed—my shaggy construct floated so enthusiastically it seemed to hover. Then I caught a couple of little creek trout and watched the fly sink like a chip of waterlogged bark. My interest in CDC sank along with the fly...for a while. Thing is, I kept seeing really good fishermen becoming fans of CDC, especially those fishermen who preferred lazy tailwaters and spring creeks where the trout are difficult. Turns out, these waters are especially well-suited to CDC flies. Todd Smith—a production fly tier and fly designer who lives in Boise, Idaho, not far from the famously challenging trout of Silver Creek—says that one

or two fish per fly is plenty on water where hooking just a few counts as a fine day.

He's right, of course. And fish slime can be washed off a CDC fly easily enough by wiping the fly with a cloth. Once the fly has had time to dry it goes right back to its stubborn buoyancy.

The most effective use of CDC seems to be in patterns that float low, such as emergers that hang partly below the water's surface or dry flies that just lie down flat upon it, like the CDC Loopwing Midge Emerger (in the chapter titled "Additional Emergers") and René Harrop's CDC *Callibaetis* Spinner. The CDC in these flies just won't let them fully sink.

Callibaetis, which René's pattern imitates, is a substantial mayfly that lives only in very slow or still water—a few lazy rivers, such as Idaho's Henry's Fork of the Snake, produce good hatches, and many clear, weedy lakes are heavy with the nymphs.

On rivers, a dead-drift presentation to rising fish is the standard approach for a *Callibaetis* spinner imitation. On lakes, I like to drop the fly in the path of a working fish, letting the fly mostly lie still, but giving it an occasional gentle twitch.

If I had to pick one size for the CDC *Callibaetis* Spinner, it would be size-14—it's the middle size, and trout always seem open to it.

The spent wings of the CDC *Callibaetis* Spinner are only one of many things the tier can do with CDC feathers.

CDC *CALLIBAETIS* SPINNER

HOOK: Light wire, standard length or 1X long (a standard dry-fly hook), sizes 16 to 12.
THREAD: Tan (or light gray) 8/0 or 6/0.
TAIL: Light-blue-dun hackle-fibers.
ABDOMEN: Goose biot dyed tan (or light-gray).
WINGS: Blue-dun, or light-gray, CDC with brown Z-lon or Antron fibers on top.
THORAX: Tan (or light-gray) synthetic dubbing, Superfine Dry Fly, Poly, Antron...

Making the Tails (two ways)

Although the fibers from a big neck hackle can do a fine job as dry-fly tails, the best fibers for this duty typically come from the short, wide hackles at the sides of a dry-fly neck, called "spade" hackles. Either hackle will serve admirably, however. To make the tails on René's spinner-fly, we'll explore two methods: one that fans the tail-fibers and my own method that creates split tails—both are manageable, both produce tails that look good and stay put.

Here is a good way to make fanned, or splayed, tails. Begin in the usual way by smashing down the barb on a light wire, 1X long, size-14 hook, and then mount the hook in your vise. (The hook in the photos is a Daiichi 1190). Now begins the splayed-tail-making method. Start the thread about three quarters up the shank from the bend, and then break or trim off the tag-end.

Pluck a suitably large hackle from a blue-dun hackle neck (or you can leave the hackle on the neck for future use, if you prefer). Stroke a small bunch of hard, straight fibers (five to eight) out to a right angle to the stem. (You are trying to even the fibers' tips, and this angle should do so, provided the fibers are all of one length.)

Measure the fibers along the hook. Determine the point on the fibers, up from their tips, where they equal the full length of the hook—the *full* length, from the tip of the eye to the far edge of the bend. Hold the fibers atop the hook with the measured point on the fibers directly over the bend (meaning, of course, where the straight shank meets the bend). Use the pinch to bind the fibers atop the shank, where you started the thread (three quarters up the shank). Add four tight thread-turns to really lock down the fibers.

Hold the fibers by their tips, and raise them slightly, under modest tension. Continue holding them in this fashion as you spiral the thread down the fibers and shank to the bend. At the bend add two tight thread-turns to really secure the fibers there.

Wind a turn of thread *behind* and *beneath* the hackle-fibers, over the bend. Pull the thread forward and tight, so that this single turn of thread pushes up against the underside of the tail-fibers and splays them out. If you want the fibers splayed further, slip a second or even third tight turn up against the underside of the fibers. Spiral the thread three quarters up the shank

Grasp the butts of the fibers, raise them, and trim them off.

Now you should have a few fibers projecting out a full hook's length from the bend, and fanned out somewhat. This method produces not really split tails, but *splayed* tails.

• • •

Here's the way I normally make split dry-fly tails. It's an approach I worked out on my own (though there are other good ones out there you can explore). Start the thread at the hook's *bend,* trying to keep the thread-turns all in one place. Cut off (don't break off) the tag-end of the thread. Build the thread up to a hard, tight little ball. The best way to build this ball is to *crisscross* the thread forward and back and forward... continuing the crisscrossing of the thread until the ball is large enough to keep hackle-fibers well spread. (If you build all the turns of thread without crisscrossing, the turns will tend to slide off to the sides.)

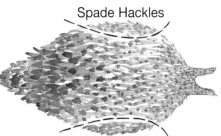

1. The standard source for dry-fly tails is spade hackles, which come from the sides of a hackle neck.

2. Splayed tails: bind hackle-fibers down the shank, so they project from the bend a full hook's length.

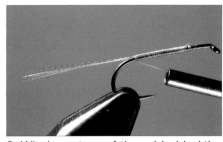

3. Wind one turn of thread *behind* the tails, and then tug it up under them.

4. This single thread-turn should push the fibers apart, for a fanned tail.

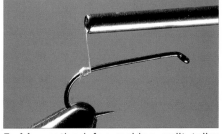

5. My method for making split tails: start the thread at the bend, and then *cut* off its end. Build a tight ball of thread at the bend.

6. Measure, and then bind a bunch of hackle-fibers down the shank to just short of the thread-ball.

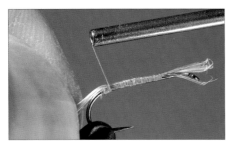

7. Hold the fibers firmly back and down as you wind the thread tightly back to the ball.

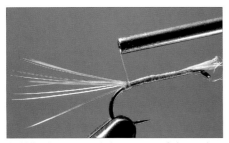

8. Wind on two tight turns of thread at the thread-ball.

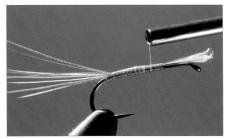

9. Spiral the thread three quarters up the shank.

When the ball is large enough (check the photos) spiral the thread steeply up about three quarters of the shank.

6. Even the tips of about 15 hackle-fibers, and strip them off the stem. Measure the fibers to find the point where they equal the full length of the hook. Bind the fibers by their butts three quarters up the shank using the pinch; add a few tight thread-turns to really secure the fibers. The measured point on the fibers should lie right at the thread-ball.

Hold the fibers slightly raised under light tension over the shank as you spiral the thread down them to just short of the thread-ball, about three to five close thread-turns short, which should be about 1/32-inch.

7. Now, holding the hackle fibers near their tips, pull the fibers firmly down behind the thread-ball. Some of the fibers will stay on top, others

8. will slide down the slides.

Continue holding the fibers down firmly as you wind the thread

9. *tightly* back to the ball in close turns. Make sure the thread comes right up against the thread-ball. Add two tight turns against the thread-ball, release the fibers and then wind the thread forward up the shank, *away* from the ball, in close turns. Spiral the thread about three quarters up the shank, stop, and let the bobbin hang.

Release the hackle-fibers. They should splay out behind the thread-ball in a fan. If any outside fibers angle downward, pull them out to the

10. sides and snip them off close to the shank. To do this, you can grasp the fibers with your thumb and finger, tweezers, or English hackle pliers. You don't want tails that point down, but rather tails that project outward, horizontally.

Push the point of your bodkin in to separate out two or three fibers from the near side of the fanned bunch. Push them straight out to the

11. side, or even a little forward, firmly. You want these fibers to stand away from the others.

Catch two or three fibers sticking out on the *far* side of the hook with

12. your bodkin and push them sharply out, just as you did with the fibers on the near side.

10. Grasp any fibers that angle down, pull them out, trim them off.

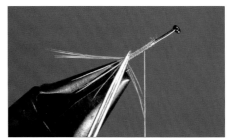

11. This is a partial top-view. Push a few fibers out from the near side of the hook using your bodkin; push hard so they'll stay out.

12. Push a few fibers out on the *far* side, as you did on the near.

Now you should have a splayed bunch of fibers in the middle, between the angled-out fibers on both sides of the thread-ball. Slip your open scissor-tips in around the middle group of fibers, close to the thread-ball—make sure the fibers you tugged out to the sides are *outside* the scissor-tips—and snip.

There should be two small groups of two or three fibers spreading out to the sides and forming a "V". *Voila*—split tails! All the fibers previously between the tails should now appear only as a cut stub.

Trim off the butts of the hackle-fibers.

I use the method I just described because, when compared with other methods, it's quicker (once you get used to it) and easier, and it makes good-looking tails (though such results might take a little practice) that *stay* neatly split.

Now you have two ways to make tails for the CDC *Callibaetis* Spinner—both are efficient and provide excellent results. Take your pick. Or try both before deciding which one you prefer.

Making the Tails (two ways)— Problems, Solutions, and Suggestions

1. Your tail-fibers may well be too short to reach from three quarters up the shank (where I told you to bind them on) out to extend a full hook's length off the bend. The solution is simple: just bind the tails on a little further back, two thirds up the shank may do it, and halfway will almost certainly work. This will leave a thin spot behind the wings, but you can build it up with thread or, if the dubbed thorax will cover it, leave it as is. You can also fill the thin area by *not* trimming the butts of the tail fibers, just binding their torn-off ends up the shank.

2. If, using the first method for *splayed* tails, you want the tails more widely spread, you can accomplish this one or more ways: (1.) *spin* the bobbin before adding the turn behind the tails, to make the thread stand high, (2.) after adding the turn, slide your thumbnail up the *underside* of the bend until it pushes the thread-turn tightly up against the tails, or (3.) add more than one thread-turn.

3. When using the second method, which creates *split* tails, make sure you keep the thread consistently tight as you bind the fibers back to the thread-ball, and as you wind the thread forward again—even a moment's slack will leave the thread less than tight and the tail-fibers less than properly spread.

Mounting the CDC and Making the Biot-Abdomen

Find two blue-dun or light-gray CDC feathers with fairly clean, even tips. The main thing is to find feathers that are symmetrical (not ragged and thin on one side and full on the other) and look similar to one another.

Hold the CDC feathers back to back, tips evened. The feathers should curve apart. Measure this set of feathers alongside the hook—find the point where the feathers, down from their tips, reach from the far edge of the hook's eye down to the middle of its bend (between the beginning of the bend and its far edge).

Stroke back all the fibers below the measured point on their stems, so that you're holding these fibers back over the butts of the feathers.

13.

13. Trim out the center fibers, leaving split tails. Trim off the butts.

14. Find two CDC feathers that are similar in form.

15. Hold the feathers back to back, curving apart, tips evened.

16. Measure the feathers against the hook. Find where they run from the eye to the middle of the bend.

14.

15.

16.

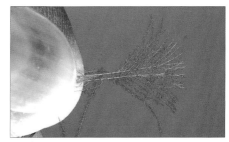

17. Stroke the fibers from the measured point back down along the butts of the CDC feathers and hold them there.

17.

18. Use the pinch to bind the CDC feathers three quarters up the shank.

19. Trim the butts of the CDC to taper partway back to the bend.

20. Bind the taper-cut butts of the CDC feathers.

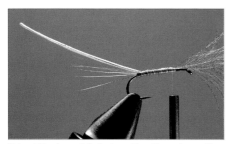

21. Bind a biot by its tip atop the bend. Wind the thread up the shank.

22. Clamp your English hackle pliers onto the butt of the biot.

18. With the thread hanging about three quarters up the shank, use the pinch to bind the feathers atop the hook. The feathers should now lie back-to-back atop the hook, on their edges. Add several tight thread-turns to really secure the feathers.

19. Trim the butts of the feathers—the stems and fibers—straight across, about one third up the shank from the bend. Now trim the cut butts to taper down to the shank. This leaves no butts over the rear third of the shank. Keep the butts you trimmed off if there are any fibers remaining on them—CDC is expensive, and even a few fibers can be useful with some of the CDC tying approaches.

20. Hold the tapered butts of the CDC back as you bind them down against the shank. Wind the thread back to the bend.

21. Here, I'll use a dyed-tan goose biot, as René prefers for the abdomen of his CDC *Callibaetis* Spinner. (But the real *Callibaetis* spinners I normally encounter have abdomens of light-gray, so I tied the finished fly at the start of this chapter with a gray biot.) Find a long dyed-tan (or, of course, light-gray) goose biot and snip it from the quill. Snip closely—you want as much length from the biot as possible. Bind the tip of the biot atop the shank right in front of the tails, using a light turn. The biot should project back over the tails, its flats facing straight up and down.

Wind the thread tightly forward up the tip of the biot and then up to just short of where the CDC feathers are bound on, three quarters up the shank.

Goose biots have a slightly convex side, and a slightly concave side. Whichever side is facing down once you've bound on the biot will show when you wind the biot. There seems to be very little difference in appearance from one side to the other. But I prefer to bind the biot with its concave side up—in other words, with the biot curving upwards—because when the biot is then wound, it may be a shade tougher because it is bending towards its natural arch. If you bind the biot too close to its point, the resulting body will be fragile; but if you bind the biot too far up from its point, the segmentation of the body will be wide and appear coarse. I generally bind the biot at least 1/16-inch up from its point. The length of the shank and the length of your biot may tempt you to use less tip than 1/16-inch; do so at your own risk—that very tip is thin and fragile.

Some tiers prefer *turkey* biots for fly-bodies. Advocates claim that turkey is both longer and tougher than goose, and looks just as good. From what I've seen, turkey biots *are* longer than goose biots, and do look good in a finished body. I can't tell you about toughness, but clearly, turkey biots are worth a try.

22. Lock the cut butt-end of the biot in the jaws of your English hackle pliers—you want the jaws in line with the biot.

Raise the biot and begin winding it—the narrow, bound tip of the biot should fold, so that the underside shows on the shank. Be careful to keep the tension on the biot firm and consistent, but without pulling hard on it—the tip of the biot will pull out if you do pull hard, even for a moment. Wind the biot up the shank in touching turns.

When the biot reaches the hanging thread, just short of the CDC, bind the butt of the biot with a few tight thread-turns. The result should be a neat, tapered abdomen (because you tapered the butts of the CDC) with clean segments that widen as they work up to just short of the CDC feathers. Very natural.

Trim off the butt of the biot closely; then bind its cut edge.

Mounting the CDC
and Making the Biot-Abdomen—
Problems, Solutions, and Suggestions

1. Rather than stripping the base of the stems of the CDC feathers, you can just stroke all the fibers forward and bind them together—the result will be thicker, shaggier wings, which you may find you prefer.

2. As you bind the taper-cut butts of the CDC, keep stroking them back and down, or just slide your left-hand grasp down them, as you add turns of thread—you'll get the neatest results this way.

3. You can bind on the wings *after* winding the biot for an abdomen if you like. But if you do, make sure you bind the butts of the CDC short enough that you can hide them under the thorax you'll dub later.

Completing the Wings
and Dubbing the Thorax

Pinch the CDC feathers together between your left-hand thumb and first finger. Try to catch up all the fibers. Draw the feathers up and firmly back. If any too-short CDC fibers project forward, trim them off closely. Push your right-hand thumbnail straight down onto the shank, and then push the nail back against the feathers' stems, creasing them upright.

Build lots of tight thread-turns back up against the base of the feathers so that when you release them, they stand erect on their own.

Carefully tug the feathers apart and down, until they project straight out to the sides of the shank. You'll need to use a *little* force in order to make them stay down, and try to hold the feathers so their flats don't twist—the flats should remain horizontal, in line with the shank, throughout this step. If one wing does wind up out of line, twist it carefully and firmly back in line. Now the feathers should stick straight out to the sides, their flats level.

23.

23. Wind the biot up to just short of the base of the wings.

24.

24. Bind the biot just behind the wings. Trim off the butt of the biot.

25. Raise the CDC feathers. Press your thumbnail back firmly against the base of the feathers.

25.

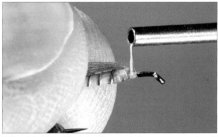

26. Build tight thread-turns against the front of the feathers.

26.

27. Pull the feathers apart and down to the sides of the hook.

27.

28. Wind crisscrossed turns of thread over the base of the CDC feathers to lock them down to the sides.

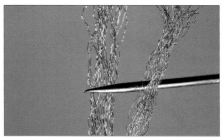

29. Divide some Antron yarn in half. Cut off a short length of one of the halves.

30. Bind the yarn atop the wings with crisscrossed turns of thread.

31. Trim the ends of the Antron at the tips of the CDC wings.

28. Wind crisscrossed turns of thread around the base of the wings to lock them down and in position. These turns should pass around the shank from the rear of one wing to the front of the other, around the shank again, but this time from the *front* of one wing to the *rear* of the other. Keep alternating turns of thread in this manner. Typically, it will take about eight to ten such turns to secure the CDC wings, but that can vary considerably.

29. Split a few inches of brown Z-lon or Antron into two equally thick bunches. (Antron yarn comes on a card or spool. The Antron you want comes as loose strands—do not use the very fine, fuzzy yarn woven like wool-yarn. (Check the photos.) Trim a two-inch length off one of the halves.

You are going to bind the Z-lon or Antron strands atop the wing so that the strands project straight out to the sides atop of the wing-feathers. The trick is to get the strands firmly mounted without knocking the CDC wings out of position. Patience and care, and a willingness to back up and try a step over, are the keys to success here.

30. Wind the thread back to *immediately* behind the base of the wings. Hold the Antron (or, of course, Z-lon) atop the shank and wings with the center of the strands over the base of the wings. The Antron should project out to the sides, over the CDC wings. Wind the thread forward from the rear of the near wing, over the strands, and down in front of the far wing. Use only light thread-tension for now.

Wind the thread under the shank, then up in front of the near wing. Wind the thread *back* over the top of the Antron and down *behind* the far wing. The thread should now be hanging behind the far wing.

Now the Antron strands are lightly bound crossways, extending out atop the CDC wings—good.

Crisscross the thread firmly, and then, for the last few turns *tightly,* around the base of the CDC wings and the center of the Antron. Add all the crisscrossed turns over the top of the Anton and shank that you feel you need in order to lock on the Antron and really secure it out over the wings. (Normally, I find that six to eight turns are enough to secure the Antron, but feel free to use more.) The Antron should now project straight out to the sides on top of the CDC wings.

31. Raise the Antron over one wing slightly, and then trim it flush with the tip of the wing. Cut the Antron straight across, so its end is squared.

Raise and trim the Antron over the other wing in this same manner.

32. Spin dubbing onto your thread. Dub all around the base of the wings and the Antron, to build a thorax. This thorax should be considerably thicker than the abdomen, and cover a little less than the front half of the shank—but leave a little bare shank behind the eye for a thread-head.

33. So, build a tapered thread head behind the eye. Whip finish and trim the thread. Coat the head with head cement. CDC *Callibaetis* Spinner completed.

32. Dub around the CDC wings and Antron to create a full thorax.

33. Build and complete a tapered thread-head.

Completing the Wings
and Dubbing the Thorax—
Problems, Solutions, and Suggestions

1. As you're working the thread in crisscrossed turns over the base of the CDC wings, tug at the wings as needed to both position the feathers properly and force all the fibers into place.

2. As with #1 above, tug and position the Antron fibers as you bind them, so that they lie neatly and the ends of the Antron splay similarly, match.

3. If the Antron yarn kicks out of position over the CDC wings, or kicks the wings themselves out of position, just back off the thread-tension a little. *Nearly* tight thread-turns will do the job, and probably won't squeeze everything into shifting around.

4. Once you've got the wings and Antron neatly and solidly bound on, dub *carefully* around them so as not to kick or twist the wings out of position.

PARACHUTE CADDIS

New Techniques: stacking calf tail, toughening a quill with cement, making a tent-style down-wing, making a parachute wing and hackle in combination with a down-wing

Ed Schroeder's Parachute Caddis makes perfect sense. The horizontal plane of its hackle-collar helps turn the fly upright and, once the fly is down on the water, the hackle-fibers appear as a plausible splay of legs along each side of the thorax. The white parachute-wing signals the location of this dark and otherwise inconspicuous low-riding pattern. The second wing, of turkey quill, softly speckled and mottled in a natural way, displays a clean and accurate outline of a caddis wing—everything about this fly is based on sound logic.

Yet after working through the shelves of my substantial personal library of fly-pattern and fly-tying books I'm left to believe that this is the first caddis imitation tied with a parachute wing and hackle, even though parachute flies date back to the 1930s and Schroeder's fly came out in the mid-1970s. A caddis with a parachute hackle, so sensible—why did it take four decades for someone to recognize that?

I suppose the good news is that someone *did* recognize it, and then did the job right.

The original *Clear and Simple* covers how to make a parachute hackle, and you already made one earlier

on the Klinkhamer Special. But this isn't your typical parachute fly—you'll make *two* wings on the Parachute Caddis, one for the hackle and one to suggest an insect's wings, all of which complicates things. That wing of turkey quill is its own challenge; it requires a coating of cement for durability, and must be *rolled* down around the sides of the body like a real caddis wing. Lots of new tying challenges here.

I fish mostly in the West, and consequently tie the Parachute Caddis mainly in size-14 and -12 for our common *Rhyacophila* and *Hydropsyche* caddis families (which are in fact common in the East and Midwest, too). And I'm sure that a size-16 Parachute Caddis with a body of dark-olive or chocolate synthetic dubbing would be just right for spring and fall hatches of the Mother's Day caddis. Caddisflies hatch in rivers all over the world. So almost any trout stream may be right for a Parachute Caddis.

Lakes, too, hold caddisflies, so...

I haven't tried it as such, but the Parachute Caddis would almost certainly pass as any number of smaller stoneflies.

PARACHUTE CADDIS

HOOK: Light wire, standard length to 1X long, sizes 18 to 10.
THREAD: Cream 8/0 or 6/0.
PARACHUTE WING: White calf tail.
ABDOMEN: Hare's mask.
DOWN-WING: Mottled turkey quill.
HACKLE: Grizzly.
THORAX: Hare's mask (or a buoyant synthetic dubbing in tannish-brown, or any caddis-color).

Making the Parachute Wing

Using a hackle gauge, select a dry-fly neck or saddle hackle to match a size-12 hook. Strip the longer and fluffy fibers from both sides of the stem, leaving the hard fibers of about equal length running up to the hackle's tip. Set the hackle aside for now.

Smash down the barb on a light-wire, size-12 hook. A hook with a standard-length shank, rather than the typical 1X long dry-fly hook, is an option for the Parachute Caddis. (The hook shown in the tying steps is a Dai-Riki 305, a standard-length dry-fly type. The hook shown on the previous page is 1X long—this way you get to see the Parachute Caddis on both hook-styles.) Mount the hook in your vise.

Start some cream 8/0 or 6/0 thread on the hook's shank, just short of the eye. Break off the tag-end of the thread. Wind the thread tightly back (towards the the bend) to about the center of the shank in close turns.

Wind the thread forward (towards the eye) halfway up the first thread-layer in close turns. The thread should therefore be coming off the hook about three quarters up the shank now.

Snip a small bunch of hair from a white calf tail. Hold the hair by its tips and comb out the short hairs. Stack the hairs in a hair-stacking tool. This'll take a little extra time—kinky hair, such as calf-tail, stacks grudgingly.

Measure the hair against the hook's shank. Find the point back from the hair's evened tips about equalling the length of the shank. (Like many parachute wings, this one will be slightly shorter than a standard dry-fly wing; though you can make it even shorter or up to standard length if you wish, a matter of personal style.)

Using the pinch, bind the hair, tips projecting forward off the eye, where the thread is hanging (about three quarters up the shank, right?). Add a few tight turns of thread.

Trim off the butts of the hair straight across, about halfway between the wing and the bend. Now trim along the sides and tops of the hair-butts to taper them back, almost down to the shank.

1. Using your hackle gauge, find a dry-fly hackle to suit a size-12 hook. Strip the fibers from the hackle's base.

2. Start the thread just back from the hook's eye. Wind it back to the center of the shank.

Wind the thread forward to the center of the first layer of thread.

3. Cut, comb, and stack a small bunch of calf-tail.

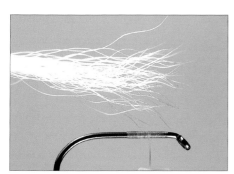

4. Find where the hair equals the length of the hook's shank.

5. Use the pinch to bind on the hair where the thread hangs. Bind the hair at its measured point.

6. Trim the butts of the hair to taper back about halfway to the bend.

7. Bind the trimmed hair-butts tightly and thoroughly.

8. Draw the hair-tips up and firmly back. Press your thumbnail back hard against the hair to crease it upright.

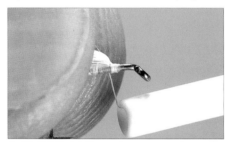

9. Build tight thread-turns against the front of the hair to hold it upright.

7. Wind the thread back in only *moderately* tight turns—not so tight as to flare or shift the hair-butts. This will gather and secure the tapered butts of the hair. Wind the thread forward again *tightly,* to really secure the butts.

8. Pull the hair-tips up and then firmly back. Hold the hair back with your left hand as you crease its base by pushing your right-hand thumb nail down onto the shank in front of the hair, and then pressing the nail back hard against the butts of the hair. This should set the hair-tips angling up.

9. Build ten to fifteen tight turns of thread up against the front of the base of the hair, to really set the wing upright.

10. Wind four tight turns of thread around the base of the *hair* (not the shank) to gather the hair into a single wing. (You can grasp the hair as often as you like to support it as you pull each thread-turn tight.) Wind the thread so that when viewed from the top, the turns run *counterclockwise.*

11. Run the thread down the *near* side of the shank, behind the wing. Pull the thread sharply back as you pull the hair straight upright. Make five tight thread-turns around the shank to anchor the thread—since the thread went down the near side of the hook, you'll have to wind the turns opposite the normal direction, away from you beneath the shank and towards you over the top.

12.

13. Wind the thread around the base of the wing again, two turns, *clockwise* (viewed from the top) this time. Now draw the thread sharply back and down the *far* side of the shank. Wind five tight turns around the shank to secure the thread—now the thread is winding again in the normal direction and the wing is locked firmly upright from two directions. This wing is set to stay.

14.

15.

10. Wind the thread around the base of the hair—counterclockwise, from the top—to gather it into a wing.

11. Pull the thread back firmly to hold the wing upright. Wind the thread down the *near* side of the hook.

12. Anchor the thread by winding it tightly around the shank *opposite* the normal direction. Add a few tight thread-turns.

13. Wind the thread around the base of the wing again, *clockwise* from a top-view.

14. Pull back on the thread and then run it down the *far* side of the hook.

15. Wind the thread tightly around the shank, in the usual direction.

Making the Parachute Wing—
Problems, Solutions, and Suggestions

1. The amount of hair you use for the wing *does* matter. If you use too much hair, the wing will overpower the silhouette of a caddisfly. Caddis have no *upright* wings, so the trout aren't supposed to even notice this one (which they won't when looking up at the fly—unless the wing is way too bushy). But if you use too little hair, the wing will bend around as you try to build a parachute hackle on it, and won't be much help when you try to spot the fly on the water.

The parachute wing in the tying photos is about as skimpy as you'd want. The wing on the completed fly at the beginning of this chapter is of typical thickness.

2. When setting the wing with thread-turns in both directions, just grasp and pull the wing around as much as you need to in order to end up with a wing locked evenly and firmly upright.

Building the Abdomen
and Making the Down-Wing

Spiral the thread tightly to the bend. Add a few tight thread-turns there (to anchor the end of the dubbed body you're about to form). Draw your bobbin out to expose a few inches of thread. Stroke a stick of lightly to moderately tacky wax lightly down the thread a couple of times—the rough dubbing you'll be spinning onto the thread will go best onto *waxed* thread. (Unless you choose to substitute a more buoyant but softer synthetic dubbing, in which case wax will be optional.)

Spin natural hare's mask dubbing onto a few inches of the waxed thread. Spin the fur on modestly heavy. (You can buy a hare's mask and trim off all the fur around the nose, eyes, and ears, then blend it, but nowadays it's much easier to buy hare's mask pre-cut and pre-blended in little packs.) Wind the dubbing-covered thread forward to build a somewhat stout dubbed body to the rear of the hair-wing. Wind the dubbing on a little thinner over the bound butts of the wing-hair; the resulting body should be fairly consistent in diameter. Again, you want to build a thick body, like the body of a real caddisfly (and like the dubbed body in the photos). You have three options for accomplishing this:

1. Keep winding the dubbing forward, then back over itself, forward and back repeatedly, as you work up the shank until you've built a body that is appropriately thick.

2. Spread out the turns of dubbing slightly, to make a thinner layer, as you wind the dubbed thread up the shank to the wing; then wind the dubbed thread back to the bend in the same way; and, finally, wind it forward in slightly spread turns up the shank to the wing again—all three thin layers together will build the body to the proper thickness.

3. Spin dubbing onto the thread more heavily than I described earlier; then just dub up the shank once for a thick, shaggy body.

• • •

16.

16. Spiral the thread to the bend. Swipe wax along a stretch of thread.

17.

17. Spin hare's mask dubbing onto the thread. Dub a body up to the wing.

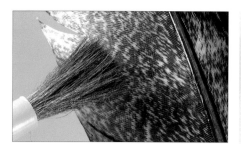

18. Toughen a turkey quill feather with Tuffilm or Dave's Flexament.

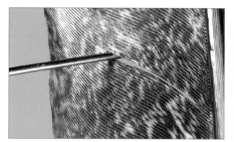

19. When the coating is set, separate a line of fibers with your bodkin.

20. Slide your bodkin out the fibers again to free a section about two thirds as wide as the hook's gape.

18. Toughen a turkey-quill feather by brushing a light coat of thinned Dave's Flexament over it (there is a thinner made specifically for Flexament) or by spraying it with an artists' fixative such as Tuffilm. You want to strictly avoid inhaling the vapors these products release, so work with them in a well-ventilated area—ideally, outdoors, keeping your face back from your work, with a cross-breeze to pull the vapors off to your side. Do not get either the spray fixative or the Flexament on your skin.

Once the feather is treated, the coating will release vapors for hours up to days afterwards, so keep the feather outside until its coating is fully cured and you can detect no odor.

You can tie the Parachute Caddis with untreated turkey, but the wing will likely split, perhaps even before the fly is fished.

19. Once the coating on the feather is cured, push the point of your bodkin straight into either row of fibers along the coated quill. You want the point of the bodkin to go in close to the quill. Slide the bodkin out along the line of the fibers to separate them.

20. **21.** Push in the bodkin again and separate the fibers again resulting in a section that is two thirds as wide as the hook's gape (no wider than three quarters of the gape). Cut the section off at the stem.

22. **23.** Fold the section *lightly* in half along its length. Cut its tip at an angle, so that when you unfold the feather it will have a "V"-notch in its tip.

24. Measure the section alongside the hook. Trim the base of the section so that when it abuts the rear of the wing, the notched tip will extend a gape's width past the rear edge of the bend (or, to look at it another way, 1 1/2 gape's widths past the rear of the abdomen).

25. Hold the trimmed section atop the abdomen and against the rear of the parachute wing. Push the sides of the section down around the abdomen. Take a light turn around the butt of the wing, then pull the turn tight to secure the wing. Add a few tight thread-turns to really lock the wing in place. Bind the wing's butt thoroughly with a few more thread-turns, but only bind back from the parachute wing about 1/16-inch and no further—if you bind the wing back too far, it won't look much like a wing.

21. Snip the section free of the quill.

22. Fold the section lengthwise. Trim its thin tip at an angle.

23. The section, when opened, should now be notched like this one.

24. Trim the thick butt of the section. It should abut the upright wing and extend back as a caddis wing.

25. Use a sort of pinch to bind the turkey-section up against the calf-tail wing.

Building the Abdomen and Making the Down-Wing— Problems, Solutions, and Suggestions

1. Nothing wrong with hare's mask for dubbing the abdomen (and, later, the thorax), and if you like the shaggy effect this coarse dubbing produces, all well and good. But, personally, I prefer a synthetic dubbing for my *Parachute Caddises* and, in fact, for all my dry flies—I've generally found natural dubbings to be absorbent and synthetic dubbings stubbornly buoyant.

2. This bears repeating: keep the coating, whether Flexament or fixative, light. A heavy coating will lie atop the fibers and tear in a ragged way when you try to separate out a section for a wing. And a heavy coating makes a wing of heavy weight—undesirable in a dry fly.

3. As an alternate to treated turkey, consider a synthetic wing-material.

4. An option: slide one scissor-blade out to separate out the wing section from the treated turkey quill—the blade's sharp edge may cut more cleanly and easily than the bodkin's needle.

5. For the finished wing, try to use the turkey section near its outer end, not down near its heavy butts, where it was cut from the stem—the thick butts of a turkey-section tend to split up when tightly bound.

6. The trick with mounting the down-wing is to bind it back just far enough so that it's locked on securely and rolls down around the body, but not so far that it looks less like a wing than a bustle (though the trout won't care either way). However, if you err one way or the other, I suggest you make a short wing bound too far back but secure, rather than a longer wing bound short that is not secure.

7. If you don't like the position of the wing after you tighten the first thread-turn, try momentarily loosening the turn to let the wing's butt straighten itself out. Then immediately retighten the thread-turn and add a few more tight turns to really secure the wing.

8. If you have trouble getting the wing to the proper length, try making the wing a little long and then trimming its end to a notch only *after* the wing is bound on.

Adding and Winding the Hackle

Wind the thread *lightly* up the calf-tail wing. You are preparing the base of the wing for the parachute hackle, so wind the thread in close turns up the wing at least 1/16-inch—enough space for five to ten turns of hackle. If you use truly light thread-tension, you won't have to hold the hair-wing at all, but can simply point the bobbin-tip straight down and orbit the wing with it to apply the thread.

Wind the thread back down the wing in close turns, *slightly* tighter than the previous turns working up the calf. You can use more tension now because the first layer stiffened the wing a little. And you still shouldn't have to hold the wing.

Hold the hackle you prepared earlier up along the base of the wing, with the fibered tip-section of the hackle up and the bare stem down. The bare stem should give way to fibers just slightly above the top of the thread-turns around the base of the hair-wing. Wind the thread in close turns up the base of the wing and the stem of the hackle—but use even a little more thread-tension than last time.

Wind the thread down the hackle-stem and wing—you can now wind the thread tightly because the previous three layers of thread and the stem of the hackle have stiffened the wing greatly. And you still shouldn't have to hold the tip of the wing as you wind the thread.

26.

27.

28.

29.

30.

26. Wind the thread in close *light-tension* turns up the base of the calf-tail wing.

27. Wind the thread back down the wing in close turns of slightly higher tension.

28. Hold the hackle you sized and prepared earlier up along the base of the wing.

29. Wind the thread in close turns up the wing and bare hackle-stem with even heavier tension.

30. Wind the thread back down the wing and stem—you should be able to apply lots of tension now.

31. Bind the hackle's stem forward a bit, and then trim it off.

32. Dub over the thread-bindings holding the down-wing. Dub all around the thorax-area.

33. Wind the hackle in close turns down the base of the wing.

31. Draw the bare butt-end of the hackle-stem forward and bind it along the shank a little ways, only about 1/16-inch—now the hackle is locked on. Trim off the bare hackle-stem closely.

32. Spin dubbing onto the thread. Dub thinly over the thread-turns that hold the turkey-quill down-wing; then dub around the base of the wing and in front of it. But leave a little bare shank behind the hook's eye for the thread-head.

33. Clamp the tip of the hackle in your hackle pliers. Wind the hackle down the base of the wing in close turns to a little way into the dubbing. If you were to stand and look straight down onto the wing (go ahead and do so if you like), you should see the hackle winding on *counter*clockwise—this way, when you tighten the thread over the hackle's tip, you'll tighten, not loosen, the hackle.

34. Bind the tip of the hackle just behind the eye. Tug the wing and hackle to angle back and allow you clear access to the hook. Trim off the hackle's tip and build a thread-head. Whip finish and trim the thread. Add head cement to the head.

35. Later, when the head cement is fully set, tug the wing and hackle back into position. (If you need help with any of the steps for making a parachute hackle, refer back to the chapter titled "Klinkhamer Special.")

Adding and Winding the Hackle— Problems, Solutions, and Suggestions

1. When you wind the thread in its fourth, final, layer of thread down the base of the calf-tail, make the turns of thread as tight as the wing will take without bending over—the turns need to be tight, yes, in order to hold everything together for keeps, but not to the *extreme*. If the wing gives too easily, just do the best you can and then make a thicker wing next time, one that will stand more firmly.

2. Don't hesitate to really pull the hackle and wing up and back so that you're free to make a neat tapered head. I often stroke all the hackle-fibers in front thoroughly back, as though I were using the triangle. When the head cement is set, the wing and hackle will go back to a correct and neat position with a little tugging, and stay there.

3. Having trouble getting a whip finish onto the head of your parachute fly? Try using a half-hitch tool to add a few hitches instead.

34. Bind the tip of the hackle at the hook's eye. Trim off the tip, build a thread-head, whip finish and trim off the thread, add head cement.

35. When the head cement is set, tug the hackle and wing back into position.

36. Top view of the Parachute Caddis. Note the notched wing and the disk of hackle-fibers.

CHERNOBYL ANT

New Techniques: building a layered foam-body, tying with and securing foam, making rubber-strand legs, making a foam strike-indicator

The name "Chernobyl Ant" suggests a freak ant, giant and malformed as a result of the Chernobyl nuclear disaster. Grim humor. Often tied on size-8 and -6 hooks, making it many times the size of any real North American ant, its eight legs crossing unnaturally at the fly's center, and now tied in layers of garish colors with striped legs inset with sparkles, well, it just makes no sense on a trout stream.

But it works. And sometimes it works when little or nothing else will. It's a true attractor fly in most of its versions—but when the time is right, unnatural attractor flies sometimes impressively out-fish imitative flies. It's just a fact of fly-fishing life.

The Chernobyl wasn't always an attractor. Allan Woolley developed the fly to imitate the big "Mormon Cricket" of certain western grasslands and tied it in black with orange thread. But once the fly caught on, new versions layered with garishly colored foam, flanked with striped legs that sparkle, topped with parachute hackles or yellow elk-hair wings began showing up—the fly continues to get weirder and weirder. I rarely see the original black version any more.

In my experience, big is usually best with Chernobyls. I like at least a size-8 hook and often fish a -6. (Though smaller ones do have their believers). It's a fly for trout rivers, rather than lakes (in my experience). You can throw it on wild or flat water, against the bank or well out from it, and watch big trout come up in earnest (if those trout are in a Chernobyl mood).

The Chernobyl Ant also serves as a good introduction to tying with foam. This, however, is only one of many ways to tie with foam-sheeting—it can also be formed into segments along a shank or a needle (then slipped off the needle), folded into a buoyant wing-case, cut to wing-shapes, and more. And sheeting is just one form of foam; there are foam-dowels; pre-cut foam-bodies; foam heads for noisy, floating bass and saltwater flies called "poppers"... Buoyant foam can fill out the thick body of a dry stonefly imitation or hold an emerger-fly up to hang from the water's surface or raise an imitation dragonfly-nymph above a sinking line and lake-bed snags. Foam has truly caught on with tiers. It's a material offering real advantages in fly-design and a material I know well—I wrote a book on it titled *Tying Foam Flies*.

My advise: use foam marketed for fly tying, unless you want to sort through a lot of it that floats poorly or is too easily cut by thread or trout-teeth.

CHERNOBYL ANT (variation)

HOOK: Light to standard wire, 2X long (a slow-curve shank is optional), sizes 10 to 6.

THREAD: Yellow 6/0 or 3/0.

BODY: Brown, yellow, and tan foam-sheeting (or whatever colors you like).

LEGS: Bronze flat rubber-strand with black markings (or any sort of rubber-strand you like).

STRIKE INDICATOR: A short strip of yellow foam-sheeting.

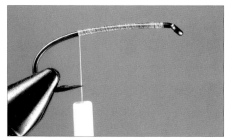

1. Start the thread near the eye. Wind a tight layer of thread back to 1/16-inch short of the bend.

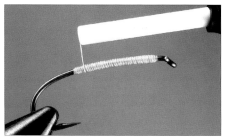

2. Wind the thread forward to where you started it. Wind a layer back, then forward, then back—five layers in all.

3. Cut three strips from foam sheeting, one tan, one yellow, one brown.

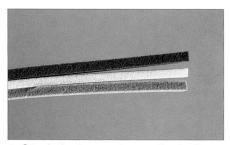

4. Stack the layers, tan on the bottom, then yellow, then brown.

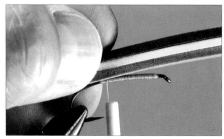

5. Hold the foam-layers securely atop the shank.

Cutting the Body-Foam and Binding it Once

Smash the barb on a size-6 light- to standard-wire 2X long hook. (The hook shown is a Tiemco 2302.)

1. I got an update on the Chernobyl Ant a couple of years ago from Montana fly tier Weston McKay for a magazine article I was writing. Wes is a big believer in building a tight thread-foundation on the hook's shank for all Chernobyls, to keep the body from twisting on the hook. This foundation gives the thread-turns securing the body something they can really grip. So, start some yellow 3/0 thread *just* short of the eye, break or cut the tag-end of the thread, and wind a tight layer of thread back to 1/16-inch short of the bend. (With the slow-curving shank of the Tiemco 2302 shown here, it's hard to say where the bend starts. So on this hook, wind the thread back to directly over the hook's point.)

Wind a second tight layer of thread forward almost to the eye (where you started the thread).

2. Wind the thread back again, and then forward again—now the shank is covered with four tight thread-layers, and the thread is hanging near the eye.

Wind the thread tightly back to 1/16-inch short of the bend (which means 1/16-inch short of the end of the other layers of thread). Now you have five thread-layers.

3. Cut a strip of tan foam-sheeting. The width of the strip should equal 1/2 the length of the entire hook (not just the shank). The length of the strip should equal twice the *full length* of the hook. The foam-sheeting should be buoyant, of course, but also fairly supple and about 1/16-inch thick—right now, several companies market such foam for tiers.

Cut another foam-strip, same dimensions as the first strip but this one should be cut from yellow foam-sheeting.

Cut a third strip, same dimensions as the first two, from brown foam-sheeting.

4. Stack the strips of foam-sheeting—brown on top, yellow in the center, tan on the bottom. Make sure the edges and ends of the strips are evened.

5. Hold the strips together atop the hook. Hold the strips by their rear end. The rear end of the strips should extend at least 1/4-inch (if not 3/8-inch) behind the *rear edge* of the hook's bend.

You are about to bind foam; time for a strategy-session. The thing is, really tight thread-tension will weaken, even cut through foam. Light thread-tension won't properly secure the foam. You need to bear down on the thread enough to really compress the foam, but stop short of digging down into it to the maximum—so use *firm* thread-tension. Since you can't use tight thread-turns to secure the foam, use lots of thread-turns (and sometimes, add some glue or cement).

Wind a light turn of thread over the butts of the three foam-layers (the thread is coming up from 1/8-inch ahead of the hook's bend, right?). Hold the foam firmly in place as you tighten the thread down (only to firm, okay?). Add 15 additional firm thread-turns to really nail down the foam-strips. Try to keep the thread-turns close, as a narrow collar.

Cutting the Body-Foam and Binding it Once—Problems, Solutions, and Suggestions

1. The purpose of binding the foam-body ahead of the bend is to expose the hook's point. The bound foam-body swells down below the shank to partially block the point, and the extended body tends to interfere with the point's work—but binding the body ahead of the bend reduces both effects so that your Chernobyl will find a solid bite and hold the trout that takes it.

2. Once the foam is bound atop the shank, tug at the foam-butt to see how easily it shifts and rolls around the shank—though it isn't yet fully secure, it shouldn't move too easily.

3. Three-ought thread has real advantages here: it covers the shank faster than finer thread would, and because it's thick, is less likely to cut the foam. So prefer heavy thread when tying with foam (although smaller fly patterns, other than the Chernobyl Ant, may require finer threads than 3/0).

4. Wes winds *seven* tight layers of thread on the hook as a foundation. He's something of a Chernobyl Ant specialist, so consider following his lead.

5. You can taper the ends of the thread-layers, making the fly a little neater, by stopping each layer barely short of the previous one.

6. Some tiers glue the foam-layer together, laminate them, with contact cement or a glue that adheres to rubber. This does make the fly a bit neater, with the foam-layers holding tight together when bound rather than spreading apart. Overall, it's a minor difference, and I haven't found that it has any influence on the fly's effectiveness.

If you do want to try laminating the foam, cut three good-sized squares of it, paint a thin layer of glue over the top of the tan foam, lay the yellow atop it, paint a thin layer over the top of the yellow and then lay the brown over that. Set something heavy and flat atop the layers (perhaps a board with a brick or other weight on top of it. Wax paper between the board and foam and under the foam will insure that only foam will be glued to foam). Follow the safety instructions that come with whatever adhesive you use.

Adding the Legs and Binding the Rest of the Body

Cut two 3-inch lengths of rubber-strand. Loop one strand over the thread; hold the loop by its ends. Slide the looped strand down to the near side of the thread-collar that is holding the foam-layers.

Swing the bobbin, and thread, away from you and slightly down. When the thread is tight, the rubber-strand should be locked in place on the near side of the hook. Wind tight thread-turns over the strand and thread-collar to really secure the strand. (Yes, you can make *tight* thread-turns, because they aren't really over the foam, but over the thread-collar.) Now one length of rubber-strand should be bound at its center on the near side of that shank, resulting in two rubber-strand legs making a "V" shape.

6. Bind the foam with plenty of *firm* thread-turns 1/8-inch up from the bend. Keep the turns gathered.

7. Double three inches of rubber-strand over the thread.

8. Slide the strand down the thread to the *near* side of the shank, against the bindings holding the foam.

9. Bind the strand at its center, with tight thread-turns.

10. Bind another length of rubber-strand on the far side of the shank. This is a top view.

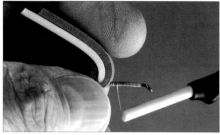

11. Hold the foam and rubber-strands back. Wind the thread forward to mid-shank.

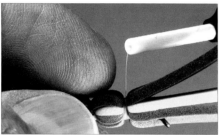

12. Lower the foam and bind it again, with *firm* thread-turns.

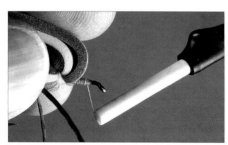

13. Raise the foam-layers again and wind the thread to 1/16-inch short of the eye.

10. Double the other length of rubber-strand over the thread and bind it on the *far* side of the shank, over the thread-collar holding the foam.

Add eight to ten more tight thread-turns over the center of both rubber-strands, over the thread-collar, to really secure them.

11. Raise the front of the foam-strips and hold the rubber-strand legs back out of the way. Wind the thread forward to the center of the thread-layers covering the shank.

12. Lower the foam to the shank and hold it firmly in place. Still holding the strands back, wind 20 *firm* thread-turns as a collar. Now the foam is bound with two thread-collars. Normally, a Chernobyl Ant is bound at the bend and again just behind the hook's eye—in two places only. But Wes McKay is convinced that a Chernobyl-body bound in three places is less apt to spin on the shank than one bound in two. Okay...makes sense to me.

13. Draw the front of the foam-strips up and back again, and hold the rubber-strand legs back, as you spiral the thread forward to about 1/16-inch short of the hook's eye.

14. Lower the foam again and bind it as before, with a thread-collar.

15.
16. Bind a length of rubber-strand tightly against each side of the thread-collar, as before.

Each pair of legs should spread at about a 45-degree angle.

Adding the Legs and Binding the Rest of the Body— Problems, Solutions, and Suggestions

1. The only way I know to push a set of rubber-strand legs further out from a foam fly-body, as on the Chernobyl, is to bind the strand more tightly. If it's too late, no problem—unlike fly tiers, trout don't obsess over leg-angles.

2. If a set of legs doesn't spread widely enough, push firmly against the base of the set, against the thread-collar, to spread the legs. If the leg-sets on *both* sides of a thread-collar need spreading, just pinch the collar firmly at the sides.

3. If your rubber-strand curves, which some may, you can put the curve in or out as you prefer—but be consistent. Your fly will look best if all the legs curve in the same way.

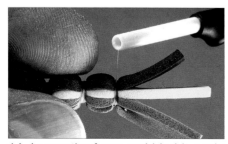

14. Lower the foam and bind it again with gathered firm thread-turns.

15. Loop another section of rubber-strand around the thread, and bind it against the near side of the thread-collar.

16. Bind another section of rubber-strand on the far side of the hook. (This is a top-view.)

Completing the Chernobyl Ant (variation)

Cut a strip of yellow foam-sheeting. The strip should be 2/3 as wide as the body-foam and 3/8-inches long.

With the thread still coming from the last, forward-most thread-collar, hold the strip of yellow foam atop the bound foam-body. Hold the yellow strip in line with the layered foam-body. The center of the yellow strip should lie directly over the last, front thread-collar. Hold the rear of the yellow foam-strip firmly. Wind the thread over the strip, and then pull the thread tight.

Bind the yellow strip of foam with plenty of firm thread-turns. You should be winding the thread over the yellow foam-strip, the layered foam-body, the thread-collar, and between the two forward sets of rubber-strand legs.

Whip finish the thread over the thread-collar and between the two sets of legs. Trim the thread.

Trim the rear end of the foam layers to about 1/2 inch from the thread-collar.

Trim off the corners of the square end of the foam.

Trim the front end of the foam straight across, about 1/4 inch past the front thread-collar. Trim off the corners of the foam, as you did with the rear end of the foam.

Trim all eight legs to length. There really is no set length for Chernobyl legs, but the idea is to make them long enough to sway or quiver in the water without making them spidery long. I trim them to a full hook's length each.

Add head cement (or low-odor epoxy glue) to the whip finish over the front thread-collar.

Remove the Chernobyl Ant from your vise. Turn the Ant upside down and run head cement or low-odor epoxy glue up the shank—add enough cement or glue so that it will bond with both the thread-covered shank and the underside of the foam-body. This step isn't required, but it does make a Chernobyl tougher.

17.
18.
19.
20.
21.
22.
23.
24.
25.

17. Cut a short, narrow section of yellow foam-sheeting.

18. Bind the yellow foam atop the last, front thread-collar holding the foam-layers and legs.

19. Whip finish the thread over the yellow foam, the thread-collar, and the leg-sections. Cut the thread.

20. Trim the rear of the foam-strip body straight across, about 1/2-inch out from the rear thread-collar.

21. Trim the corners of the foam.

22. Trim the front of the foam-strips about 1/4-inch past the forward thread-collar. Trim the corners.

23. Trim all the legs to about the full hook's length.

24. Add cement or glue around the whip finish on the thread-collar.

25. Add cement or glue along the shank under the foam-body.

WOOLLY WING, ORANGE

New Techniques: working with wool in general, blending wool and fine Mylar, building a body and wing in sections, trimming a woolen wing

For my books and magazine articles over the years I've tied hundreds of fly patterns—perhaps thousands—and still, I've yet to see another fly like my Woolly Wing. The closest fly-design is undoubtedly the Mikulak Sedge. I got to know the Mikulak while fishing for weeks at a time in British Columbia as research for the book *Morris & Chan on Fly Fishing Trout Lakes*. The pattern is a big hit on Canadian lakes.

I can see why—the fly floats stubbornly and its short wing-hairs don't splay out but instead hold the shape of a real sedge, or caddisfly wing; also like a real caddis the Mikulak rests its body down on the water. A buoyant and convincing fly pattern—what's not to like? In British Columbia it's a popular fly for imitating the caddis of lakes, especially when tied on long-shank size-6 and even size-4 hooks for the traveller sedge, a stout caddis behemoth that can lure really big trout up in range of a dry fly.

So I was sold on the Mikulak Sedge, yet I had a feeling it could lead me to a dressing that would suit me better. Only took a decade or so. The breakthrough came when I discovered that wool, despite that it's almost always used in sinking flies, is really buoyant. So I made a fly with a trimmed woolen wing and watched it float all day (except when a trout took it down, but once I got the fly back and snapped it dry it would be up bobbing again on the current). I also liked the neatness of the wing—its outline was clean.

I questioned my discovery of wool's buoyancy—why did I seem to be the first to notice? Was I mistaken when I observed my woolen-winged dry flies bobbing so high for so long? Was I going mad? I wrote to my friend John Rohmer, owner of Arizona Flyfishing, Inc., a company that produces dubbings and synthetic streamer hair. I've come to trust John's deep understanding of both natural and synthetic tying materials.

Judging by his reply, I'd say either I was correct or we're both mad. He said:

> Wool is one of the natural fibers that tends to shed water. Once it gets soaked it will sink, of course, but it will also shed water on backcasts, so it has been a staple dry fly dubbing for those who prefer natural materials.

Actually, this makes sense to me. I mean, if wool makes buoyant dubbing that easily throws off moisture, it should make wings that do the same, right? Trust me—it does.

I'm a fan of the parachute hackle—its hackle-fiber legs spread convincingly around the fly's thorax, and the horizontal plane of the fibers helps the fly light upright on water. Using a parachute hackle on my Woolly Wing also allowed me to perch a bright dome of yarn up where the trout couldn't see it but where it would catch my eye on dark water—this made it an easier fly to spot than the all-dark Mikulak Sedge.

But this isn't a contest between fly patterns—the Mikulak remains an excellent and original fly that will always have its followers, and should. I still fish it myself. It's just that now I fish my Woolly Wing more often.

Mostly, I fish Woolly Wings to imitate caddisflies and stoneflies—which both look very similar to one another from below, where trout see them. Sometimes, however, I throw a Woolly Wing out on a river or lake if I just think the trout are in the mood for a stout dry fly.

The Woolly Wing, Orange imitates two huge western insects: the salmonfly stonefly and the October caddis. Tied on a size-8 or -6 hook it'll cover the adults of both hatches—trout don't seem to quibble about size with giant insects. Tied in other sizes and colors it imitates many different caddis and stoneflies, from big to small.

WOOLLY WING, ORANGE

HOOK: Light to heavy wire, 2X long (standard length or 1x long for smaller hooks), sizes 8 to 4.

THREAD: Orange 8/0, 6/0, or 3/0.

BODY AND WING: Bunches of dyed-brown wool mixed with fine strands of brown Mylar (Ice Dub, Lite Brite, Angel Hair...) between short sections of somber-orange synthetic dubbing (I prefer Antron or Poly dubbing).

PARACHUTE WING: Dyed-yellow or -orange wool (or egg-yarn or Poly yarn).

PARACHUTE HACKLE: Brown.

Building the Wing and Body

Smash down the barb on a size-8 light- to heavy wire 2X long hook with or without a slow-curve shank. (The hook shown is a Daiichi 1260.) Mount the hook in your vise.

Use your hackle gauge to find a size-8 brown dry-fly neck or saddle hackle. (Yes, this is a 2X-long-shank hook, so theoretically it takes a size-*4* hackle—two sizes larger than the hook size. But with big hooks like these, I usually find the hackle looks just right when it matches the hook's designated size. Strange, but with smaller Woolly Wings tied on conventional standard-length or 1X long dry-fly hooks, matching the hackle-size to the hook-size also looks correct to me. Must have something to do with an anomaly in the space-time continuum.) Strip the longer, softer fibers from the lower half or so of the hackle's stem. Set the hackle aside for now.

Start the thread about two thirds up the shank, and then wind the thread in fairly close tight turns to the bend. This creates a foundation for the wing-sections to grip. (Tough to say exactly where the bend is on a slow-curve hook like this one, but just imagine the shank is straight and you'll be close enough. Note that on the Daiichi 1260 I guessed the bend to be where the thread will hang about halfway between the hook's point and barb.) Spin dubbing onto the thread. Dub a short butt from the bend forward—keep the butt short and thick.

Snip off a 2-inch-long section of wool. The section should be, when lightly rolled to round, about 1/4- to 5/16-inch in diameter. (Use the photos as a guide.)

Spread the section of wool out to its sides, so it forms a thin layer and a rectangle.

Snip off some fine Mylar strands (or Ice Dub, whatever that's made of), same length as the wool. Distribute the strands across the woolen rectangle. The strands should roughly align with the wool-fibers.

Roll the wool from one side. You should be rolling the wool not *up* the fibers but *across* them, so the fibers remain straight. When you're done, you should have a little bundle of wool with Mylar layered all through it.

Trim off the very *front* end of the wool-section, so that the fibers all end at the same place.

Wind the thread forward to about 1/16-inch ahead of the dubbed butt. Use a light turn (or the pinch) to bind the section (by the end you just trimmed) atop the shank. Add some tight thread-turns to really secure the wool.

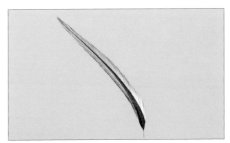

1. Strip the fibers from the base of a dry-fly hackle, set the hackle aside.

2. Start the thread two thirds up the shank. Wind it back to the bend, and then build a ball of dubbing there.

3. Spread out a two-inch-long section of wool into a sheet.

4. Cut fine Mylar strands to two inches long. Spread them over the wool.

5. Roll up the wool and mylar, from the side of the fibers.

6. Trim off the end of the woolen bundle cleanly.

7. Bind the end of the wool atop the shank, with the wool sweeping back.

8. Trim the ends of the wool to a short taper. Bind the wool thoroughly.

9. Take one medium-tight turn of thread around the wool only.

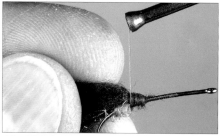

10. Hold the wool back and bind it back to the dubbed butt.

11. Dub a short, stout body-section over the bound wool-butts.

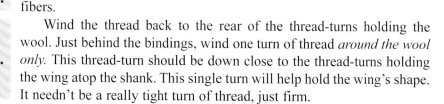

8. Trim the front end of the wool to a slight taper and bind the trimmed fibers.

9. Wind the thread back to the rear of the thread-turns holding the wool. Just behind the bindings, wind one turn of thread *around the wool only.* This thread-turn should be down close to the thread-turns holding the wing atop the shank. This single turn will help hold the wing's shape. It needn't be a really tight turn of thread, just firm.

10. Stroke your grasp back over the wool a little, to even the tension on all the fibers. Hold the wool firmly back and slightly elevated as you wind tight thread-turns down it and the shank just a little way to the dubbed butt. Add a few tight turns at the rear of the thread-windings to really secure the wool.

11. Dub again, this time over the bound ends of the wool. This section of dubbing should be as thick as the dubbed butt (though it can be a little thicker if you like), and *barely* over 1/8-inch long.

The idea here is to make four (or three or five) wing-sections and four (or three or five) dubbed sections (including the butts) for the body/wing—and to still have one third of the shank remaining in front for the thorax (though this front one-third will have bound woolen wing-butts over most of it). Keep this goal in mind as you build the body/wing.

12. Stroke this first wing-bunch of wool back horizontally off the bend. Cut the bunch 1/2-inch away from its bound base (this will leave a wing-section about 1 1/2 times the width of the hook's gape). Cut straight across. Now you have the wool for the second wing-bunch in your left hand.

13. Use a light turn (or the pinch) to bind this second wool-and-Mylar bunch atop the shank in front of the dubbing. Bind this second wing-bunch just as you did the first.

14. Dub another short body-section over the bound butts of the wool.

12. Stroke the wool back and cut it in half—now you have wool with Mylar for the next wing-section.

13. Bind on the next wing-section as you did the first.

14. Dub another short body-section over the bound butts of the wool.

Cut another section of wool like the first one. Spread out the wool, top it with fine Mylar, and roll the whole thing up, all as before. Resume making sections of the dubbed body with woolen wing-bunches until, as I mentioned, you have four wing-bunches and four body-sections (or three wing-bunches and three body-sections or five and five) and one third of the shank remains in front. *Do not* dub in front of (and over the butts of) this final wing-section. That's it—you've made the wing and abdomen. Now you need to trim the wing to shape.

15. Keep making wing- and dubbed body-sections until two thirds of the shank are covered.

Building the Wing and Body— Problems, Solutions, and Suggestions

1. A hook-shank is smooth and slick; that's why you wound a layer of thread over the shank before binding on the woolen wing-sections—the thread-layer provides something for the wool and its securing thread-turns to grip. So make sure those foundation thread-windings are indeed tight and not too spread over the shank.

2. You may prefer a wing made with the thickest bunches of wool for the rear two wing-sections and slightly thinner bunches for the front two wing-sections—this is logical, since the rear of the final, trimmed wing is much broader than the front and therefore needs more wool to fill it out.

Also, keeping the front wing-sections thinner will create less taper in the thorax-area, which will later make building the parachute hackle easier.

3. When you roll up the wool and Mylar, you'll tend to get a bunch of Mylar sticking out of one side of the rolled bunch. To eliminate this inconsistency, keep the Mylar strands short of the far edge of the flattened wool as you roll up the wool; then the last, clear edge of the wool will roll up over the Mylar-strands.

16. Whip finish and cut the thread.

4. The single turn of thread around the base of each wing-bunch, added before binding back over the base to the previous dubbed section, isn't required. But it does tend to make neat wing-sections. If you do add the turn of thread though, make sure you tug it forward, close to the bindings holding the bunch to the shank—if any part of the single thread-turn is back too far, it may be exposed even after the dubbing is applied. This exposed thread-turn will be the weak link of all the thread-turns holding the fly together, dangling out there for trout teeth to cut. Besides, the fly will just look a little sloppy with thread showing where it shouldn't (though, of course, the trout won't care. Trout aren't big on aesthetics).

The best way I've found to make sure the single turn is well forward is to raise the wool-bunch high and really tug the thread down and forward.

5. It's okay—and you may even prefer the results—if you wind the thread *back* a few close turns over each dubbed body-section and the base of the wool. Winding back will insure that there are no gaps in the body, where the thread might show.

Trimming the Wing

Whip finish the thread out in front of the wool. Cut the thread.

Remove the hook from your vise. Hold the hook carefully by its bend as you trim the wing.

17. Remove the hook from your vise. Hold it by the bend as you trim the woolen wing.

18. Trim the end of the wing straight up.

19. Trim the top of the wing to taper from low in front to higher in back.

20. Trim the sides of the woolen wing to close in front, tapering to wider in back.

21. Trim the rear of the wing along the underside.

22. Return the hook to your vise. Restart the thread.

18.

First, check the rear of the wool, and if you think another snip would make it cleaner on the end, go ahead and snip away. (But remember that you want the wing to terminate back from the body a distance equal to 1 1/2 times the gape, so don't snip off too much wool.)

19.

Trim the top of the wool to taper from low in front to higher back at the bend. Use good scissors, with fine serrations in the blades, and cut from the rear of the woolen wing forward.

20.

Trim the sides of the wool to taper from close to the dubbed body in front to wider (though still somewhat narrow) at the rear end.

21.

You'll probably need to trim the underside of the rear of the wing, so it's about level with the line of the shank (even though it's a curving line with the slow-curve shank hook in the photos). You just want a clean, straight underside on the rear of the wing.

22.

Return the hook to your vise and restart the thread just in front of the trimmed wing. Break or trim off its tag end.

The finished wing should be small and fairly close in front, tapering slowly along the sides to noticeably wider at the rear—but not really wide. The top of the wing should angle up at a modest angle. Pay close attention to the photos as you trim the wool and your wing will have a realistic shape and help the fly float long.

Trimming the Wing— Problems, Solutions, and Suggestions

1. For your first couple of Woolly Wings, I suggest you follow the instructions by whip finishing and cutting the thread before trimming the woolen wing. However, it's only a little tricky to hold the hook, and trim the woolen wing without cutting the thread—as long as you trim the part of the wing that is on top as you rotate the hook, you can't cut the hanging thread.

2. It is easy enough to trim the woolen wing with the fly still in the vise, if your vise is the rotary kind so that you can flip the fly over to work on both sides of the wing. But you'll wind up with a lot of wool and Mylar trimmings on the base of your vise. I prefer to hold the hook and trim over a trash can for this reason, and because I tend to get a neater trimming this way.

3. I find it easiest to trim the wool if I cut against the cant of the fibers, that is, from the rear of the wing forward. Cutting from the front of the wing back can work, but the fibers tend to dodge the scissors' blades.

4. Trim the woolen wing fairly closely in front, and close enough so that it looks similar to the wing of a real caddisfly adult. The wing can be a little oversize. If you cut too closely, however, the wool sections will look like individual tufts rather than part of a single wing. The trout may not notice, but your friends' smiles will sour whenever you open the fly box containing the Woolly Wings you tied.

5. Never hurts to turn over a Woolly Wing right after the wing is trimmed. When viewed from below, the woolen wing should lie close to the edges of the dubbed body, especially in front, and extend well beyond the rear end of the body.

Making the Parachute Wing and Mounting the Hackle

Because we covered this style of wing thoroughly in the chapter titled "Klinkhamer Special," I won't go into a lot of detail here—but refer back to that chapter freely whenever you feel the need.

Cut a section of dyed-yellow wool about two inches long. The section should be a little thinner than the bunch of wool you used for the first wing-section (slightly under 1/4-inch wide when lightly rolled).

Use the pinch to bind the section atop the shank right in front of the woolen wing with eight to twelve *tight* turns of thread as a narrow thread-collar.

Raise the ends of the yellow wool firmly upright. Hold the wing firmly upright as you execute this next step: pass the bobbin from hand to hand as you work about eight *tight* turns of thread around the base of the parachute wing.

Without holding the wing at all, wind a light-tension layer of thread up the base of the wing about 1/8-inch for a moderately full parachute hackle-collar (wind the thread higher for a heavier collar, of course, making the finished fly more buoyant for rough water). Wind thread up the wing far enough so that you can later wind five to nine turns of hackle down the layer of thread.

The base of the wing is now stiffened by the layer of thread. Using slightly more thread-tension, wind another layer of thread back down the wing's base.

Hold the hackle's stripped stem against the base of the parachute-wing. Wind the thread up the wing and hackle-stem using moderate thread-tension. Wind the thread back down the base of the wing and the hackle's stem—this time you can apply considerable tension on the thread.

Pull the butt of the hackle-stem forward (since the parachute wing is back against the front of the other wing, there isn't room to bind the stem *back*). With the stem angling forward and down along the near side of the shank, bind the stem tightly against the shank one quarter to halfway to the eye, and then trim off its end. Bind the cut end of the stem.

Making the Parachute Wing and Mounting the Hackle— Problems, Solutions, and Suggestions

1. Try to make the butts of the last woolen wing-section taper evenly down to just short of the eye over the front third of the shank. If the wing-bindings over the thorax-area taper too steeply at some point, the dubbing and even the parachute wing may slide forward over them.

2. Try to keep the final section of the *down*-wing as thin as you can while still making it thick enough to blend with the rest of the wing—this way the taper atop the thorax-area will be lower and easier to work on when you make the parachute wing and hackle and dub the thorax.

3. Make sure you bind the parachute-wing well back, against or right in front of the trimmed woolen wing—if the parachute-wing is forward much at all, the parachute hackle will be harder to make and the fly will look unbalanced.

4. Bind the wool for the parachute-wing atop the thorax-area in earnest—really nail it down with *tight* thread-turns.

23.

23. Bind a two-inch section of yellow yarn atop the shank at the front of the trimmed woolen wing.

24.

24. Raise the ends of the yarn and bind them tightly with a few turns of thread.

25.
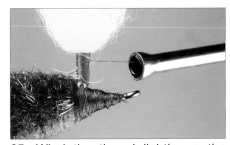
25. Wind the thread lightly up the base of the yarn and back down it.

26.

26. Hold the stem of the hackle against the base of the wool. Wind a firm layer of thread up and a tighter one down the yarn and stem.

27.

27. Pull the stem forward and bind it partway to the eye. Cut off the stem.

28. Dub around the base of the upright wing and thorax-area—but try not to dub much in front of the wing.

29. Wind the hackle down the base of the wool-wing in close turns.

30. Drape the hackle over the shank, and let the pliers hang.

31. Draw the hackles-fibers up in front, bind the hackle-tip, and then cut it off.

32. Dub in front of the parachute-hackle and -wing. Build and complete a thread-head.

5. Keep the thread-turns holding the wool for the parachute-wing gathered, not spread, as a narrow thread-collar. It will be difficult to make both ends of the wool into a tight, single post for the hackle otherwise.

6. Some tight thread-turns down at the very base of the parachute wing—right down against the bindings over the butts of the trimmed woolen wing—can really lock the *parachute*-wing firmly upright. The key is to make these thread-turns tight and at the very base of the parachute-wing.

7. If you can't find a size-8 dry-fly hackle with enough usable length to make a full parachute hackle-collar (big dry-fly neck-hackles tend to have a lot of overlong and over-soft fibers, and most long saddle hackles are for small hooks) a good solution is to size, strip the bases of, and bind *two* big hackles onto the base of the parachute-wing. You can later wind one hackle in slightly open spirals down the wing's base, secure the hackle's tip with thread-turns, and then wind the second hackle down in the space between the turns of the first hackle.

8. To keep the wool parachute wing up and out of your way as you wind the hackle, stroke a little dubbing wax up through the tips—the tips only!—of the wool before winding the hackle.

9. Since you want a smooth foundation over which to wind the dubbing, trim the thick stem of the hackle at an angle. A blunt-cut stem would make a shelf—it's always awkward to dub or work thread over a shelf.

10. If you have trouble with the steep taper of thread over the front third of the shank, lengthen the taper to lower the taper—you can make the front thorax-area stretch over almost half the shank. Trout won't care, and the fly will still look good.

Winding the Parachute Hackle and Completing the Woolly Wing

28. Dub the area from the front of the rear *trimmed woolen wing*—the tapered one back over the body—forward to just in front of the *parachute*-wing and hackle. But try not to dub much in front of the parachute wing.

29. Mount the tip of the hackle in the jaws of your hackle pliers. Wind the hackle down the base of the parachute wing in close turns, winding the hackle *counter*clockwise, viewed from the top.

30. When the hackle reaches the dubbed thorax, drape the hackle over the far side of the hook and let the hackle pliers hang.

31. Draw back the hackle-fibers in front of the wing, and then wind the thread over the tip of the hackle.

Trim off the hackle's tip and any bound fibers projecting forward.

32. Dub the area in front of the parachute-wing. Leave a little bare shank behind the eye for a thread head. Build a thread-head, whip finish and then trim off the thread.

Pull the parachute wing firmly up, and slide your grasp up the wool fibers a little to even out your tension on them.

Use the closed tips of your scissors to push down any hackle-fibers that angle upward rather than out to the sides of the parachute wing.

With one crisp snip, cut off the top of the wool parachute wing about 3/16-inch above the hackle. The result should be a little dome of yarn atop the hackle—now *that*'ll show up on the water. Add head cement to the thread-head.

Once the cement is set, pull the hackle and parachute wing back into position.

33.

34.

33. Pull the parachute-wing straight up, and snip it straight across. Add head cement to the thread-head.

34. Tug the parachute wing and hackle back into shape and position.

Winding the Parachute Hackle and Completing the Woolly Wing— Problems, Solutions, and Suggestions

1. When you dub around the base of the parachute wing, be sure to cover all the thread in the thorax-area with dubbing. This is not quite as easy as you might assume. So wind on the dubbing-covered thread at various angles as you keep checking both sides of the parachute-wing's base, and the thorax-area in general, to make sure dubbing covers everything it should.

2. You *can* tie the Woolly Wing with a more conventional hackle—such a hackle is easier to make than the parachute hackle and the resulting fly is perfectly effective. (I prefer the parachute hackle myself, however, but only by a shade.)

To make this more-or-less conventional hackle, bind a hank of dyed-yellow wool in front of the trimmed woolen wing. The yellow wool should lie back atop the trimmed wing. Find a size-8 hackle, strip its base, bind the hackle atop the the shank directly in front of the trimmed woolen wing. Dub to just short of the eye. Wind the hackle in a few spirals to the eye, bind and trim the hackle's tip, build and complete a thread-head. Trim the fibers from the underside of the hackle leaving a shallow "V". Trim the yellow wool to extend about 1/4 to 1/2-inch back over the trimmed wing.

35.

36.

37.

38.

35. To make a Woolly Wing with a spiraled hackle, bind some bright yarn or wool back over the trimmed-wool wing. Trim the yarn or wool short.

36. Bind a hackle along the thorax-area, right in front of the trimmed wing. Trim off the hackle's butt.

37. Dub the thorax-area. Spiral the hackle over the thorax, and then bind and trim off its tip. Build and complete a thread-head.

38. Trim off some of the fibers from the underside of the hackle, leaving a shallow "V". Add head cement to the thread-head.

DAVE'S HOPPER

New Techniques: making a looped-yarn butt, a yarn body, a trimmed-hackle rib, knotted hopping-legs of pheasant tail and from hackle stems, and making a flared-hair grasshopper-head and collar

Are you ready for a challenge? Wait, let me answer for you: yes, you are. That challenge will be the Dave's Hopper. While it truly is a complex fly with a lot of steps, most of those steps aren't especially difficult, and you'll have plenty of photos and instructions and suggestions to help you manage them. Besides, the trickiest operation of the whole fly is creating the flared-hair head and collar, and you've already worked that out with the Marabou Muddler. So, a challenge, yes, but one you're prepared to tackle.

The Dave's Hopper has been a hot fly ever since it first appeared in Art Flick's *Master Fly-Tying Guide*. The *Guide* came out way back in 1972. Yet today the Dave's Hopper remains the standard imitation for grasshoppers. Remarkable. But not surprising—it's an excellent fly.

Grasshoppers, or, as fly fishers refer to them, "hoppers," can be important from midsummer into fall on trout streams that are bordered by grassy meadows. (And, I've occasionally found, on grass-edged lakes.) Thrown onto the water by wind or bad luck, a big stout hopper can send a trout rushing for a mouthful.

Grasshoppers fall into the category fly fishers call "terrestrials," insects that live out their lives entirely on land: beetles, ants, flying ants, inchworms, moths, grasshoppers (of course), and others less common. "Aquatic" insects, those that live in and may emerge from water (caddisflies, mayflies, stoneflies, and scuds, to name a few) are the main event on trout streams most of the time. But when terrestrials have the trout's attention, you'd better have imitations handy.

Want more help with tying this pattern, and more options? Go to the master himself—get Dave Whitlock's video, "Tying and Fishing the Dave Whitlock Originals, Volume One," which includes both the Dave's Hopper and an equally interesting bullet-head variation, the Whit Hopper.

Grasshopper size varies, but I tend to think of the Dave's Hopper as an imitation of larger specimens, so I've always tied and fished it in sizes 8 and 10 on 2X and 3X long hooks.

The Dave's Hopper presented in *Art Flick's Master Fly-Tying Guide* published so long ago is a very different fly from the one in Dave's recent video. I've been tying the fly for a couple of decades, so the version that follows is a blend of old and new that I know is sound and effective.

DAVE'S HOPPER

HOOK: Light to heavy wire, 2X or 3X long, sizes 14 to 6.
THREAD: Yellow 3/0, 6/0, or 8/0. White or gray size-A rod-thread for the head and collar.
TAIL (OPTIONAL): Elk or deer hair dyed red.
BUTT: Yellow Poly yarn.
BODY HACKLE (RIB): One brown hackle, trimmed.
BODY: Poly Yarn or yellow synthetic dubbing.
UNDER-WING: Yellow deer hair.
WING: Mottled-brown turkey quill.
LEGS: Pheasant tail.
HEAD AND COLLAR: Natural-gray deer hair.

Creating the Tail

Smash down the barb on a size-10, 2X or 3X long, light to heavy wire hook. (The hook shown is the one Dave prefers for his Dave's Hopper: the Tiemco 5263. It's 3X long with *heavy* wire—Dave clearly expects the big trout that take this fly to mangle fine-wire hooks.) Mount the hook in your vise, and then start some yellow 3/0 (or lighter) thread about two thirds up the shank. Break off the end of the thread.

Spiral the thread tightly back to the bend. Spiral the thread tightly back up the shank to *slightly short* of where you started it (about 1/16th-inch short).

Cut, comb, and stack in a hair-stacker a small bunch of red deer or elk hair (about 20 to 25 hairs, if you want to count).

Measure the hair against the hook's gape to find where the hair-tips extend *slightly* further than the gape's width (about 1/16-inch further, no more than 1/8-inch further). Hold the hair atop the shank (slightly short of two thirds up the shank towards the eye—the point you measured on the hair should lie directly atop the bend). Use the pinch to bind the hair atop the shank. Add a few tight turns of thread.

Hold the hair-tips back and slightly above the shank under moderate tension. Spiral the thread down hair and shank to the bend.

Add a few tight thread-turns at the bend. Spiral the thread forward up two thirds of the shank. Trim off the butts of the hair. (This red tail is optional. I omit it on the Dave's Hoppers I tie for fishing, including it only for the ones I tie for display.)

Creating the Tail— Problems, Solutions, and Suggestions

1. Make sure your first two layers of thread—the ones that run down and then back up the bare shank—are *tight*. These layers provide a textured surface for the tail and body to grip. If the layers are secure, and everything over them is wound tightly, the body stays put. Tight thread-turns over the tail-hair will also help secure the body.

2. You can bind heavy monofilament (I use at least 15-pound test, but the thick butt of an old tapered leader works) from the bend forward up two-thirds of the shank before adding the tail and making the body. This mono will act as a stopper, a brace, against the hair you'll flare and compress for the head—this mono will insure that the body won't slip down the shank when you compress the hair back. (The mono needn't go all the way back to the bend.)

1.

2.

3.

4.

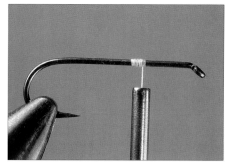

1. Mount a hook in your vise, and then start the thread about two thirds up the hook's shank.

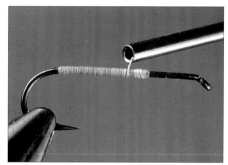

2. Spiral the thread tightly down the shank to the bend, then back up.

3. Cut, comb, and stack a small bunch of red deer hair.

4. Bind the hair down the shank to the bend; then add a few thread-turns there. Spiral the thread up the shank. Trim off the butts of the hair.

5. Using the pinch, bind the end of some poly yarn two thirds up the shank. Trim off the stub-end of the yarn.

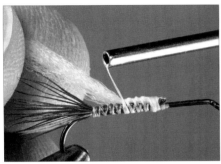

6. Raise the yarn and spiral the thread down yarn and shank to the bend.

7. Add tight thread-turns at the bend. Double the yarn to make a short loop. Bind the yarn to secure the loop.

8. Strip the extra-long, softer fibers from the base of the stem of a big dry-fly hackle. Stroke the remaining fibers out from the stem.

Creating the Yarn-Butt

5. Using the pinch, bind the end of about five inches of yellow Poly yarn atop the shank *slightly* short of two thirds up the shank. Add a few tight thread-turns to really secure the end of the yarn. Trim off the front stub-end of the yarn.

6. Hold the yarn up and back over the shank as you spiral the thread down yarn and shank to the bend. At the bend, add a few tight thread-turns.

7. Double the yarn forward at the bend. Lower the yarn down atop the shank (and atop the yarn that is bound along the shank) leaving some yarn extending back—the result should be a yarn-loop, like the one in the photos. This loop should be upright, and extend back as far as the gape is wide. Use the pinch to bind the end of the yarn-loop atop the bend. Add eight to ten *tight* thread-turns as a narrow thread-collar, to really secure the yarn.

Creating the Yarn-Butt— Problems, Solutions, and Suggestions

1. Here's a good way to make a neat loop of yarn: bind the yarn-loop *lightly,* push the tip of your bodkin into the loop from the side, and then draw the loop back out to size. The bodkin's needle will pull the yarn fibers equally and in one direction—the result, a neat and even yarn-loop.

2. Because the tail is *slightly longer* than the gape is wide, and the yarn-loop is *slightly shorter*, the tail should extend a little past the end of the loop—if it doesn't, back off the thread and redo the hump, tail, or both; or just get it right on the next Dave's Hopper. (This, however, is about aesthetics. The fish won't care either way.)

The Palmered Hackle and the Body

Find a big dry-fly neck hackle or dry-fly saddle hackle with at least fairly long fibers.

Strip the softer, longer fibers from the butt of the feather, leaving only the hard shiny fibers of consistent length running up to the tip (usually, this means stripping the fibers from the lower half of the stem).

Hold the hackle firmly by the last 3/4-inch or so of its pointed tip and pinch the feather lightly just below this with your other hand. Stroke the pinching hand down the fibers a few times until they stand well out from the stem—stroke *lightly,* or you'll weaken or even strip off fibers.

Trim along a row of fibers so that the row ends up about two thirds as wide as the gape. Trim the fibers along the other side of the feather also to two thirds the gape's width. (In other words, the full width of the trimmed hackle should end up about one-and-a-third times the width of the gape.) You'll find it easiest to cut from the tip of the feather towards its butt, rather than cutting *up* from the butt—and scissors with fine serrations along the blades (most good tying scissors have such serrations) really help with this step.

Tug the yarn lightly to the far side of the hook and let it hang there, out of your way. Use the light turn to bind the feather by its stem against the near side of the bend. This light turn should be over the thread-collar holding the end of the yarn loop. The flat of the feather should face you (I prefer the *convex* side facing me, so the fibers will cant back slightly after the hackle is wound, but this is a minor point and either plane of the hackle can face you). A tiny length of the bare, stripped stem should show between where the fibers start and where the stem is bound at the bend. Add a few tight thread-turns over the light turn to really secure the stem. Draw the loose end of the yarn back completely out of your way, bind the stem up two thirds of the shank, and then trim off the butt of the stem. Add a few tight thread-turns at the front of the abdomen. The bare stem should now be bound up the near side of shank and the fibered tip-end should extend back off the bend.

With the thread hanging about two thirds up the shank, wind the yarn up the shank in close turns to the hanging thread. (Try to angle the first turn of yarn back to cover the thread-collar at the bend.) Bind the end of the yarn with several tight thread-turns. Trim off the end of the yarn. Be sure to leave one third of the shank bare ahead of the body and its bindings—you'll need this bare shank for building the head and collar.

Clamp the jaws of hackle pliers onto the tip of the hackle. Wind the hackle in four to seven turns to the front of the body. Bind the tip of the hackle on the front of the abdomen (not *in front* of the abdomen). Trim off the hackle's tip.

Closely trim the hackle fibers off the top and a little down sides of the body so the wing will lie well.

The Palmered Hackle and the Body— Problems, Solutions, and Suggestions

1. Make sure the tail-hair and *all* the yarn atop the bend are bound *tightly*—otherwise the tail and yarn-butt will shift on the shank when you wind the yarn to make the body. But if the yarn-loop does want to shift, you can hold it in place as you wind the yarn up the shank.

2. You can use a long dry-fly *saddle* hackle three or four sizes smaller than the hook's size (in this case, a hackle gauged for a size-18 or -16 hook) *untrimmed* for the rib—many do—but the stubby fibers of a trimmed hackle were the original approach for the Dave's Hopper.

3. To hold the hackle stable as you trim its fibers, you can mount its butt in English hackle pliers, then hook the loop of the pliers over something firm, such as the lever or jaws of your vise. Hold the tip of the hackle out in another set of hackle pliers—and then trim away, down one side of the feather, then the other.

4. Another approach to stretching out the hackle for its trimming is to hold the butt between thumb and first finger and pinch the hackle's tip between your second and third fingers. Tricky, but it can be learned.

9.

9. Trim the fibers short along both sides of the stem.

10.

10. Bind the bare stem of the hackle at the bend, and then bind it up the shank. Trim off the butt of the stem.

11.

11. Wind the yarn up the shank. Bind the end of the yarn two thirds up the shank. Trim off the tag-end of the yarn.

12.

13.

12. Spiral the hackle up the yarn-body. Bind the hackle's tip *on* the front of the body.

13. Trim off the hackle's tip. Trim off the fibers along the top of the body.

14. Wind the thread back over the front edge of the yarn-body a little.

15. Bind a small, stacked bunch of yellow deer hair atop the body, but only *firmly*. Trim off the hair-butts.

16. Toughen a turkey quill with flexament or an artist's fixative.

17. Separate out a gape-wide section of the quill-fibers with your bodkin.

18. Snip the section from the quill. Trim the end of the section to rounded.

5. You may find it easier to make the yarn-butt and then simply *dub* the body with yellow synthetic dubbing—Antron, Poly, Super Fine Dry-Fly...—than to wind the yarn. The tail and hump are less likely to shift with a dubbed body, and you may prefer the effect.

6. If the yarn spreads too much as you wind it forward for the body, twist it a *little;* one or two twists should do it. This will gather the yarn and give you more control.

7. If you have a problem when you bind the yarn at the front end of the body—the problem being that the yarn slips forward over the cut butts of the tail-hair—try working the yarn so that its last turn at the front of the body is *beneath* the shank. This way, you're binding the last turn of yarn at the underside of the shank, where there's far less bulk and no hair-butts for the yarn to slip off of.

Creating the Wing

Wind the thread back a little, on the front of the yarn body—not *in front* of the body but back *on* the body. If this kicks any hackle-fibers off at strange angles, just trim them off. If there are any hackle-fibers now in front of the working thread, trim those off too.

14. (If you try to bind the wing-hair and wing *in front* of the body, they'll both tend to tip sharply up instead of settling down atop the abdomen.) Wind the thread only about 1/16-inch back, certainly no more than 1/8-inch—more than this and the body starts looking too short.

Cut, comb, and stack a small bunch of yellow deer hair. (About twenty hairs. It's a good idea to actually count the hairs the first time, to give you a sense of the size of the hair-bunch you need.) Hold the hair atop the front of the abdomen, so that its tips are about even with the tips of the tail. (That is, if you added the tail—if not, then just set the wing-hair so its tips extend slightly past the far edge of the loop of Poly yarn.)

15. Use the pinch to bind the hair atop the front of the body with a narrow thread-collar, only about 1/16-inch wide (slightly back from the front edge of the body). Bind the hair with only *moderately* tight thread-turns—tight turns will flare the hair, which you don't want, and it may also make the thread collar slip forward off the body. Don't worry, we'll use glue, as Dave Whitlock does, to hold the hair in place. Trim off the butts of the hair closely.

This hair under-wing is optional. I've never felt the need for it. Nice effect though.

Typically, the turkey quill for a Dave's Hopper wing is toughened

16. with a coating of thinned Dave's Flexament or a spray-on artist's fixative like Tuffilm. But you can use untreated turkey if you like—it will more likely split up after a trout has mauled the fly, but since real hoppers often land with splayed wings, well, why not?

Anyway, you can find all the details on how to toughen the turkey-quill wing—and how to do it without breathing chemical vapors—on page 112, in the chapter titled "Parachute Caddis."

Push the point of your bodkin straight into the fibers on one side,

17. then the other, of a section of turkey-quill fibers about as wide as the hook's gape. Trim the section from the quill. (All this is also covered in detail in the chapter titled "Parachute Caddis.")

18. Trim the tip of the turkey-section to rounded.

Hold the turkey section down atop the body, over the yellow hair. The rounded tip of the section should terminate directly over the far rear edge of the Poly-yarn butt. Roll the sides of the section down around the sides of the Poly-yarn abdomen.

Use a sort of modified pinch to bind the section atop the front of the body, but tighten the thread only *moderately*. (Again, you want to bind the wing on the body, not the shank.) Build a *moderately tight* thread-collar at the front of the body, over the first thread-collar holding the hair. (Remember—you're going to bind the butt of the wing only over the very end of the body, about 1/16-inch (at least 1/32-inch) back from the front of the body, as I described for the under-wing.)

Trim off the butt of the wing closely. Now the wing-butt should terminate barely in front of the thread-collar holding it. Whip finish the thread over the wing (not the shank), and then cut the thread.

Add a little head cement (or low-odor epoxy glue) to the thread-collar holding the wing.

Work some head cement (or epoxy) up under the butt of the wing in front, where this adhesive can wick back into the bindings over the hair-under-wing. Remove the half-tied fly from your vise and stick it in a turning wheel or in a board you flip over regularly until the cement or epoxy is set.

If the cement has vapors, I suggest you follow the guidelines for dealing with them I laid out on page 112 in the chapter titled "Parachute Caddis" (which essentially means applying the cement outdoors and leaving the fly there until the cement has set and has released all its vapors). Since this means you have to quit tying partway through the fly, you can keep going by building a bunch of Dave's Hoppers to this point, then returning to them when all the cement is cured, an assembly-line approach.

19.
20.
21.

19. Roll the section around the top of the body. Bind the section atop the front edge of the body.

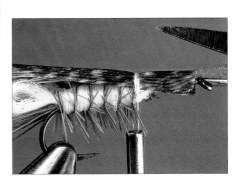

20. Trim off the butt of the wing. Whip finish and cut the thread.

Creating the Wing—
Problems, Solutions, and Suggestions

1. These points are worthy of repeating: (1.) you must mount the wing on the *body*, not the shank, otherwise the wing will angle wildly up against the front of the body, (2.) the thread-turns holding the wing can be firm, but if they are tight, the front of the body may collapse or the wing may, yet again, angle steeply up (it's the head cement or epoxy that really holds the wing on), and (3.) keep the thread-collar holding the wing slim and gathered, while watching that no thread-turns creep back over the body.

2. Now is a good time to check and make sure you left a full one third of the shank bare in front for the hair-head and -collar. That's the key to leaving any space on a fly—keep checking, and back off when you start slipping forward into it.

3. An alternate approach to the whole body-wing business here is to just taper out the front of the body-yarn and bind the hair under-wing and the turkey-section wing tightly out over the front third of the shank. This means, however, you'll have to flare the hair over the wing-bindings. The bindings will hold the hair firmly in place, making it difficult to compress the hair back much, if at all, over the bindings; and the resulting hair-head won't be nearly as dense as if it were made on a bare shank. However, as I've said before, the fish won't care.

21. Add head cement or glue to the thread-collar holding the wing.

Work some head cement or glue up under the butt of the wing. Set the half-tied fly aside for the cement or epoxy to set up.

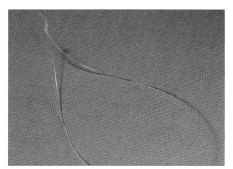

22. Double a foot of fairly heavy monofilament, and tie an overhand knot about an inch up from the ends.

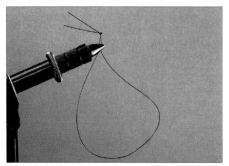

23. Mount the butt-ends of the mono-loop in your vise, so the loop hangs straight down. (I used black monofilament here, so you could really see the loop.)

24. Stroke some fibers straight out from the stem of a pheasant tail, and then cut off the fibers.

Making the Legs

It's time to make the Dave's Hopper's big legs, that represent the stout pair of legs by which a real grasshopper makes its great leaps. When these legs were added to the pattern (the original lacked them), they were formed of pheasant-tail fibers. But a trimmed hackle stem has become a popular alternative. We'll explore both styles.

To make the pheasant-tail legs, double about one foot of fairly heavy monofilament (leader or tippet) so the ends are evened, and then tie the ends in a simple overhand knot. The knot should only be about one inch up from the cut ends, leaving a large loop. Pull the loop and ends of the loop to tighten the knot.

I use a stiff mono called Mason's "Hard Type Nylon Leader Material" in 15-pound test. If you use tippet, you'll need at least 0/X, which is very heavy. But the thick middle part of an old tapered mono leader should do the job.

Clamp the cut ends of the monofilament loop in the jaws of your vise. The mono-loop should now be hanging *straight down* from the jaws of your vise.

Stroke five to eight pheasant-tail fibers out to a right angle to the stem (this should even the tips of the fibers, since pheasant-tail fibers are normally all the same length). Closely trim the bunch of fibers from the stem. Use the hard, crisply marked fibers. Some pheasant-tails have such fibers along both sides, others have them only along one side—the mottled, fragile, slightly ragged fibers found along one side of many pheasant-tail-feathers are useless.

Hold the pheasant-fibers, with their tips up and trimmed butts down, between the thumb and first finger of your right hand. Hold the fibers near their butts. Slip both sides of the monofilament loop into the tips of your right-hand thumb and first finger, next to the pheasant-fibers. Now the mono is on the left, the pheasant on the right. Hold the loop at or slightly above its center, with the sides of the loop close together, and the knot and cut ends of the loop up in the vise jaws.

The trick to making these next steps work is to really bend the mono around as needed. You are about to wind the tips of the pheasant-fibers clockwise (looking down on them) around the mono, so keep this in mind as you proceed.

Move your right hand around so the mono bends and the tips of the pheasant-fibers go across the *front* of the loop to the *left.*

Reach around from behind the mono with your left hand and grasp the tips of the fibers. You'll need to swing your left hand over the top of the vise to reach the fibers. You can bend the mono around with your right hand in any way that helps your left hand.

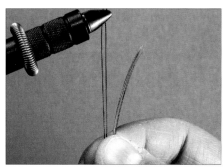

25. Hold the pheasant-fibers, tip-ends up, against the mono-loop. Mono on the left, pheasant on the right.

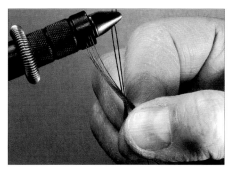

26. Move your right hand so the pheasant crosses in front of the mono to your left.

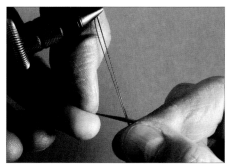

27. Reach back around with your left hand and grasp the tips of the fibers.

Pull the tips off to your right, *behind* the mono-loop.

Pull the tips down *in front* of the mono-loop. The tip-fibers should angle down and to your left. Catch the fiber-tips in your right-hand thumb and finger—the same thumb and first finger that are still holding the *butts* of the fibers.

Reach up into the mono-loop from below with your left-hand thumb and first finger. Grasp the pheasant-tips, and then pull them lightly down into the loop. (Now you know why the loop has to be large—to allow your thumb and finger to slip comfortably through it.)

Slide your right and left hands down, letting the loop slide through your right-hand grasp. (Don't let your hands shift around, but instead maintain their position as you slide them.)

When the tips of the pheasant reach the bottom end of the loop, release the tips from your left-hand. The tips will gently slide up through the rest of the coiled pheasant-fibers, creating an overhand knot. As you pass the end of the mono-loop, try not to let the knot close up.

Grasp the pheasant-tips right away, before the knot in them opens. Work the knot closed from both ends.

If you're patient and careful you can work the knot up or down the fibers as it closes. The knot should lie in the middle of the fiber-legs, or slightly nearer the butts of the fibers, that is, nearer the quill.

You just completed one pheasant-tail leg. Now make another.

When you get used to this, you can make legs right up the length of a pheasant-tail feather.

28.
29.
30.
31.
32.
33.
34.
35.

28. Pull the fibers off to your right, behind the mono-loop.

29. Pull the fibers down in front of the mono and catch them in your right hand thumb and first finger.

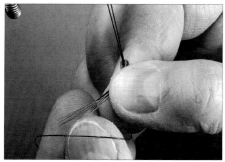

30. Reach up into the mono-loop, grasp the tips of the fibers, and then pull them down into the loop.

31. Slide the pheasant and your hands down to the end of the mono-loop. Let go of the fibers' tip with your left-hand.

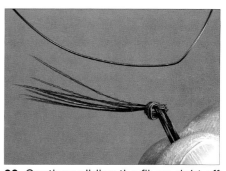

32. Continue sliding the fibers right off the end of the mono-loop, leaving a loose overhand knot in the fibers.

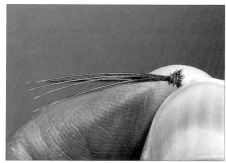

33. Work the knot firmly closed. Work from one side, then the other side of the knot.

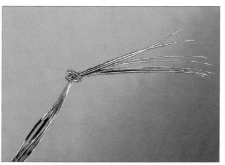

34. This is how the completed knotted leg should look. Knot another bunch of fibers to create a second leg.

35. Eventually you'll be able to knot legs right up the length of a pheasant-tail feather.

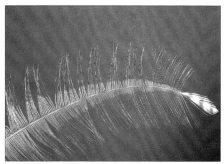

36. To make hackle-stem legs, stroke the fibers out to the sides of a big hackle.

36.

37.

38.

37. Trim both sides of the stem, so the fibers taper from narrow near the tip to wider near the feather's butt.

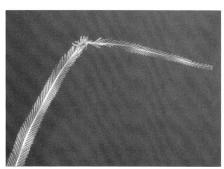

38. Trim off the tip of the hackle. Tie the stem in an overhand knot. Make a second leg in this manner.

Making the Legs, Method #2

Here's an option: make the big hopping-legs from hackle stems. It's pretty simple. You can use a big brown, dyed-yellow-grizzly, barred-ginger, ginger, or dyed-red dry-fly neck hackle. Just pluck the feather from the skin, hold it by its tip, and stroke down the feather to set the fibers out from the stem.

Trim down along one side of the stem a full two inches, then the other. You want to trim very close to the stem near the feather's tip, but taper the fibers a little—not much—so they're slightly longer near the thick base of the stem. (Look at the photos.)

Prepare two hackles in this manner. Cut off their untrimmed tips, which you held as you stroked the fibers outward—now only short, trimmed fibers remain, running down the stem.

Make an overhand knot in one stem, then in the other. Each knot should be down from the fine, cut tip of the stem a distance equalling about two thirds of the shank's length.

While some find the hackle-legs quicker and easier to make than the pheasant-legs, hackle-legs are also much thinner than pheasant-legs from the trout's view. Some see this as a drawback. I understand the logic behind their opinion, but I know that a lot of trout fall to hopper-fly patterns having *no* hopping legs at all. So, tie up a few Dave's Hoppers with pheasant legs, a few with hackle-legs, fish them, and see which you prefer.

Making the Legs (both methods)— Problems, Solutions, and Suggestions

1. The easiest and most efficient way I've found to tighten the knot in the *mono-loop* (not in the hopping-legs) is to hold the cut ends of the loop in pliers. Almost any pliers will do (except hackle pliers—too weak)—flat-nose, round-nose, or even the standard all-purpose pliers in every tool box.

2. The whole business of bending the flexible mono-loop around the pheasant is complicated if you try to figure out every aspect. But if you just concentrate on getting the pheasant to go around and then down into the loop as I described, most of the manipulation of the fibers and loop will happen on its own—focus mostly not on the details but on the results.

3. When you slide the pheasant-tail fibers down off the mono-loop, concentrate on maintaining the position of the hands, as though they were frozen. The effect is as if the hands and pheasant were stationary and the *mono-loop* were moving—this gives you real control.

4. With the hackle legs, knot them so that the two legs will curve apart, each angling away from the body after they are mounted.

5. About any kind of stiff chicken hackle can be used to make hackle-stem hopper legs: rooster neck hackle, big rooster saddle hackle, webby bass-bug rooster hackle...whatever can be knotted and looks good.

6. You can use your tweezers to grip the tip of a hackle-stem leg and pull the knot tight.

Mounting the Legs

Restart the thread over the thread-collar that is holding the wing. Get the thread securely started, but try not to kick the body off to one side or the other. Trim off the tag-end of the thread.

Hold one leg (either kind, pheasant or hackle) against the near side of the abdomen. The knotted end of the leg should angle up a little so that the leg-knot is just above the abdomen. The leg-knot should lie alongside the bend. The butt-end of the leg should angle down from the knot. Important: bind the leg to the side of the *front of the abdomen* using the light turn—do not bind on the leg *in front* of the abdomen, where the head and collar will be formed. The leg should be bound, essentially, against the narrow thread-collar securing the wing. It's critical that you keep the front one third of the hook's shank bare.

Once you've worked the leg into proper position, add a few more *firm* thread-turns—don't use *tight* turns or you'll flare the wing upwards and possibly split it.

Bind the second leg on the far side of the abdomen. This second leg should pretty much match the length and angle of the first, should mirror its position. The knots in both legs should lie directly across from one another.

Trim off the butts of both legs.

Whip finish the thread over the front of the abdomen, and cut the thread.

Add more cement or epoxy, safely as before, over the whip finish. Once the cement or epoxy is set, you can go on to the next step in tying the Dave's Hopper.

39. Restart the thread over the front of the abdomen. Secure a leg against one side of the abdomen using a light turn. Add a few *firm* thread-turns.

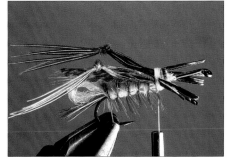

40. Bind a second leg on the other side of the abdomen, just as you bound the first.

41. Trim off the butts of both legs.

Mounting the Legs— Problems, Solutions, and Suggestions

1. This bears repeating: use only *firm* thread-turns to bind on the hopping-legs. If you use tight turns you may tip up the wing or split it, or the body may twist around the shank. Use firm turns and let the cement you add do the work of really securing the legs.

2. After you first bind on a leg with a couple of thread-turns, take a moment to consider the leg's angle—now is the time to tug the leg up or down to an angle that looks right to you, or to twist it if it is turned wrong.

Also, when you bind in the second leg, adjust it to mirror the first leg before continuing with the tying of the fly.

42. Whip finish and cut the thread. Add some head cement to the bindings.

Making the Flared-Hair Head

43. Start some size-A rod-thread tightly on the shank, directly in front of the body. Trim off the tag-end of the thread.

44. Cut, comb, and then stack a bunch of deer hair.

43. Start some size-A thread immediately in front of the body—up close to the front of the body. Trim off the tag-end of the Size-A thread.

44. Cut a medium-thick bunch of natural tan-gray deer hair (about the thickness of the bunch you used for the hair-collar on the Marabou Muddler, Brown) from close to the hide. Comb, and then stack the hair in a hair-stacking tool.

45. Hold the hair atop the shank at the front of the body with the evened tips of the hair reaching halfway to two thirds back along the body (that is, the body only, not including the yarn-loop). Work the hair down around the shank a little, wind two turns of thread around the hair, hold the hair firmly as you pull the thread tight.

46.
47. Stroke all the butts of the hair back, pull the thread forward through the hair, and then add five tight turns of thread directly in front of the hair. Compress the hair back with thumb and finger or a hair-compressing tool.

Bind on another bunch in front of the last, but you needn't stack this bunch in a hair stacker first. Just bind this second bunch as you did the first (that is, not spinning it) if you wish. Or you can spin this bunch (as described on pages 60 and 61 in the chapter titled "Marabou Muddler, Brown"), but you'll need to first add the three spiraled thread-turns over which to spin. If the compressed hair doesn't yet reach the eye, bind on and compress one or even two more bunches until hair does reach the eye.

48.

49. Make several half hitches to secure the thread (a half-hitch tool can really help with this). Trim off the thread.

For plenty of detail on flaring and compressing hair, see the chapter titled "Marabou Muddler, Brown"—making a Muddler head is very close to making the head of a Dave's Hopper, though the final shapes will differ.

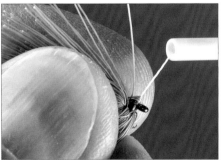

45. Bind the hair over the shank with two turns of thread. Hold the hair firmly as you pull the thread tight.

46. Pull the butts of the hair back and pull the thread forward.

47. Wind on five turns of thread. Compress back the hair.

48. Bind on another bunch of hair, compress it back, wind five tight turns of thread onto the shank.

49. Add yet a third bunch of hair if necessary; make half hitches in the thread and trim it.

Making the Flared-Hair Head—
Problems, Solutions, and Suggestions

1. For smaller hooks, you'll probably find it easiest to work with hair that has soft tips—the tips in the collar will be appropriately short to match the hook-size, and will flare more easily than tips that are hard. Hard hair-tips are normally dark and thin. But if the tan-gray color of the body of each hair extends almost to the point, you probably have soft-tipped hairs.

2. You can add cement or low-odor epoxy to the final half hitches for the thread-head (the ones in the heavy hair-flaring thread) and let it cure *before* trimming the hair if you wish; this eliminates the possibility of you knocking some of the half hitches loose while you trim.

3. Want to insure the completed head won't twist around the shank under the stresses of fishing? For starters, really pull the size-A thread tight and make sure you tighten it again before securing it in front of each hair-bunch. And throughout the hair-flaring, don't allow a moment's slack, or the thread will loosen and stay loose (although you can recover that slack if you immediately re-tighten the thread and keep it tight). Finally, you can run a line of low-odor epoxy glue along the underside of the head, where it is cut close to the shank. The epoxy will seep in, but if you blast it with a hand-held hair dryer the hot air will thin the epoxy and push it down to the shank. (But, as always, use the epoxy safely, as described on its label.)

Trimming the Flared-Hair Head

Mount the fly in a hand-vise, midge-head, old vise-head or such. View the fly at its front, so that you're looking down the length of the shank, and make a cut along the underside using scissors or a razor blade—don't cut close yet, or you may cut the thread. Cut back to just short of the hair-tip collar.

Make vertical cuts along the sides, front to back. Stop cutting just short of the hair-collar. These cuts should make a head that is constant in width, or slightly wider in front than back by the collar.

Cut back along the top of the hair. Stop cutting just short of the collar, like the other cuts. The result should be a head that looks like an upright rectangle from the front view, higher than it is wide. When viewed from the side, the head should be level, or slightly higher in front than in back, by the hair-tip collar.

Now that the hair is largely trimmed and you can clearly see the hook's bend and the location of the shank, trim the underside of the head fairly close to the shank, but don't push your luck—just one nick in the thread and you have to unravel the thread and hair and start a new head.

Trim in from the sides of the head until the head is flat in front and ends just behind the eye. Cut carefully, so as not to cut the heavy thread half-hitched in front of the hair.

Turn the fly so that you're looking at its side, so you can see how far back you're cutting. Cut into the last fibers against the hair-tip collar all the way around—the underside, sides, and top—trim these hairs down so that the rear of the head ends at the collar. You may take a few collar-hairs in the process, especially if you use a razor blade, but a few is no problem. (You can wait until the head is otherwise fully shaped and clean before trimming back to the hair-collar if you want.)

50. Mount the fly in a midge vise-head or old vise-head. Trim the underside of the flared hair back to the hair-collar.

51. Trim the sides and top back to the hair-collar, leaving a large head.

52. Trim the underside of the hair-head *fairly* closely.

53. Trim straight in from the sides of the head, to make a flat face on the head.

54. Trim the hair back to the hair-collar. Trim the edges of the hair-head to rounded.

55. Trim off the hair-tips along the underside of the head, to expose the body.

56. If required, trim the tips of the hopping legs to proper length.

57. Add epoxy or head cement to the half hitches in the size-A thread, the knots in the kicking legs, and then stroke epoxy or cement down the tip-sections of the kicking legs.

ADDING CEMENT (OR EPOXY) TO THE COMPLETED DAVE'S HOPPER

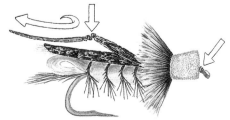

54. (cont.)

Now trim the edges of the hair to rounded, with long strokes of the blade or snips of the scissors down the length of the head. When you're finished, the head should be rounded in cross-section, though still higher than it is wide. It should also be trimmed even and close underneath and flat across its face.

55.

Trim back along the underside of the hair-collar to remove most or all the hairs—this will expose the body to the view of the trout. (This is an optional step—some tiers leave the hair-collar intact underneath—but I think that exposing the body makes sense.)

Trimming the Flared-Hair Head— Problems, Solutions, and Suggestions

1. You'll find pretty much everything you need to know about trimming a flared-hair head and collar, beginning on page 63, in the chapter titled "Marabou Muddler, Brown."

2. When you trim the underside of the flared-hair head and collar, be careful not to trim off the hackle-fibers (or, of course, cut the thread—either thread, the rod-thread or the thread holding the wing and body).

3. If you have only one bobbin and therefore have to change threads for the head, consider tying up several bodies—with tails, humps, wings, and hopper-legs—in succession. Then you can switch threads and do the flared heads and collars in assembly-line fashion. This is actually an efficient way to tie complex fly patterns anyway.

Completing the Dave's Hopper

56.

Time for the final steps (whew!). Trim the tips of the hopping legs to length, if they need it—the tips should extend back from the knots a distance about equal to three quarters of the shank's length.

57.

Add low-odor epoxy glue to the half hitches in the size-A thread, the knots in the hopping legs, and then stroke it along the tips of the hopping legs if the legs are of pheasant-tail fibers. Try to gather the pheasant-fibers together into a single bunch, by stroking from the top, underside, or sides.

ADDITIONAL NYMPHS

ANATOMICAL *CALLIBAETIS*
Skip Morris

Hook: Heavy wire, 1X or 2X long, sizes 16 to 12.
Thread: Tan or brown 8/0 or 6/0.
Head: Black metal bead, 5/64-inch for size 16 and 3/32-inch for sizes 14 and 12.
Weight: Lead or lead-substitute wire, 0.015-inch.
Tail: Mottled tan-brown turkey quill, three fibers.
Back: A slim section of mottled tan-brown turkey quill.
Rib: Fine gold wire. Wind the rib over the abdomen and the back and between the turns of gill-hackle.
Gills: One brown dry-fly neck hackle, trimmed close on one side and stripped on the other.
Abdomen: Natural tan-brown hare's mask.
Legs: Natural brown (or gray) partridge-flank fibers.
Wing Case: A section of mottled tan-brown turkey quill (clear sheeting, such as Stretch Flex or Medallion, over the wing case is optional).
Thorax: Natural tan-brown hare's mask.
   Comments: Imitates the standard mayfly of trout lakes, *Callibaetis*, which also inhabits some slow, weedy rivers.

BEAD HEAD PRINCE

Hook: Heavy wire, 2X long, sizes 14 to 6.
Head: Gold metal bead.
Thread: Black 8/0 or 6/0.
Weight: Lead wire (optional).
Tail: Brown (or black) goose quills.
Rib: Fine oval gold (or silver) tinsel.
Body: Peacock herl (or black ostrich herl).
Hackle: Brown (or black) hen hackle, as a collar.
Wing: Two white goose biots, long and forked.
   Comments: This bead-head version of the beloved Prince Nymph grows more popular by the year. The bead adds brilliance and, of course, carries the fly right down.
   To tie the Bead Head Prince, just slide a bead up a hook and, essentially, tie the conventional Prince Nymph.

COPPER JOHN, SILVER
John Barr

Hook: Heavy wire, 2X long for sizes 18 to 12, standard length to 1X long dry-fly hook for size 20.
Head: Silver metal bead.
Weight: Lead wire.
Thread: Gray 8/0 or 6/0.
Tail: White goose biots (or hackle fibers).
Abdomen: Silver copper wire.
Wing Case: One strand of pearl Flashabou over a strip of Natural Mottled Bustard Thin Skin, topped with epoxy glue.
Thorax: Pale-gray ostrich herl.
Legs: Natural-gray partridge fibers.
   Comments: Not so natural as the original, but that can be a good thing. For the details, see the chapter titled "Copper John."

DARK MOSSBACK
Dan Bailey

Hook: Heavy wire, 2X to 4X long, sizes 12 to 4.
Thread: Black 8/0 or 6/0.
Weight: Lead wire.
Tail: Black goose biots.
Abdomen: Black and olive woven horsehair, nylon hair, raffia...
Thorax: Black thread.
Legs and Antennae : Black goose biots.
   Comments: My research left holes and I had to guess at some of this pattern. Short on black and olive horsehair, I substituted Antron yarn in the fly above. An almost forgotten fly, but fascinating and fun to tie. A snapshot of a little historic corner of fly tying.

FOX'S POOPAH, OLIVE
Tim Fox

Hook: Heavy wire, 1X long, sizes 14 and 12.
Head: Gold metal bead.
Thread: Black 8/0 or 6/0.
Rib: Small gold Ultra Wire (or substitute copper wire). The rib secures the Vernille abdomen.
Under-Body: Medium flat pearl tinsel, wound up the shank.
Abdomen: Olive Vernille or Ultra Chenille. Melt the butt-end of the material before binding it on.
Legs: Mottled-brown hen-back or partridge.
Antennae: Two pale-yellow wood-duck fibers (or mallard dyed wood-duck color).
Thorax: Dyed-black ostrich herl.
   Comments: Clever design, eh? Imitates a caddis pupa. Also tied in cinnamon.

GABRIEL'S TRUMPET, GOLD
Skip Morris

Hook: Heavy wire, curved or straight shank, sizes 16 to 10.
Bead: Gold metal, 1/32- to 1/8-inch.
Thread: Gold or yellow 8/0 or 6/0.
Weight: Lead wire, 0.015-inch.
Tail: Two gold or amber goose biots.
Rib: Fine red copper wire.
Abdomen: Gold Flashabou.
Wing Case: Mottled turkey quill (or Thin Skin or some other sheeting).
Thorax: Tan or amber ostrich herl.
Hackle: Ginger or tan hen neck.

Comments: This attractor can be deadly. As can the pink version, with pink thread, abdomen, and thorax; white or cream tail and hackle, red wire rib; and the brown version, which is brown, brown, brown with amber wire for the rib.

KILLER CADDIS, OLIVE
Dennis Brown

Hook: Heavy wire, humped shank (scud/pupa hook), sizes 18 to 12.
Abdomen: Three to five olive small or "midge" glass beads.
Thread: Chartreuse for the butt; wine color for the rest, 6/0 or 8/0.
Butt: Olive Antron dubbing.
Thorax: Dyed-black or -brown rabbit, or other natural dubbing.

Comments: Slide on the beads, start the thread and dub a short butt at the bend—a stopper for the beads. Whip finish and cut the thread. Push the beads back and restart the thread in front of them and then dub the thorax.

Other standard colors for the Killer Caddis include brown, dark-green, amber, and tan. This is just one of many ways to tie with glass beads.

POXYBACK LI'L YELLOW STONE
Mike Mercer

Hook: Standard or heavy wire, 2x long, slow-curve shank, sizes 18 to 14.
Thread: Tan 8/0.
Weight: Lead wire (optional).
Tail and Antennae: Dyed-yellow pheasant-tail fibers, split.
Rib: Fine copper wire.
Abdomen: Turkey-tail section over Haretron Golden Stone dubbing (or dark-gold rabbit fur).
Wing Case: Turkey tail, topped with epoxy.
Thorax: The same dubbing as in the abdomen.
Legs: A short section of natural-brown partridge flank, bound in front to lie back atop the thorax.
Head: The same dubbing as in the abdomen.

Comments: Imitates nymphs of the little yellow stonefly complex.

TFS WD Brassie, Brown
The Fly Shop (Redding, CA)

Hook: Heavy wire, humped-shank (scud/pupa hook), sizes 20 to 16.
Thread: Brown 8/0.
Tail: Natural brown or gray partridge-flank fibers.
Abdomen: Small-diameter brown copper wire.
Wing Case: Pearl Flashabou.
Thorax: Natural dark-gray squirrel.
Legs: Natural brown or gray partridge flank, in one bunch per side.

Comments: Also tied with thread and an abdomen in olive, amber, or chartreuse. Tim Fox, of The Fly Shop, told me the TFS WD Brassie is a blend of two nymphs you see all the time: the WD40 and the Brassie. He fishes it as an attractor, below a dry fly, or deep below an indicator.

WIRED STONE
Brad Befus

Hook: Standard to heavy wire, 2X long (slow-curve shank preferred), sizes 16 to 8.
Head: Gold metal bead.
Thread: Olive 8/0, 6/0, or 3/0.
Tail: Dyed-ginger goose biots split around any kind of ginger dubbing.
Abdomen: Hot-yellow and black (or brown and black) Ultra Wire, wound together. Use the "small" wire for the smallest hooks, graduating to "large" for the biggest hooks.
Legs: Dyed-ginger goose biots, one pair at the rear of each thoracic segment.
Wing Case: A section of mottled-brown Medallion Sheeting (three wing cases).
Thorax: Three sections of peacock herl, each section with it's own legs and wing case.

Comments: Both the bead and wire pull this convincing fly down to the fish.

WOVEN DRAGONFLY NYMPH
Darrel Martin

Hook: Heavy wire, 3X long (slow-curve shank, usually) size 6.
Thread: Brown 3/0.
Foundation: Thick leather.
Abdomen: Brown and chartreuse or olive Vernille, woven.
Thorax and Legs: Dyed-brown rabbit fur in a dubbing loop.
Eyes: Two loops of black or brown Vernille.
Wing Case and Top of Head: A small feather, laquered, a notch trimmed in the end. Bind on the feather at the eye, dub around the eyes, and pull the feather back and bind it behind the eyes with a thread-collar.

Comments: The foundation can be formed of shoe leather, a teardrop shape, split. For lakes.

ADDITIONAL STREAMERS

CONEHEAD MUDDLER MINNOW

Hook: Heavy wire, 3X or 4X long, sizes 12 to 2.
Nose: A gold, bronze, or silver metal cone.
Thread: White or gray 8/0, 6/0, or 3/0. White or gray size-A rod-thread for the head.
Tail: A single section of mottled turkey quill.
Body: Flat gold tinsel.
Wing: Dyed-brown calf tail inside two sections of mottled turkey quill.
Head and Collar: Undyed gray-brown deer hair.
  Comments: Really, the original Muddler Minnow but with a cone head for weight.
  I like to smear head cement (or epoxy glue) on the thread and then make the whip finish behind the cone. I break a double-edge razor blade in half and break one of the halves to a point using two pairs of pliers—the pointed blade helps in trimming the hair behind the cone.

MORRIS MINNOW, BROOK
Skip Morris

Hook: Heavy wire, standard length to 3X long, ring (straight) eye, sizes 10 to 2.
Thread: Dark- or medium-green 6/0 or 3/0.
Weight: Lead or lead-substitute wire.
Body: Fine Mylar strands (Angel Hair, Lite Brite) bound in sections up the shank. The Mylar should be dark-green on top, medium-green along the sides, red or orange under the shank for the belly. Trim all the Mylar to fish-body shape.
Head: The working thread, or a short length of gold (or bronze) Mylar tubing bound on behind the eye, and then pushed back to turn inside out over the body. Complete the head as described in the chapter titled "Morris Minnow, Brown." Paint the head as in the photo with a dark-green top, medium-green sides, light-green squiggles on the top, red underside, white eyes with black pupils, red or black gills; mix the paints as needed to get the colors right. Coat the head with epoxy glue.
  Comments: You can tie the Morris Minnow to imitate not only a small brook trout, as here, but any trout species and even smallmouth and largemouth bass by varying the colors of the Mylar and paint. This fly really dances when tied on with a loop knot.

RED-FINNED CLOUSER MINNOW
Bob Clouser and Lefty Kreh

Hook: Heavy wire, 2X or 3X long (slow-curve shank is optional), sizes 10 to 6.
Thread: Light-brown (or tan) 8/0, 6/0, or 3/0.
Eyes: Lead or lead-substitute barbell eyes pre-painted red with black pupils.
Belly: Dyed-orange squirrel tail.
Under-Wing: Silver Flashabou.
Wing: Undyed gray squirrel tail.
  Comments: This small Clouser Minnow can suggest all sorts of little fishes to catch all sorts of bigger ones—trout, smallmouth bass, pan fishes, and various saltwater species. Squirrel tail is softer than buck tail, so squirrel and similar materials make sense for Clouser wings on smaller hooks.

WHITE AND BLUE LEFTY'S DECEIVER
Lefty Kreh

Hook: Heavy wire, short to standard length, sizes 8 to 4/0.
Thread: White 6/0, 3/0, or flat waxed nylon.
Tail: White saddle hackles, six to ten, divided into two sets cupped together. Bind the hackles atop the bend. Ten strands of pearl Flashabou outside each set of hackles.
Wing: Dyed-blue buck tail atop white buck tail.
Throat: Red Flashabou.
Head: A large thread head painted blue with poster paints (or a kids' water-based paint). Coat the head and eyes with epoxy glue.
Eyes: Painted white with black pupils.
  Comments: For trout, largemouth and small-mouth bass, striped bass, many saltwater fishes.

WOOLHEAD SCULPIN, OLIVE
Mike Lawson

Hook: Heavy wire, 3X long, sizes 10 to 4.
Thread: Olive 6/0 or 3/0.
Weight (optional): A gold metal cone.
Tail: Dyed-olive Zonker strip over a few strands of pearl Flashabou.
Body: A dyed-olive Zonker strip wound up the shank, and then trimmed along the sides and underside.
Pectoral Fins: Dyed-olive hen-back feathers, two per side.
Gills: A bushy collar of dyed-red rabbit, dubbed.
Head: Dyed-olive wool, bound up the shank and trimmed to a wide, flat head.
  Comments: Bind on the wool in close bunches, but don't compress the wool back. Trim the wool as you did in the chapter titled "Woolly Wing."

ADDITIONAL EMERGERS

CDC LOOPWING MIDGE EMERGER

Hook: Light wire, humped shank (pupa/ emerger hook), sizes 18 to 10.
Thread: Black 8/0.
Shuck: Pearl Krystal Flash, one to three strands.
Rib: One strand of pearl Krystal Flash.
Abdomen: Dyed-brown rabbit fur.
Thorax: Dyed-dark-brown rabbit fur (or Haretron).
Wing: Two natural-gray CDC feathers. Bind the feathers close by their tips, over the thorax. Push the butts of the feathers back to make two loops, bind the butts, trim off the butts, and build a thread head.

    Comments: The CDC Loopwing Midge Emerger imitates, of course, a hatching midge. The tiny sizes are for rivers, the larger ones for lakes. CDC emerger patterns abound these days.

OLIVE MARABOU QUIGLEY CRIPPLE
Bob Quigley

Hook: Light wire, standard length or 1X long (standard dry-fly hook), sizes 20 to 12.
Thread: Light-olive (or olive) 8/0 or 6/0.
Tail (shuck): Dyed-olive marabou.
Rib: Fine gold wire.
Abdomen: Dyed-olive marabou.
Thorax: Dyed-light-olive or -yellow deer hair, flared and shaped, or dubbing.
Wing and Burst Shuck: Undyed tan-brown deer hair.
Hackle: Dyed-yellow-olive grizzly or dyed blue-dun grizzly.

    Comments: A general imitation of olive or just pale mayflies. Practically everything you need to know about tying the Olive Marabou Quigley Cripple is in the chapter titled "PMD Quigley Cripple."

E/C CADDIS
Ralph Cutter

Hook: Standard length to 1X long, standard or slightly heavy wire, sizes 20 to 12.
Thread: Olive 8/0 or 6/0.
Shuck: Amber Antron or Z-lon fibers in a loop.
Body: Any brown dubbing for the rear half; green, yellow, or tan dubbing for the front half.
Hackle: One, grizzly.
Wing: Undyed tan-gray deer or elk hair. Bind on the hair with tips rearward. Trim the butts to stubby, and then wind the hackle around the base of all the hair—under both the tips and butts.

    Comments: Here's an original wing and hackle. Sound concept. While the E/C Caddis is primarily for caddis hatches, it can be good for imitating hatching mayflies too, especially if you tug the wing up high.

OVERLEY'S SPOTLIGHT CADDIS, BLACK
Steve Overley

Hook: Light wire, humped shank (pupa/emerger hook), sizes 20 to 12.
Thread: Black 8/0 or 6/0.
Rib: Fine copper wire, securing the abdomen.
Abdomen: Black Ultra Chenille or Vernille, melted on the rear end, secured with the rib.
Down-Wing: Medium-dun (grayish-brown) Sparkle or Antron yarn.
Parachute Wing: White calf tail or body.
Parachute Hackle: Medium-blue-dun.
Thorax: Black Mottled Nymph Blend dubbing (or black rabbit).
Legs: Natural-brown partridge or hen back.
Antennae: Wood-duck or substitute, long, two.

    Comments: A low-riding caddis-emerger imitation. Also tied in olive and tan.

MORRIS EMERGER, GREEN DRAKE
Skip Morris

Hook: Light wire, humped shank (pupa/emerger hook), sizes 12 to 8.
Thread: Green or olive 8/0 or 6/0.
Tail: Dark-olive or brown hen back.
Abdomen: Ostrich herls, two dyed-olive and one dyed-brown, twisted in a dubbing loop, trimmed top and bottom.
Thorax: Olive buoyant synthetic dubbing (Poly dubbing, Superfine Dry Fly...). Optional: a yellow rib of twisted flat waxed nylon.
Burst Shuck and Wing: Natural-dark (or dyed-dark-gray) coastal deer hair as a fan, angling slightly forward. The butts should be cut straight across over the rear of the thorax, and trimmed a little along the sides.

    Comments: Though this version imitates the western green drake, in other sizes and colors the Morris Emerger can imitate most any mayfly.

POM POM EMERGER, PURPLE
Skip Morris

Hook: Light wire, humped shank, sizes 16 to 12 (standard wire, 2X long, slow-curve shank for sizes 10 to 6,).
Thread: Brown 8/0.
Tail: White goose biots.
Rib: Fine silver wire.
Abdomen: Purple Flashabou or Krystal Flash.
Parachute Wings: Yellow or orange wool, Poly yarn, or egg-yarn, short.
Parachute Hackle: Brown, one for each wing.
Thorax: Purple synthetic dubbing (Poly, Superfine Dry Fly...).

    Comments: This is the only attractor emerger fly I know—and it works. It can also be tied in pink, gold, and brown. Really move each wing around to help with winding the hackle. The hackle-tips should come forward *between* the wings to the head.

ADDITIONAL DRY FLIES

CARD'S CICADA
Charles Card

Hook: Light (or standard) wire, standard length or 1X long (standard dry-fly hook), sizes 12 to 8.
Thread: Black 6/0.
Under-body: Medium-brown Wing n' Flash (or Ice dub or another fine Mylar), dubbed.
Body: A strip of buoyant black foam-sheeting, extending back over the shank.
Head: The strip of foam for the body, doubled and bound, the hook-eye poking through.
Wing: White calf tail over "rainbow" Flashabou Accent (or substitute pearl Krystal Flash).
Legs: Black rubber-strand over barred-orange rubber-strand.

Comments: After dubbing the shank, push the eye up through the foam and right back out. Bind foam, add the wing, double back the front of the foam and bind it. A proven imitation of the cicada, so important on some trout and smallmouth rivers.

CDC FLYING ANT

Hook: Light wire, standard length or 1X long (standard dry-fly hook).
Thread: Six-ought or 8/0 in a color to blend with the thorax color.
Abdomen: Antron dubbing (or another synthetic dubbing) in black, amber, or cinnamon. Make the abdomen full and a bit short.
Wing: Gray CDC around gray Antron or Z-lon yarn fibers.
Hackle: One dry-fly hackle, spiraled over a slim waist of the working thread.
Thorax: Same dubbing you used in the abdomen. Make the thorax full, but shorter and not so full as the abdomen.

Comments: Simple and effective, the CDC Flying Ant is yet another angle on tying with CDC. There are many.

CDC RUSTY SPINNER
René Harrop

Hook: Light wire, standard length or 1X long (standard dry-fly hook), sizes 20 to 14.
Thread: Brown 8/0 or 6/0.
Tail: Light-blue-dun hackle-fibers.
Abdomen: Goose biot dyed rust (a reddish yellow-brown or orange-brown).
Wings: Light-blue-dun CDC with light-blue-dun Z-lon or Antron fibers on top.
Thorax: Rust synthetic dubbing, Super Fine Dry Fly, Poly, Antron...

Comments: You'll find tying instructions in the chapter titled "CDC *Callibaetis* Spinner." The spinners of many mayflies have rust-colored bodies, making this a versatile version indeed.

MIKULAK SEDGE
Art Mikulak

Hook: Light to heavy wire, 1X to 3X long, sizes 10 to 6.
Thread: Eight-ought, 6/0, or 3/0 in a color similar to the hackle's or body's color.
Tail: A bunch of natural-light to -dark elk hair, the tips evened in a hair-stacker. The tail is really part of the wing.
Wing and Body: Two to four stacked bunches of elk hair between short dubbed sections. Use a buoyant synthetic dubbing (Antron, Poly, Superfine Dry Fly) in any reasonable caddis (or stonefly or attractor) color: olive, green, orange, brown, tan...
Hackle: One dry-fly hackle wound over a thread collar between the front wing-section and the head.
Head: The butts of the front wing-section, trimmed straight across.

Comments: Making of the wing and body of the Mikulak Sedge is similar to making the wing and body of my Woolly Wing—it ought to be; Art's fly provided the inspiration for mine. The main differences between the wing of the Mikulak Sedge and the Woolly Wing are that the former has a sort of tail and the latter does not, and that the Mikulak Sedge's wing-sections are stacked rather than trimmed.

Originally designed to imitate the huge traveller sedge caddis of western lakes, the Mikulak Sedge now imitates all sorts of caddisflies on lakes and rivers. I also use it as an attractor. It probably makes a good imitation of a stonefly too, though I've seldom tried it as such.

OSWALD'S FOAM PARA-ANT
Duncan Oswald

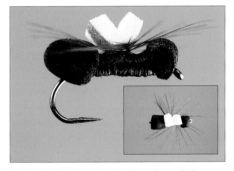

Hook: Light wire, standard length to 1X long (standard dry-fly hook), sizes 18 to 12.
Thread: Black 6/0 (or 8/0).
Abdomen: A strip of buoyant black foam-sheeting.
Thorax: The same strip of foam used for the abdomen.
Strike Indicator (and hackle-post): A short strip of yellow foam-sheeting.
Parachute Hackle: Brown, sparse.

Comments: Bind the foam-strip down to make the center of the fly narrow. Double each end of the strip and bind the end down the shank. The doubled ends of the foam should abut one another. Foam is a natural in ant and flying-ant imitations. No reason I can think of that the Oswald's Foam Para-Ant can't be tied in the other common ant-colors, red and cinnamon.

PARACHUTE HOPPER
Ed Schroeder

Hook: Light to standard wire, 2X long, sizes 18 to 10.
Thread: Cream 8/0, 6/0, or 3/0.
Abdomen: Golden-brown Antron dubbing (or another synthetic dubbing).
Parachute Wing: White calf tail.
Down Wing: Toughened turkey quill.
Hopping Legs: Knotted pheasant-tail fibers.
Parachute Hackle: Grizzly.
Thorax: Same dubbing as in the abdomen.

Comments: Tying instructions for the down-wing and hopping legs are in the chapter titled "Parachute Caddis" and "Dave's Hopper." The Parachute Hopper is a perfectly logical and reliably effective follow-up to the Parachute Caddis.

RAINEY'S GRAND HOPPER, TAN
Rainey Riding

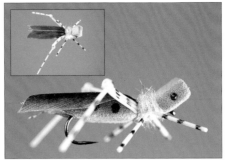

Hook: Light to standard wire, 3X long, sizes 16 to 6.
Thread: Tan 8/0 or 6/0.
Body: Thick tan foam sheeting, cut to about gape-wide, dotted with a black marking pen. The body is partially slit down its center and then glued to the thread-covered shank.
Wing: One coated undyed-brown hen-back feather, flat atop a few strands of Pearl Krystal Flash.
Hopping Legs: Three connected strands of tan round rubber-strand. Knot the strands, trim off two strands behind the knot, dot the legs with a black marking pen.
Legs: Tan round rubber-strand, one section bound tightly on each side of the foam body, angling outward. Bar the legs with a black marking pen.
Collar: Tan Rainey's Sparkle Dub, or another shiny, coarse, tan dubbing (such as Antron).
Eyes: Premade black plastic barbell eyes, pushed into the sides of the head by their cut stems with glue. (Rainey uses a Bug-Eye Stick, melting one end, pushing the stick through the foam, and then carefully melting the other end.)

Comments: Unusual in its tying, and no pushover at the vise, the Rainey's Grand Hopper is nonetheless easier to make than the Dave's Hopper. Rainey also ties her fly in yellow, brown, olive, red, and chartreuse. Foam is a natural for imitating grasshoppers and other large, plump insects.

SILVEY'S ADULT MIDGE, BLACK
Brian Silvey

Hook: Light wire, standard length or 1X long, sizes 20 to 16.
Thread: Black 6/0 (or 8/0).
Rib: Pearl Flashabou Accent (or another narrow pre-twisted Mylar strand).
Abdomen: The working thread.
Wings: Clear Wing (or another clear synthetic wing-material) trimmed to two wings spread in a "V".
Gills: A tuft of white CDC (trimmed or tied short).
Hackle: Grizzly.

Comments: Silvey's Adult Midge—which imitates exactly what it's name denotes—is tied in black, as here, and olive and tan. Fish it dead drift to trout in rivers feeding on freshly hatched or egg-laying midge adults.

STIMULATOR, ORANGE
Randall Kaufmann

Hook: Light (or standard) wire, 2X or 3X long (straight or slow-curve shank), sizes 16 to 4.
Thread: Orange (or *fluorescent* orange) 8/0, 6/0, or 3/0.
Tail: Natural-dark elk hair.
Rib: Fine gold wire.
Abdomen Hackle: One furnace (or brown) saddle hackle.
Abdomen: Bright- or rust-orange synthetic dubbing (Antron, Poly, Super Fine Dry-Fly...).
Wing: Natural-dark elk hair.
Thorax Hackle: Grizzly.
Thorax: Dyed-amber goat hair (or amber synthetic dubbing, such as Poly or Antron).

Comments: Tying instructions are in the chapter titled "Stimulator, Yellow." This orange version, aside from being an attractor, suggests various caddis and stoneflies, particularly two western giants: the salmonfly stonefly and October caddis.

WOOLLY WING, GREEN
Skip Morris

Hook: Light to heavy wire, standard length to 2X long (straight or slow-curve shank), sizes 14 to 8.
Thread: Green 8/0 or 6/0.
Body and Wing: Bunches of dyed medium-gray wool mixed with fine strands of fine pearl Mylar. Add wing bunches between sections of green synthetic dubbing (Poly, Antron...).
Parachute Wing: Dyed-yellow or -orange wool (or egg-yarn or Poly yarn).
Parachute Hackle: Brown.

Comments: Tying instructions are in the chapter titled "Woolly Wing, Orange." This size-range and coloring can suggest green-bodied caddis and the greener varieties of little stoneflies. Of course, all the Woolly Wings make solid attractor dry flies.

OTHER FLIES

ARTICULATED LEECH

Rear Hook: Traditional loop-eye heavy wire Atlantic salmon/steelhead hook, sizes 10 to 2.
Thread: Six-ought or 3/0 in the tail's color.
Tail: Zonker strip. Natural-gray, dyed black, olive, brown, or purple.
Rear Section: A crosscut rabbit strip, the tail's color, wound up the shank.
Front Hook: Any hook with a big eye. Cut off the bend. This hook can be inexpensive.
Connection: Fly-line backing, through the eye of the rear hook, around the shank, and back out the eye, doubled back through the eye of the front hook and bound.
Front Section: A crosscut rabbit strip, in the tail's color, wound up the shank.
Weight (optional): Lead or lead-substitute barbell eyes.
Comments: This long, billowing, hinged leech-fly—or leech-like fly—got popular for steelhead, then big trout. It's a fairly new design and will probably prove itself on all sorts of fishes.

BASS BUG

Hook: Heavy wire, short shank (standard bass-bug hook), sizes 10 to 2.
Thread: For the tail: three-ought in the tail's color. For the body: size-A rod-thread in white, or the body's color.
Tail: Buck tail in the body's color (or a complimentary or contrasting color).
Body: Deer hair in natural tan-brown, olive, yellow, gray, green, black, brown, purple—really, almost any color—flared and trimmed.
Comments: A bass bug may have a hackle or rubber-strand tail, rubber-strand legs, eyes, a monofilament snag-guard—and no matter what it has or doesn't have, it's still just a bass bug. Usually, a white (or yellow) face, for visibility. Different colors of hair can create banding.

A standard pattern for largemouth and small-mouth bass.

BEADHEAD CRYSTAL BUGGER

Hook: Heavy wire, 3X or 4X long, sizes 14 to 2.
Head: Gold metal bead.
Thread: Eight-ought, 6/0, or 3/0 in a similar color to the body's color.
Tail: One dyed marabou plume, a few strands of Krystal Flash, in pearl or the body's color, trimmed to the tail's length.
Rib: A saddle or neck hackle spiraled up the body. Normally, in the body's color.
Body: Shiny plastic chenille (commonly called Crystal Chenille).
Comments: The stunningly popular Woolly Bugger—a fly for about any fish under 20 pounds—has inspired an abundance of variations. This one, with its metal bead head and sparkling body, is among the most successful. Common colors are olive, black, purple, claret, brown, and white.

DAVE'S EELWORM STREAMER
Dave Whitlock

Hook: Heavy wire, 1X to 3X long, sizes 4 to 1/0.
Thread: Three-ought in the body's color.
Eyes: Silver bead-chain or metal barbell eyes, mounted atop the shank.
Tail: Four long dyed or undyed grizzly hackles, in two sets cupped together, a shorter hackle curving out on each side.
Rib: Fine copper wire, counter-wound forward through the hackle. Bind on the hackle behind the eyes, spiral it back over the body, and wind the wire forward though the hackle.
Body: Almost any dubbing, natural or synthetic.
Hackle: Dyed-grizzly, in the body's color.
Head: The body-dubbing, around the eyes.
Comments: My slight variation. Name aside, this largemouth bass fly isn't really a streamer to me. Common colors are black, blue, purple, brown, and green. Rides inverted.

FATHEAD DIVER
Jack Ellis

Hook: Standard to heavy wire, short shank to 1X long, sizes 10 and 8.
Thread: Red 3/0 for the tail and snag-guard; size-A rod-thread for the hair.
Snag-Guard (optional): Mason or Maxima monofilament of 0.012-inch diameter, bound down the shank and later at the eye.
Tail: Brown marabou over red marabou over squirrel-tail hair.
Collar: The stacked tips of the first hair bunch.
Diving-Collar and Body: Undyed tan-gray-brown deer hair. Trim the hair close beneath, tapered on top and sides, a collar with trimmed tips behind the body.
Comments: A miniature version of the popular Dahlberg Diver bass fly, for bluegill, green sunfish, and other pan-fishes.

GLO-BUG, PINK
The Bug Shop

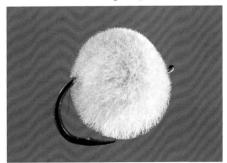

Hook: Heavy wire, short shank, sizes 16 to 4.
Thread: Pink 8/0 or 6/0.
Body: Pink egg-yarn, flared and trimmed.
Comments: Simply bind one or two sections of the yarn beneath the center of the shank, and one or two atop it, whip finish the thread and trim it, and then raise all the yarn and cut it closely in one snip.

This soft, bright, and simple imitation of a fish egg can work wonders on moody trout. It's normally much bigger than a real trout egg, but that doesn't seem to matter. Other fishes will go for this fly. I've caught steelhead and huge dolly varden char on Glo-Bugs It is also tied and fished in orange and red, and even chartreuse and black.

JANSSEN LEECH
Hal Janssen

Hook: Heavy wire, 2X long, sizes 12 to 2.
Thread: Eight-ought, 6/0, or 3/0 in the tail's color.
Weight: Ten to 12 turns of 0.020-inch lead wire.
Tail: Marabou fibers from the side of the plume, in black, brown, olive, gray, or tan.
Wing: Three bunches of marabou fibers of the tail's color, from the side of the plume. Bind the butts of each bunch up the shank.
Head: The butts of the front marabou-bunch, twisted around the thread.
Comments: The tail- and rear wing-bunches should each equal about two shank-lengths. This very lively leech imitation was designed for trout in lakes. But I've caught some fine trout in rivers with the Janssen Leech, and it's a natural for smallmouth bass, maybe largemouth bass.

McGINTY

Hook: Heavy wire, standard length or 1X long, sizes 14 to 10.
Thread: Black 8/0 or 6/0.
Tail: Barred teal over red hackle-fibers.
Body: One strand each of black and yellow chenille, wound together for a banded effect.
Hackle: Brown hen neck.
Wings: Naturally white-tipped mallard primary quill sections.
Comments: Bee-like but not quite a bee, the McGinty is an old wet fly that has become, more than anything else, a pattern for bluegill, crappie, and other pan-fishes. Toss it out, let it sink, and twitch it back.

MURRAY'S HELLGRAMMITE
Harry Murray

Hook: Heavy wire, 2X or 3X long, sizes 10 to 4.
Thread: Black 6/0 or 3/0.
Weight: Lead wire, about the diameter of the shank, covering the middle three quarters of the shank.
Tail: About 20 dyed-black ostrich herls, their tips pinched off, a full hook-length.
Antennae: Two lengths of fine black rubber-strand.
Rib: A big soft dark-blue-dun hackle spiraled up the body.
Body: Black chenille.
Comments: The hellgrammite, which Murray's fly imitates, is abundant in some smallmouth rivers.

PINK CRAZY CHARLIE
Bob Nauheim

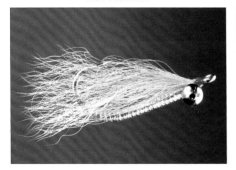

Hook: Heavy wire, standard length, stainless steel (standard saltwater hook), sizes 8 to 4
Thread: Pink 6/0 or 3/0.
Eyes: Silver bead-chain eyes.
Body: Clear V-Rib (or another gelatinous body-material such as Scud Back or D-Rib) over pearl Flashabou.
Wing: Dyed-pink calf tail.
Comments: The Crazy Charlie is a standard for the tropical bonefish that cruises clear shallow flats and streaks wildly across them when hooked—the speed and distance of a bonefish's run are legend. Lots of popular bonefish flies are based on the Crazy Charlie. It is often tied in tan, brown, yellow, and white.

RACCOON, PINK
Skip Morris

Hook: Heavy wire, 1X long sizes 12 to 6, to 2X long sizes 10 to 6.
Bead: Metal, gold (usually), black, or silver.
Thread: White 8/0, 6/0, or 3/0.
Tail: The fluffy base-fibers from a grizzly "soft hackle," a webby, supple rooster hackle.
Body: Dyed-pink rabbit and fine silver, pearl, and pinkish Mylar strands blended (or Arizona Flyfishing's Sparkle Nymph Dubbing in "Skip's Pink").
Hackle: Grizzly soft hackle (or any soft, full hackle).
Comments: Slip a line of dubbing into a dubbing-loop for the shaggy body. The Raccoon is for Pacific salmon and sea-run cutthroat trout. Other colors include yellow, black, orange, and red. The hackle and tail are always grizzly.

UNDERTAKER
Warren Duncan

Hook: Standard heavy or light-wire, up-eye steelhead/Atlantic salmon hook, sizes 6 to 2.
Thread: Black 8/0, 6/0, or 3/0.
Tag: Fine oval or flat gold tinsel behind fluorescent-green floss behind fluorescent-orange floss.
Rib: Fine gold oval tinsel.
Body: Peacock herl.
Hackle: Dyed-black saddle.
Wing: Natural black bear (or dyed calf tail or buck tail).
Cheeks (optional): Jungle cock.
Comments: If there is a typical classic steel-head and Atlantic salmon fly, the Undertaker is about as reasonable a candidate as any.

INDEX

OTHER TITLES BY SKIP MORRIS

Fly Fisher's Guide: Western River Hatches

You'll be amazed at the amount of detailed information Skip Morris has packed into this handy-sized book. This booklet helps you identify a hatching insect, select an appropriate fly to match it, and fish that fly effectively. Skip provides useful information, such as: important insect stages; seasons; hatch times; hatch conditions; habitat; imitation size; size of natural, including minimum and maximum sizes; effective fishing strategies; 2 clear photographs of important stages; actual insect size chart; beautiful artwork; fly plates; seasonal hatch chart with major western hatches; and more. This book was written and designed to bring more trout to your flies. 5 x 4 inches, 32 pages.

SB: $4.95   ISBN-13: 978-1-57188-363-6
                           UPC: 0-66066-00197-2

The Art Of Tying The Dry Fly

This is the finest book ever published on how to tie dry-flies, featuring over 400 clear, color photos demonstrating all the techniques and materials you need, plus clear, concise tying instructions from display-fly tier Skip Morris. Contains the information you need to tie the very best 100 dry-flies—a dry-fly for virtually ANY stream. Printed on bright, glossy paper, large format which stays open easily. 8 1/2 x 11 inches, 112 pages.

SB: $29.95   ISBN-13: 978-1-878175-36-6
                           UPC: 0-66066-00123-8
HB: $29.95   ISBN-13: 978-1-878175-37-3
                           UPC: 0-66066-00124-5

Tying Foam Flies

The first book done on how to tie fascinating, productive foam flies and all photos are in color. Master fly tier Skip Morris shows you step-by-step in clear photos and descriptive text how to make buggy-looking foam flies that are at the forefront of fly-fishing development. With this easy-to-understand book you will be able to create any number of new patterns after you have learned the tying steps. Thorough information about types of foam, best threads, knots, etc. 8 1/2 x 11 inches, 48 pages.

SB: $16.95   ISBN-13: 978-1-878175-89-2
                           UPC: 0-81127-00130-9

Concise Handbook Of Fly Tying

This is a basic, all-color fly-tying guide that teaches all the necessary techniques needed to tie excellent flies for trout and other fish. Tying materials are explained and tying techniques demonstrated. An excellent introductory book to the wonderful world of fly tying! 5 1/2 x 8 1/2 inches, 40 pages.

SB: $7.95   ISBN-13: 978-1-57188-214-1
                           UPC: 0-66066-00428-4

Morris & Chan On Fly Fishing Trout Lakes
by Skip Morris and Brian Chan

From two of the biggest names in the industry comes this all-encompassing guide to fly-fishing trout lakes. Combining their vast knowledge on fly-fishing, fly-tying, entomology, and aquatic biology, Skip Morris and Brian Chan have created a book full of information for lake fly-fishers of all levels. They share: general techniques; reading a lake; cycles of a trout lake; insects and other trout foods; productive lake flies; casting; watercraft; equipment; knots; trout species; learning a new lake; courtesy and safety; and more.

With the teaming of Skip Morris and Brian Chan, you are getting the advice of top experts in the fields of fly-fishing, fly-tying, entomology, and fish biology. This is your guide for improving and perfecting your skills as a lake fly-fisher. All-color, 8 1/2 x 11 inches, 96 pages.

SB: $24.95   ISBN-13: 978-1-57188-181-6
                           UPC: 0-66066-00392-8
HB: $39.95   ISBN-13: 978-1-57188-182-3
                           UPC: 0-66066-00393-5

Morris on Tying Flies

Skip Morris has assembled his favorite flies and how to tie and fish them for trout and other fresh water species. Important writing on fishing and tying techniques from one of America's top five fly masters. Discover some great new patterns for your fishing. 8 1/2 x 11 inches, 112 pages, all-color.

SB: $19.95   ISBN-13: 978-1-57188-378-0
                           UPC: 0-81127-00212-2

Fly Proportion Chart

This handy, full-color, laminated chart shows you the proper fly-tying materials' dimensions for tying traditional dry-flies, parachute dry-flies, comparadun dry-flies, stoneflies, caddisflies, soft hackle flies, nymphs, streamers & bucktails and steelhead & Atlantic salmon wet-flies. Double-sided. 4.25 x 9 inches.

$3.95   ISBN-13: 978-1-878175-69-4
                           UPC: 0-66066-00157-3

Fly Tying Made Clear And Simple

With over 220 color photographs, expert tier Skip Morris shows all the techniques you need to know. 73 different materials and 27 tools. Clear, precise advice tells you how to do it step-by-step. Dries, wets, streamers, nymphs, etc., included so that you can tie virtually any pattern. 8 1/2 x 11 inches, 80 pages.

SPIRAL SB: $19.95   ISBN-13: 978-1-878175-13-
                           UPC: 0-66066-00103-
SB: $19.95   ISBN-13: 978-1-57188-231-
                           UPC: 0-81127-00131-
DVD: $26.95   ISBN-13: 978-1-57188-365-
                           UPC: 0-81127-00199-

The Art Of Tying The Nymph-DVD

Trout, and other fish, feed heavily on nymphs, which makes artificial nymphs deadly effective. Through this DVD, tying nymphs becomes logical, fun, and fascinating.

Learn to tie all nymphs from simple to the very complex. Skip Morris carefully guides you step-by-step. Morris is also one of the world's finest display fly tiers, guaranteeing you learn from a master. 112 minutes.

DVD: $26.95   ISBN-13: 978-1-57188-433-
                           UPC: 0-811127-00267-

Flies For Sea-Run Cutthroat Trout-DVD

In this DVD of nearly two hours, fly fishing celebrity Skip Morris will teach you to tie some great fly patterns for sea-run cutthroats and show you where and how to fish them. He'll take you from tying the patterns at the vise to walking a beach or wading a river and working them for sea-run and salmon. Discover these remarkable fish and the fascinating flies that consistently take them.

DVD: $29.95   ISBN-13: 978-1-57188-406-
                           UPC: 0-81127-00240-

The Art Of Tying The Bass Fly-DVD

Skip shares his 30 years of experience tying the flies needed to catch these fish. Skip covers: essential techniques, floating and sunk flies, divers, insects and crustaceans, pan-fish flies, plus the tools and materials you'll need for both. Bass flies are very popular for many reasons—they are durable, attractive, and fun and challenging to tie. In this book you will learn from one of the world's expert fly tiers! 105 minutes.

DVD: $26.95   ISBN-13: 978-1-57188-366-
                           UPC: 0-81127-00200-